AF479247

CONTEMPORARY GOVERNMENT REFORM IN JAPAN

Contemporary Government Reform in Japan

The Dual State in Flux

Eiji Kawabata

CONTEMPORARY GOVERNMENT REFORM IN JAPAN
© Eiji Kawabata, 2006.

First published in 2006 by
PALGRAVE MACMILLAN™
175 Fifth Avenue, New York, N.Y. 10010 and
Houndmills, Basingstoke, Hampshire, England RG21 6XS
Companies and representatives throughout the world.

PALGRAVE MACMILLAN is the global academic imprint of the Palgrave Macmillan division of St. Martin's Press, LLC and of Palgrave Macmillan Ltd. Macmillan® is a registered trademark in the United States, United Kingdom and other countries. Palgrave is a registered trademark in the European Union and other countries.

ISBN-13: 978–1–4039–7112–8
ISBN-10: 1–4039–7112–9

Library of Congress Cataloging-in-Publication Data

Kawabata, Eiji.
    Contemporary government reform in Japan : the dual state in flux / Eiji Kawabata.
        p. cm.
    Includes bibliographical references and index.
    ISBN 1–4039–7112–9
    1. Japan—Politics and government—1989– 2. Japan—Economic policy—1989– I. Title.

JQ 1631.K392 2006
320.952—dc22   2006041844

A catalogue record for this book is available from the British Library.

Design by Newgen Imaging Systems (P) Ltd., Chennai, India.

First edition: September 2006

10 9 8 7 6 5 4 3 2 1

Printed in the United States of America.

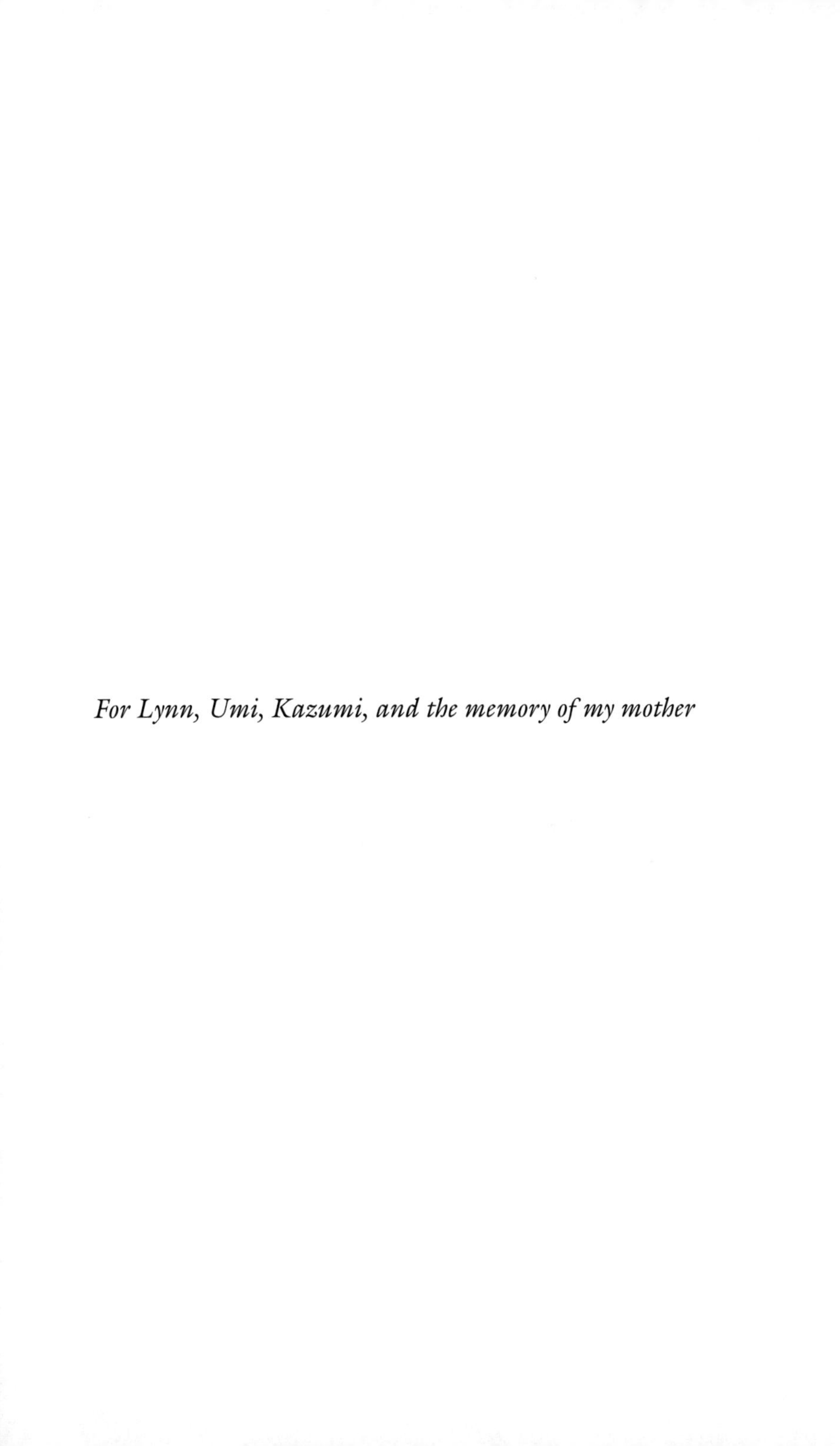

For Lynn, Umi, Kazumi, and the memory of my mother

Contents

List of Tables and Figures   ix

Acknowledgments   xi

Abbreviations   xv

Introduction   1

1   Japanese Government Reform from
a Comparative Perspective   17

2   The Politics of the Dual State   39

3   The Dual State and Government Reforms   65

4   Postal Business: Old Guard Politics Die Hard   93

5   Reforms in Transportation: Trains, Planes, and
Automobiles   125

6   Telecommunications Regulatory Reform:
Bureaucracy-Led Liberalization?   147

Conclusion   179

Notes   193

Index   217

List of Tables and Figures

Tables

3.1 Government structure proposed in the
    Administrative Reform Council's interim report   74
3.2 The structure of old and new government
    ministries and major agencies   78
4.1 Progress of the liberalization of large-scale
    deposit interest rates   106
4.2 Computation of the *teigaku* deposit interest rate   111
4.3 Chronology of small-scale deposits
    (over ¥10 million per account)   114
4.4 Major MPT–MOF agreements on tax reform and
    financial liberalization and major concessions   115
4.5 MPT's independent investment   118
6.1 Internet users in select countries in 1998   166

Figures

1.1 Patterns of government reform   33
4.1 The Postal Savings Fund and the
    Fiscal Investment and Loans Program   96
4.2 PSF account balance, fiscal year 1980–2000   117
4.3 Total assets (PLI and private sector life insurance)
    in the 1990s   121
6.1 Integration of major long-distance, mobile, and
    international New Common Carriers   163

Acknowledgments

This book project first started as my dissertation dealing solely with specific policy issues, but its focus has been significantly broadened to discuss Japan's government reform, and includes updated analyses of dramatic reform events that occurred in the last decade. Consequently, it took a very long time to finish the entire manuscript. In the process of this long journey of research and writing, I received advice and assistance from numerous individuals. Ellis Krauss, Bert Rockman, and John Campbell made crucial contributions to my project. Ellis's cheerful intellectual advice and personal encouragement kept me going on this project. In the early stages, he helped me develop my analysis for the dissertation. In the mid-stages when I was revising the dissertation into a book, he pressed me to clarify a broader general theme for the project, which I present here as the dual state. In the final stages, he shared his knowledge about the logistics of book writing, guiding me as a first-time book writer through the process. Similarly, Bert has not only provided invaluable suggestions that helped me to incorporate comparative aspects in the project but also consistently gave moral support in the development of my career as a scholar. John consistently showed his enthusiasm for my project, and in the final stages, read all the chapters and made helpful and constructive criticisms, which helped me to significantly improve the quality of this project. I am particularly grateful to these three mentors/ friends.

In addition, the following scholars offered me invaluable suggestions about various aspects of the book project: Davis Bobrow, Karen Cox, Rich Friman, Glen Fukushima, Kozo Kato, Mari Miura, Koichi Nakano, Greg Noble, Skip Orr, Simon Reich, Len Schoppa, Mitchell Smith, Brian Taylor, Mark Tilton, Steve Vogel, and Tony Walters. Many government officials and Diet members in Japan agreed to be interviewed. Since I assured them their anonymity, I cannot name them individually here, but their insight clarified many aspects of the government reform process. Toby Wahl at Palgrave MacMillan recognized the potential of this project and encouraged me to pursue publication. Kat Sparks and Umi Kawabata provided editorial and research assistance. I owe a lot to them as well as to those who I failed to mention here. I thank them all but I have to remind the reader that any flaws that this book still has are of course mine.

This project would not have been possible if I did not have the fortune to be affiliated with two first-rate research institutions in Japan, the Institute of Social Science at the University of Tokyo (*Shaken*) and the Institute of Comparative Culture at Sophia University, and two universities in the United States, the University of Oklahoma and Minnesota State University, Mankato. The two Japanese institutes not only provided access to their library and other resources but also opportunities—research seminars, lunches, and drinking parties—to interact with Japanese and international scholars. I especially thank Nobuhiro Hiwatari at *Shaken* and Koichi Nakano at Sophia who arranged my affiliation at the respective institutes. At the University of Oklahoma, I developed my scholarship through interactions with university members, particularly those of the comparative politics section in the Department of Political Science, that is, Charlie Kenny, Russell Lucas, Mitchell Smith, and Brian Taylor. The warm environment (even during the severe Minnesota winter) in the Department of Political Science and Law Enforcement at Minnesota State University, Mankato, greatly helped me finish my manuscript. I particularly thank Department Chair Doran Hunter and my colleagues in the international relations program, Abdalla Battach, Tom Inglot, and Jackie Vieceli, for their encouragement and friendship.

The following institutions provided funding for this research project. Japan Society for the Promotion of Science, the Northeast Asia Council of the Association for Asian Studies, the College of Arts and Sciences and the Research Council at University of Oklahoma, and the Office of Research and Sponsored Programs Minnesota State University, Mankato. A part of this book was published in "Dual Governance in Contemporary Japanese Policymaking," *Social Science Japan Journal*, April 2004, volume 7, no. 1.

Last but not least, my friends and family need to be acknowledged because they made my life worthwhile during this project. Elaine and Jerry Donohoe have always made my life in the United States very enjoyable. Also, my casual discussions with them about politics and business led me to recognize the importance of my project to a broader audience. My family members always (albeit painfully) reminded me of the importance of life beyond academia. Lynn was not yet born when the project started, but I hope that she now understands at least what this book is about. In the early stages of this project, Umi, as a teenager, used to wonder who would read my writings, but she grew up so fast and ended up proofreading my manuscript. My wife, Kazumi, has been so anxious about my finishing this project. She cheerfully or sometimes not so cheerfully pressed me to work on the project. My parents have been supportive of me for a long time. Unfortunately, my mother passed away just before the completion of this book project, but I can imagine in my mind how she would smile at the front cover of this book. I thank my family for their patience and support.

Abbreviations

ANA	All Nippon Airways
ARC	Administrative Reform Council
CGP	Clean Government Party
DDI	Daini Denden Incorporated
DPJ	Democratic Party of Japan
DSL	digital subscriber line
EU	European Union
FCC	Federal Communications Commission
FILP	Fiscal Investment and Loans Program
FIRG	Financial Issue Research Group
GTSRC	Government Tax System Research Council
HC	House of Councillors
HR	House of Representatives
IDO	Nihon Ido Tsushin
JAL	Japan Airlines
JH	Japan Highway Public Corporation
JNR	Japan National Railways
JRCPC	Japan Railway Construction Public Company
JSP	Japan Socialist Party
KDD	Kokusai Denshin Denwa
LDP	Liberal Democratic Party
LDS	Letter Delivery Service
LTSRC	LDP's Tax System Research Council
MITI	Ministry of International Trade and Industry
MLIT	Ministry of Land, Infrastructure, and Transport
MMC	money market certificate
MOC	Ministry of Construction
MOF	Ministry of Finance
MOT	Ministry of Transport
MPT	Ministry of Posts and Telecommunications

MPHPT   Ministry of Public Management, Home Affairs,
         Posts, and Telecommunications
NCC   new common carrier
NPM   new public management
NTT   Nippon Telegraph and Telephone
NTTEW   NTT East and West
PARC   Policy Affairs Research Council
PHCs   Public Highway Corporations
PLI   Postal Life Insurance
PSF   Postal Savings Fund
SDP   Social Democratic Party
TDA   Toa Domestic Airlines
TRL   telecommunications-related law
TWJ   Nihon Kosoku Tsushin
VAN   value added network

Introduction

Japan's Struggling Government Reform

After Japan's defeat in 1945, major cities were in ruins and major industries were destroyed. However, the Japanese economy achieved remarkable economic development in the period leading up to the early 1990s. In the 1950s, thanks to an economic boom created by the Korean War, Japan recovered quickly from the destruction of the economy caused by the war, and enjoyed rapid economic development in the 1960s. In the 1970s, however, the Japanese economy encountered major turbulence. The yen's appreciation against the dollar was a critical blow for Japan, whose economic development had been heavily dependent upon exports to the United States; it made Japanese exports more expensive and lessened their price competitiveness. Also, the dramatic increases in oil prices pushed up the cost of raw materials, and this was another blow for Japan, which lacked natural resources and depended heavily on imports of raw materials. However, Japan overcame these difficulties by shifting the focus of production to high-tech high-value-added products.

As a result, the 1980s was the most prosperous period for Japan. Japanese products, such as autos, VCRs, and semiconductors, flooded the U.S. (and world) market, bringing about an enormous trade surplus for Japan. Domestically, the 1980s was the so-called bubble period because of the inflated wealth that the Japanese enjoyed. Although skyrocketing land prices made it difficult for many Japanese to own houses, citizens possessed abundant funds with which to invest in the stock market and to consume luxury goods. Japan came to be recognized as a model of economic success, and many attributed its success not only to business, but also to the government, in particular the government bureaucracy. Those scholars and pundits known as revisionists even went so far as to suggest that the United States, seemingly in decline, should emulate Japan to regain economic competitiveness.

The early 1990s, in which the bubble burst, was a big turning point for the Japanese economy. It marked the beginning of Japan's lost decade(s); the Japanese economy has been moving downhill ever since. The Nikkei stock price index—which hit a historical high of 38,915 in 1989 and was predicted to eventually reach some 80,000 during the bubble period—has been in a long-term downward spiral since the early 1990s.[1] The government's direct and indirect measures to resist stock price declines kept the Nikkei above the 10,000 mark throughout the 1990s, but it sank below the mark with the chaos created by the September 11 attack in 2001. Securities companies that prospered in the 1980s have been in serious financial trouble, as exemplified by the bankruptcy of Yamaichi Securities, one of the four major Japanese broker houses that had been thought to be infallible, in 1997. Commercial banks have been burdened with an enormous amount of nonperforming loans that originated from their aggressive lending in the 1980s, a time in which banks had abundant funds. Because of nonperforming loans whose national total is too large to be fully known, some banks have gone bankrupt, while others have been trying to survive by consolidating operations through mergers.

Japan's economy as a whole also fell into a downward trajectory in the 1990s. Although Japan's per capita GNP had topped the world in the mid-1990s, its growth stagnated, and it fell to a lower place, sixth in 2003.[2] Japan's industrial competitiveness was esteemed to be the highest in the world in the 1980s, but the International Institute for Management Development has recently been ranking Japan's industrial strength below tenth place. Most companies have downsized their operations and relocated production overseas to take advantage of low operation costs. Those companies unsuccessful in turning around simply went bankrupt or became controlled by foreign capital, as exemplified by Renault's takeover of Nissan management, the establishment of Shinsei Bank by GE Capital, and the acquisition of Sea Gaia, a gigantic resort facility, by Ripplewood, a U.S.-based investment bank. Although many of the Japanese companies, such as Toyota, Honda, and Sony, still fare very well in the global market, the decline of Japanese business as a whole is palpable.

Consequently, unemployment is steadily rising. As of 2003, Japan's unemployment was about 5 percent, extremely high for a country in which unemployment had been virtually nil before the burst of the bubble. Homelessness is becoming a major problem. In the public parks of major cities, such as Tokyo, Osaka, and Kobe, hundreds of people set up and live in shacks made with blue vinyl sheets and cardboard. The prevalence of unemployment and homelessness is not unusual for advanced industrial countries, including the United States, but its social impact is stronger in Japan, where people were more used to job security. The number of suicides committed by those who suffered from business failures or job losses is increasing. In Tokyo, every so often trains are delayed when someone jumps into the path of a train and gets killed. The long-lasting depression is clearly taking a toll on Japanese society.

The ailing economy has taken a toll on the Japanese government as well. The stagnant economy not only reduces government revenue, but also presses the government to increase spending to stimulate economic recovery. The end result is an ever-increasing national debt, amounting to two and a half times gross domestic product, which is unusually high for a peacetime economy. More importantly, however, many claim that the government is an important factor in the exacerbation of Japan's economic problems, for a number of reasons. The government has been extremely slow in coping with the nonperforming loan problem, and endorses regulations that protect incumbent companies and discourage competition among them, distressing new entrants and prohibiting business expansion. The government also continues to fund pork barrel projects that benefit uncompetitive economic actors much more than the general public. These government measures all serve to preserve economic inefficiency, and delay economic recovery by imposing costs on growth-oriented new businesses.

The government, once hailed as the entity that effectively promoted Japan's rapid economic development, is now at the center of Japan's economic problems, and, government reform is therefore an essential part of Japan's economic reform. In fact, problems with the government have long been recognized among reformist politicians, business leaders, and scholars, and these reformers embarked upon major government reforms in the early 1980s. Even though the conservative Liberal Democratic Party (LDP) was in power during this period, except for a brief descent from power in the early 1990s, the downsizing of government was constantly on government agendas, and many reform attempts were made. Some of the crucial issues pertinent to government inefficiency were left untouched, however, and bureaucrats and politicians succeeded in aborting reform attempts that would undermine their influence on politics. However, many government activities were undertaken as a result of reforms, indicating that reform attempts did enjoy a certain measure of success. For example, major government corporations, such as Nippon Telegraph and Telephone (NTT) and Japan National Railways (JNR), were privatized. The government also eased regulations in various business areas, enabling companies to engage in freer business activities. In addition, the number of government agencies was drastically reduced in the late 1990s. As politicians and bureaucrats often altered reform measures to their favor, one should not exaggerate the overall effectiveness of reform; however, it is fair to say that changes have been occurring in Japanese politics.

In this book, I analyze Japan's government reform, which is crucial for an understanding of Japan's current economic problem. I identify both successes and failures of each government reform, and trace the impact of each on the three major economic sectors: telecommunications, postal business, and transportation. Interestingly, none of these sectors has been extensively analyzed, despite their relevance and importance to government reform. Through the analyses, I argue that two economic factors, development and distribution, are key to an understanding of government reform and, therefore, the reason why government reform has been staggered in Japan.

Alternative Explanations of Contemporary Government Reform

Despite the importance of government reform to the current economic problems, the cause of government reform's stagger in Japan remains unanswered. In general, the three actors central to reform are citizens who ultimately determine government policy, politicians (or elected officials) who formulate government policy, and bureaucrats who not only interact with politicians in formulating policy but also implement it. Therefore, it is necessary to examine the relationship between each actor and government reform in order to determine the cause of current economic difficulties.

One may argue that the long-lasting economic problem has not had a deep impact on the society as a whole, despite its serious blow to the social segments identified above; in other words, one may argue that the lives of citizens in general are not threatened seriously enough to prompt them to strongly demand government reform. On the surface, this seems to be reasonable, considering the contrast between Japan's continued social stability and the social instability in East Asian countries that faced economic difficulties in the late 1990s. When the financial crisis hit high-flying East Asian countries in 1997, disgusted citizens and workers in many countries took to the streets and showed their anger toward the government. In contrast, despite the ongoing crisis, Japanese society shows no sign of panic, and remains stable, or at least not substantively less stable than pre-crisis days. Few large-scale demonstrations or work stoppages, let alone riots, occur in Japan. Citizens are still buying luxury goods, and major upscale brands, such as Louis Vuitton, Chanel, and Calvin Klein, have recently added mega stores to their already extensive nationwide sales networks in Japan. Entertainment districts in major cities are crowded with jarred businesspeople after dark. Since few citizens seem to have the sense of urgency to solve the economic crisis, some analysts conclude that government reform is not gaining momentum.

It is true that the economic problem has not deteriorated Japanese society to the point of prompting citizens to call for some sort of revolution. However, the general public's frustration with the government has still become clear, particularly recently. The election of reformist Prime Minister Koizumi Junichiro in 2001, for example, shows the growth of support for government reform. Koizumi lacked strong support from LDP leaders, but won the LDP presidential election with support from local rank and file LDP members, who benefited most from current protective government measures and were therefore likely to go against reforms. This is indicative of the prevalence of demand for government reform among the Japanese public. Besides, strong support for government reform has existed among business leaders since the late 1970s, prompting Prime Ministers Nakasone Yasuhiro and Hashimoto Ryutaro to embark upon government reforms in the 1980s and the 1990s, respectively.

Since demand for reform exists among the public as well as among business leaders, the major deficiency that inhibits progress in government reform seems to lie in the political process, which may be incapable of responding to public preferences. Aurelia George Mulgan attributes the failure of government reform attempts to Japan's political structure, which prevents prime ministers from exercising strong leadership, standing in stark contrast to the British parliamentary system after which the Japanese system was modeled. The Japanese and British systems are especially different in terms of the prime minister's leadership vis-à-vis the government party as well as the bureaucracy. Unlike in Britain, where either of the two major parties has a top–down decision-making structure that enables the prime minister to strongly pursue his or her agenda, the decision-making system of the LDP is fragmented, and the party president/prime minister needs to accommodate demands from internal factions. As for the bureaucracy, the Japanese government is much less receptive to the prime minister's directions than its British counterpart.[3] Therefore, unlike in Britain, where a strong leader such as Margaret Thatcher is able to pursue government reform, it is nearly impossible for a reformist prime minister with solid public support such as Koizumi to accomplish fundamental reform, due to resistance from his own party and the bureaucracy.

The prime minister's weak leadership is definitely a part of the problem, given that the strongest resistance to reform attempts came from Koizumi's own party and the bureaucracy in major government reforms. However, reform is possible, at least theoretically, if the interests of the reformist prime minister, the LDP, and the bureaucracy happen to converge, leading the three policy actors to cooperate in the pursuit of reform. In reality, of course, this does not happen, but the executive's limited power alone does not explain why. An explanation of government reform therefore needs to go beyond the weak executive and identify the broader societal factors that prompt LDP politicians and bureaucrats to fight against reforms.

Based on the analysis of economic, political, and social practices peculiar to contemporary Japan, Edward Lincoln provides a comprehensive explanation for the lack of progress in economic reform in Japan, illustrating a very slow shift to an American-style economy that boasts free market competition, enhancing economic efficiency and competitiveness, and which Japanese reformers use as a desirable system. In particular, Lincoln identifies the interconnectedness of business organizations, vested interests deeply enrooted in the existing system, and the bureaucracy's initiatives in the reform process, resulting in the alternation of reform, among other things, as major factors that bring about the degeneration of reform.[4] Although Lincoln's analysis provides useful background information about government reform, especially with regard to counterreform elements prevalent in Japanese society, the analysis is unclear about how these factors stall government reform, and how government reform progresses more rapidly in certain policy areas than in others.

These analyses primarily focus on the lack of progress in reform and identify actors—voters, politicians, and bureaucrats—who inhibit reform attempts. There are two analytical shortcomings common to these and other analyses of reform in Japan. One shortcoming is that the analyses place too much emphasis upon the degeneration of reform attempts, and fail to pay attention to the success of certain reform attempts. Indeed, although each of the major reforms since the early 1980s failed to fully achieve goals that reformers had initially set out, this does not mean that these reforms made no substantive impact. In fact, in telecommunications and transportation, reforms resulted in privatization and deregulation, making freer economic activities possible. Therefore, the analysis of government reform needs to examine not only how reform attempts were aborted or stalled but also how and to what extent certain reform attempts succeeded. The other shortcoming is that, although the analyses rightly identify the actors influential for reform outcomes, they do not explain how interactions among these actors generate reform outcomes. Therefore, the argument on government reform that I present in this book incorporates an analysis of the variance in the progress of government reform and shows the dynamics among the actors.

Argument in Brief: Politics of the Dual State

In this book, I analyze government reform in its relationship to the fundamental characteristic of the Japanese political economy—the dual state. The Japanese political economy consists of two distinctive sectors: developmental and distributive. The developmental sector seeks to create economic value and to maximize efficiency and competitiveness, whereas the distributive sector is primarily concerned with the transfer of value created by the developmental sector. Development and distribution are two fundamental elements of economic activities, and the existence of this duality itself is not peculiar to the Japanese political economy. In Japan, however, distinctive networks covering politicians, bureaucrats, and business leaders have developed on the basis of each of the two sectors, and each network has different political dynamics. Both inter- and intra-network interactions are crucial for the development of specific government reforms.

Economic actors in the distributive sector engage in value-creating activities, but they are both uncompetitive and inefficient, depending heavily upon the government-backed distributive mechanism. The most direct method of government distribution is government spending, whereby the government, through taxation, collects wealth generated by the developmental sector and reallocates it to the distributive sector. In Japan, a major transfer of value is directed toward rural areas, and most direct beneficiaries are construction companies. Nonetheless, government spending sustains rural economies and benefits the distributive sector as a whole.[5] Government regulation also serves as a distributive tool. Restrictions on market entry protect incumbents from new competitors, and formal and informal price controls ensure handsome profits. Those who benefit from this regulatory protection and redistribution look to politicians and bureaucrats to maintain these mechanisms. In return for their contribution to the maintenance of the distributive network, politicians, particularly old guard LDP politicians whose districts are in rural areas, gain monetary contributions and electoral support, and bureaucrats take lucrative post-retirement jobs in private sector companies or government-affiliated organizations in the network. Although the protective mechanism imposes a social cost that is borne by society as whole, and particularly by the developmental sector, the distributive networks are deeply embedded in Japanese polity and highly resistant to reform attempts.

Similarly, in the developmental networks, major members—bureaucrats in charge of developmental sectors, reformist LDP leaders concerned with the well-being of the Japanese state as a whole, and leaders of big business—maintain constant interactions. However, the internal political dynamics of the developmental networks are different from those of the distributive networks. Although business executives and bureaucrats in the distributive sector share a common immediate interest in maintaining protective regulations, business–bureaucracy relations in the developmental sector are more ambivalent. In the developmental sector, as analyzed by Richard Samuels,[6] the bureaucracy and business maintain a symbiotic relationship of "reciprocal consent" in which business accepts the bureaucracy's jurisdiction and the bureaucracy allows for flexible business operation and refrains from unilateral intervention. Although business actors may need government protection or approval of their activities, they try to minimize the governmental intrusions that often constrain their activities.

In this context, the bureaucracy is engaged in policymaking that conforms to business interests, but as long as the bureaucracy merely confirms business practice, the bureaucracy cannot claim importance to the economy distinctive from, if not contradictory to, short-term business interests. As a result, the bureaucracy pursues forward-looking vanguard policies in order to remain relevant and maintain its autonomy and legitimacy. These bureaucracy–business interactions occur against the backdrop of elected politicians. In contrast to the crucial role of government regulation in the distributive sector, the expected benefit of political involvement is smaller for both business leaders and bureaucrats. Involving politicians in the activities of the developmental sector increases uncertainty, leading business and the bureaucracy to work to contain conflict (which might encourage political intervention) through compromise. However, politicians are occasionally invited to participate in the interactions between business and the bureaucracy when they cannot solve conflicts, or when party leaders voluntarily intervene in interactions that concern issues crucial for society as a whole. Accordingly, in the developmental sector, participation by politicians is less direct and more sporadic, but policymaking is nonetheless of interest to politicians who make crucial decisions.[7]

Both intra- and inter-network dynamics are crucial for the development of government reform. In the distributive networks, since political actors share the interest of maintaining the distributive mechanism, intra-network interactions do not result in major changes. However, in the developmental networks, due to the transfusion of the neoconservative anti-state ideology that Margaret Thatcher and Ronald Reagan utilized to pursue government reform in Britain and the United States, respectively, big business seeks to minimize the role played by the government bureaucracy. Big business and reformist LDP leaders pursue government reform through deregulation and privatization of government operations. Since the major target of government reform within the developmental networks is the bureaucracy, and the reform requires the bureaucracy to make major changes in their policymaking, the bureaucracy tends to resist changes at the early stage of the reform. However, once the bureaucracy is given a proper role in the new format, it stops interfering and sometimes even promotes reform. Thus, government reform progresses, albeit slowly and oftentimes rather incrementally, in dealing with issues that involve adjustments in the developmental networks.

Reform attempts deriving from inter-network dynamics entail the fundamental reformation of the dual state, and, therefore, are important and controversial. Since the end of the rapid economic period in the early 1970s, firms in the developmental sector faced increased competition from both newly industrialized economies in the international market and the rise of protectionism in the U.S. market, the sector's major export market. Their profits fell accordingly, leading the developmental sector to demand a reduction of their burden of the maintenance of the dual state. In addition to government reform within the developmental networks, business leaders' and reformist LDP leaders' targets include issues pertinent to the distributive mechanism, and old guard politicians and bureaucrats from the distributive networks fiercely resist reform attempts impacting these issues. Reform, therefore, stalls because of inter-network dynamics.

Policy Issues

In this book, I directly apply the argument of government reform as a result of the politics of the dual state to the analysis of the Nakasone, Hashimoto, and Koizumi reforms, and discuss both reform processes and outcomes in terms of their relationship to interactions among political actors from the developmental and distributive sectors. In addition to the analysis of these politically heated periods, I provide a more longitudinal analysis of three policy areas central to government reform: telecommunications, postal business, and domestic transportation. Unlike finance, manufacturing, and agriculture, these areas are relatively under-researched. More importantly, each of them exists in the intersection of the distributive and developmental sectors, and is therefore suitable for the examination of intra- and/or inter-network dynamics. As briefly summarized below, each area is important for the Japanese economy as a whole, and is involved in major government reforms. However, the pace and extensiveness of reform vary among them. Through the case analyses, I aim at explaining interactions within and between the developmental and distributive networks as the source of the variations.

Telecommunications before the 1980s was regarded as a natural monopoly, and NTT, a government corporation, operated all telephone services. It also had some distributional function, in that it constructed and maintained nationwide telecommunications networks, providing valuable infrastructure to rural areas. However, the completion of the building of the networks decreased NTT's distributive functions. When technological progress made telecommunications no longer a natural monopoly, reformers embarked upon fundamental changes in the format of the operation and regulation of telecommunications. Although telecommunications reform sought drastic measures, such as the privatization of NTT and the liberalization of the telecommunications market, reformers faced relatively weak opposition from politicians and bureaucrats. This lack of opposition is likely due to the fact that interactions, although extensive and conflict-laden, were contained within the developmental networks. The political actor at the center of the reform interactions was the Ministry of Posts and Telecommunications (MPT). The MPT was in charge of the postal businesses crucial to the distributive networks, as described below, and was commonly viewed as a second-class conservative ministry. However, with the transformation of the telecommunications policymaking arrangement, the MPT took over the leading role from NTT, and aggressively promoted market competition as well as the upgrading of the use of telecommunications technology in Japan. Telecommunications, the crucial business in the age of information technology, shows the current political dynamics of the developmental networks.

The MPT's approach to the reform of the postal business was totally different from that of the reform of telecommunications. In postal business reform, the MPT acted as an old guard and worked vigorously to block the progress of the reform, because the business was an integral part of the distributive mechanism. The most important component of the Japanese postal business was the postal savings fund (PSF). The PSF was a consumer banking operation that consistently absorbed about one-third of the total savings in Japan, and its total deposit amount had been over ¥200 trillion (about $1.66 trillion at $1 = ¥120) since 1995. This vast amount was generally transferred to the Fiscal Investment and Loans Program (FILP) operated by the Ministry of Finance (MOF) and often referred to as Japan's second budget. During Japan's rapid economic development period, this program was used to fund projects to stimulate economic development, but its primary function was to provide funds to pork barrel projects and government affiliated organizations that were in charge of distributive projects. Therefore, old guard politicians were adamant about reforms that would weaken the PSF operation. In addition, so-called *Tokutei* (special) local postmasters were politically important. *Tokutei* post offices account for about 18,400 out of the total of about 24,000 post offices in Japan. The position of the *Tokutei* postmaster has been transferred by inheritance, and *Tokutei* postmasters have been at the center of social activities in rural areas.[8] In Diet elections, *Tokutei* postmasters actively campaigned for LDP candidates. This made it even more important for old guard politicians to defend the postal business. Enmeshed in the distributive networks, politics in postal businesses show the strength of antireform old guard political forces.

Just like telecommunications and postal business, transportation provided infrastructure crucial for regional economic development. Since improvements in railway, road, and airline transportation in rural areas made shipping and travel more convenient, politicians often used transportation improvement measures as campaign slogans to attract support from their constituents. More specifically, transportation was central to the distribution mechanism because many of construction projects were for the improvement of transportations systems; the building of high-speed bullet train lines, the construction of toll ways, and the expansion of airports had been the important projects. In particular, the first two types of government projects had been crucial for the distributive mechanism, providing a number of construction companies with business opportunities. Government reform measures to fundamentally alter them were therefore opposed and modified by old guard politicians. The privatization of the JNR during the Nakasone reform did not change the system to build new bullet train lines, and old guard politicians and bureaucrats from the Ministry of Land,

Infrastructure and Transport (MLIT) stalled the privatization attempt of the Japan Highway Public Corporation (JH) during the Koizumi reform. Deregulation measures not pertinent to the distribution mechanism, however, progressed steadily, if not rapidly.

The analysis of government reform in these areas demonstrates the importance of the dual state in contemporary Japanese politics, and provides a vantage point from which to look at reform in other major policy areas, such as finance. Moreover, it explains the nexus between the two fundamental features—development and distribution—of the Japanese political economy, laying the basis for the analysis of political economies of other advanced industrialized countries.

Implications to Japanese and Comparative Political Economy

This analysis of government reform aims at contributing to the development of the discussion of the Japanese political economy, whose major approaches are the state-centered, the society-centered, and state–society approaches, particularly on the relationships among the bureaucracy, politics, and society. For the state-centered approach, which hailed the effectiveness of the Japanese government's economic management, Japan's inability to cope with current economic problems is a big puzzle. The approach illustrates the importance of the economic bureaucracy's industrial policy, which effectively stimulated the expansion of advanced industrial sectors and contributed to the upgrading of the Japanese economy as a whole, while transferring resources away from obsolete sectors.[9] My analysis of the developmental sector shows the bureaucracy's continued pursuit of economic development in an evolved way, but it also points to the state-centered approach's major deficiency. The approach fails to recognize that the distributive sector has political dynamics quite different from those of the developmental sector, and that it behaves as a major obstacle to a transformation of the Japanese economy that would help Japan regain her competitiveness.

Contrary to the state-centered approach, the society-centered approach emphasizes the fundamental supremacy of societal interests, such as business and district-based local interests, as well as the primacy of politicians who, as agents for societal actors, insert societal interests into economic policymaking.[10] My analysis of government reform is consistent with this approach in that politicians make crucial decisions that set the fundamental course of action. However, the analysis focuses on an important aspect of Japanese policymaking that the society-centered approach has left underdeveloped, that is, bureaucratic discretion, or agency slack. By distinguishing between the developmental and distributive sectors, the analysis clarifies that each sector has a different pattern of interactions between politicians and bureaucrats. The analysis shows that politicians get deeply involved in issues related to the distributive mechanism while allowing the bureaucracy to make crucial decisions for issues in the developmental sector. Thus, this analysis points to the society-centered approach's deficiency: due to its overemphasis on politics, the approach tends to neglect the bureaucracy's inherent importance to public policymaking in Japan.

The state–society approach, on which my analysis is based, recognizes the strength of the Japanese bureaucracy in its relationships with politicians, but argues that the state-centered approach exaggerates the bureaucracy's strength while overlooking the importance of politicians in policymaking. According to this approach, leading politicians have also been influential, having first created a policy environment favorable for the bureaucracy. Leading politicians wield particularly strong influence over policymaking through their coordinating roles. Furthermore, societal actors, such as business leaders, maintain constant direct communications with government ministries and are thus in a position to insert their preferences into policy. The state–society school has contributed to our understanding of Japanese politics by highlighting the important roles that the LDP and business play in policymaking. However, this approach is logically indeterminate as long as it simply says that both bureaucrats and societal actors are strong; it is necessary to identify under what condition bureaucrats are more (or less) forceful than society actors. My analysis attempts to contribute to the development of this approach by arguing that the sectoral divide between the developmental and distributive sectors is an important factor that determines the bureaucracy's mode of interaction with societal actors.

In addition to furthering the discussion of the Japanese political economy, the analysis in this book is also pertinent to broader discussions of comparative political economy. Though this book exclusively discusses government reform in Japan, government reform is a primary political agenda in other advanced industrialized countries as well, such as the United States, Britain, Germany, and France. The book also discusses government reform in Japan in terms of its relationship to the two fundamental elements of the political economy: development and distribution. In this sense, the analysis of Japanese government reform lays the basis for further comparative research of government reform and its relationship to the two elements.

Preview of the Book

In Chapter 1, I start with an overview of government reform efforts in advanced industrialized countries. In each of the two dimensions of government reform—civil service/regulatory reform and structural reform—I show that Japan's progress in reform is comparable to, if not ahead of, that of many other advanced industrialized countries, and that government reform involves structural adjustment in coping with a new international economic environment. At the same time, I highlight that the distinctive feature of government reform in Japan lies in sectoral variations in the progress of reform. I attribute this sectoral variation to the historically developed politics of the dual state that is made up of developmental and distributive networks.

In Chapter 2, I explain the dual state and its two major economic aspects—development and distribution. These two aspects were the most important for the advanced industrial states seeking political stability after World War II, particularly those that had suffered from wartime devastation. A state-led approach was used to balance development and distribution in France, for example, whereas Germany adopted a social market economy. In Japan, the LDP and the government bureaucracy developed the dual state in response to political instability between the end of the war and the mid-1970s. The dual state they developed has two components—developmental and distributive networks—and each has distinctive internal dynamics, involving LDP politicians, government bureaucrats, and societal actors. Toward the late 1970s, developmental networks began to find it difficult to bear the costs of sustaining the dual state, and called for the reform of the arrangement. The interaction between the two components of the dual state was at the core of a series of government reforms that began in the late-1970s.

Chapter 3 discusses the three major government reform efforts that have taken place since the early 1980s. I describe how Prime Minister Nakasone's reforms of the 1980s accomplished the privatization of several major government corporations while leaving the sources of other government inefficiencies intact. I show that Prime Minister Hashimoto's reforms of the 1990s drastically reduced the number of government ministries and agencies but failed to reduce the overall scale of government activities. I then discuss Prime Minister Koizumi's ongoing reform efforts and show that, despite his popularity with the public, his reform attempts have been stalled by old guard politicians.

In Chapter 4, I discuss the postal service, and show that, in this period, the postal savings fund has continued to maintain its business advantage and has expanded its business base. I also discuss the development of the postal service and the postal life insurance system, each of which put substantial pressure on corresponding private sector competitors. I then analyze the impact of the reforms attempted by Prime Ministers Hashimoto and Koizumi. This chapter lays out the essence of the old guard politics of the distributive networks.

Chapter 5 discusses various aspects of transportation, another core industry in the distributive networks. National highway construction was closely related to the development of the distributive network, prompting old guard politicians and bureaucrats to resist reforms. Regarding the privatization of the national railways, although reformers succeeded in infusing a more efficient management style through the suppression of left-wing unions, the distributive mechanism was largely sustained. In contrast, the national airline was less extensively connected to the distributive mechanism, and reform therefore proceeded without inciting major controversies.

In Chapter 6, I focus on telecommunications, one of the most important industries for economic development, to examine the contemporary politics of developmental networks and, more specifically, the impact of reform on the industry, dealing with the regulatory aspect of developmental politics. After the privatization of NTT, which also significantly liberalized the market, the MPT pursued the breakup of NTT in order to stimulate competition, but, at the same time, subjected new entrants to the field to its tight regulation. Due to growth of demand for deregulation, the MPT eventually eased its regulation of the industry; however, LDP intervention stalled the MPT's pursuit of NTT's break up. In the conclusion, I summarize my findings and reevaluate my argument about the dual state and government reform. I draw out the argument's implications for analysis of the overall recovery of Japan and explore possibilities for future reform.

Chapter 1

Japanese Government Reform from a Comparative Perspective

Frustrated domestic and international observers tend to emphasize the lack of progress in Japanese government reform when analyzing Japan's inability to render its economy more efficient and dynamic and overcome the current economic difficulties. However, Japan's government reform actually began relatively early and has achieved remarkable accomplishments. Nakasone's administrative reform began in the early 1980s, roughly concurrent with reforms commonly considered acts of pioneering, that is, the Regan reform in the United States and the Thatcher reform in Britain. Although it has experienced both upheavals and downturns, the Japanese reform movement has lasted more than two decades. In the long process of Japanese government reform, various issues were discussed, including government reorganizations, privatizations, and deregulations, and reform measures were implemented in such areas as finance, telecommunications, and railway transportation. These reform measures, however, did not go as far as to completely satisfy reformist politicians and business leaders.

As long as one compares the reality with the ideal, one's assessment of government reform in Japan will be negative. One must also remember that it is possible for those who participate in reform movements to overemphasize reform results as their political feat. In order to assess the progress of government reform accurately and realistically, as opposed to idealistically, it is therefore necessary to compare Japanese government reform with government reforms in advanced industrial countries, particularly Britain, the United States, France, and Germany. In these states, as in Japan, a great deal of pressure for government reform developed, and reform measures were implemented. Through this comparison, I evaluate Japan's speed of government reform in relation to that of the other advanced industrial countries. At the same time, I identify the patterns of government reform in the advanced industrial countries and explain these patterns through the use of two institutional determinants—the extent to which the state is embedded in the economy, and the state's decision-making structure. Based on this comparison, I illustrate the general dynamics of Japanese government reform to lay the basis for the next chapter's analysis of Japan's dual state.

In the next section, I analyze the pre-reform politicoeconomic arrangement that developed in the post–World War II period in the advanced industrial countries, including Japan. This arrangement allowed the government to play an active role in the economy and expanded the size of the government. The arrangement did generate social stability; however, it also incurred social costs and caused government reform pressure to develop. In the third and fourth sections, I discuss civil service and regulatory reform, the two fundamental components of government reform. Although these aspects are not totally mutually exclusive, but rather interrelated, each of them has a different focus; civil service reform is concerned with improvement in pursuing policymaking, regulatory reform deals with the evolution of bargaining between the state and society; and economic adjustment involves the state's (forced) adjustment to changes in both domestic and international economic environments. Therefore, in each section, I draw a general picture of civil service or regulatory reform in the four advanced industrial countries and show that Japan's reform is comparable to them. Then, I demonstrate the relationship between the institutional factors and the patterns of government reform in these countries, including Japan, thereby placing Japan's government reform in a comparative context. I remind the reader that since the main purpose of these analyses is to place Japan's government reform in the comparative context, each of the discussions on specific aspects of government reform in each country is concise.

Post–World War II Government Expansion: Precondition of Government Reform

The government reform that began in the late 1970s to the mid-1980s in advanced industrial countries was largely a reaction to the politicoeconomic arrangement that allowed growth in the governments' sizes and involvement in the economy. This arrangement emerged in 1929, when the Great Depression compelled advanced industrialized states to abandon pre-Depression free-market policies of classical economics and experiment with nonliberal market interventionist approaches to economic activities, including neo-mercantilism, deficit spending, nationalization of industries, and so on. When these unorthodox attempts were reorganized during World War II, there emerged a pattern of political economy, common to advanced industrial countries, in which the politicoeconomic system accommodated the interests of major social actors, including business and labor. In general, this arrangement included three major components—Keynesian fiscal policy manipulation, welfare programs, and economic regulations. Keynesian fiscal policy manipulation provided labor with employment and generated demand for business; social welfare programs ensured labor, along with security and protection for the underprivileged; and regulations that restricted competition increased business stability and reserved certain industries/firms with extra profits.[1] As briefly described below, the details of the arrangement differed across the four advanced industrial countries, but the essence of the arrangement was always the same; in all four states, the government played an important role in each of these aspects, and therefore incurred costs generated by nonmarket activities.

In Britain, which has a liberal tradition minimizing government intervention in the economy, government involvement in the economy was less intrusive than elsewhere, but the government still had a great deal of influence on economic management in the post–World War II period. For example, Keynesian policy measures were used to stimulate the economy and secure employment. These measures included macroeconomic demand manipulation through government spending and tax policy, income policies such as wage and price controls, and attempts at industrial restructuring through government–business–labor cooperation.[2] The government's commitment to employment was coupled with provisions for social welfare programs, particularly in housing and health care.[3] Although British regulatory policy had traditionally focused on competition enhancement, the British economy included a government monopoly in telecommunications, restrictions on financial transactions, and the ad hoc promotion of industrial development before the early 1980s.[4] Thus, the British government's role in the economy was somewhat larger than might be expected in a liberal state.

The United States, another liberal state, also developed a politicoeconomic arrangement, known as the New Deal, that increased government involvement in economic activity after the Great Depression, and maintained this arrangement through the late 1970s. As in Britain, Keynesian macroeconomic policy was adopted, and deficit spending was tolerated. The government also provided Social Security, Medicare, and assistance programs for the poor. Although these social welfare programs stabilized business–labor relations, regulatory policy stabilized business interactions by increasing predictability in business activity through regulatory rules designed to restrict competition, as found in transportation, financial, and energy markets.[5] These policies expanded not only the government's role in the economy, but also its physical size, due to the necessity of establishing and maintaining organizations to operate the programs. Understandably, this arrangement imposed extra costs on economic activity.

France experienced considerably more overt government expansion after World War II, and the government pursued interventionist policy measures. The French right-wing coalition government engaged in strategic planning and identified target industries that it deemed essential to the enhancement of industrial competitiveness. Utilizing tight control over major banks, the government assisted target industries by channeling financial resources to them.[6] These microeconomic controls were combined with macroeconomic policy to spur industrial development through the expansion of demand.[7] The French government also established a comprehensive social security system, including pensions, unemployment insurance, and family support, which covered almost all of the population and accommodated various interests.[8] The French government maintained its interventionist stance a little longer than the British and U.S. governments; until the mid-1980s, the French socialist government continued to maintain and strengthen its involvement in the economy through expansionary fiscal policy, whose major beneficiaries were low-income households, and the nationalization of major industrial firms.[9]

Although neither French nor German economies adhered to Anglo-American liberal economic principles, (West) Germany's approach to post–World War II reconstruction was significantly different from France's *dirigisme*. Although the government was an integral part of economic management, leading roles were played by societal actors, such as banks, industrial management, and labor. These societal actors developed cooperative relationships amongst themselves to minimize disturbances caused by cyclical economic downturns while pursuing long-term economic development. In this arrangement, the most important government actor was the central bank, the Bundesbank. The bank's biggest concern was the containment of inflation, which had been a major cause of political instability and the Nazis' ascent to power in the pre–World War II period. To counterbalance the inflationary pressure derived from the overvalued currency and wage increase, the bank maintained a tight monetary policy. The Bundesbank also counteracted the Social Democratic government's late and short-lived use of Keynesian fiscal policy after the mid-1960s.[10] Instead, in order to stabilize society, (West) Germany maintained a comprehensive social welfare system derived from nineteenth-century social policy, which covered such various areas as pensions, unemployment, and healthcare, while remaining flexible enough to contain cost increases.[11] As for regulations, although the government itself did not maintain restrictive regulatory measures, quasi-public organizations, such as industrial and labor associations, engaged in coordinating activities and steered companies away from price competition and toward quality competition.[12] German capitalism also included extra-market factors that imposed costs on economic activities.

Japan's post–World War II politicoeconomic arrangement is similar to that of the other advanced industrial countries. Although the Japanese government's current budget deficit is prohibitively large, Japan's government spending expansion started later than that of the other advanced industrial countries. During the mid-1950s, spurred on by the demand generated by the Korean War, the Japanese economy began to recover from its wartime destruction, and achieved rapid economic development until the currency appreciation and oil price increases of the 1970s. During the rapid economic development period, the government maintained a fiscally conservative stance, and financial resources were allocated mainly for economic development, leaving social overhead capital undeveloped and frustrating the general public. In response to this, in the early 1970s, the LDP government began to engage in expansionary fiscal policies, particularly through increases in spending on public works. In the same period, the government changed its minimalist approach to social welfare, expanding the public pension and national healthcare systems.[13] With regard to the regulatory aspects, while the Japanese government's involvement was much less directive than that of the French government in the same period, it still played an important role in enacting export-led economic development measures, whose major component was the minimization of price competition among domestic manufacturers and an emphasis on quality competition, as found in West Germany, as well as the channeling of financial resources to the developmental industries.

Since each of the advanced industrial countries had different economic ideologies and historical backgrounds, their post–World War II politicoeconomic arrangements were varied. For example, these arrangements developed earlier in the United States and Britain than in France, (West) Germany, and Japan. The state played a much more active role in microeconomic management in France than in other countries. The use of Keynesianism was extensive in Britain and the United States whereas (West) Germany (and Japan until the early 1970s) was fiscally conservative. The expansion of social welfare began very late in Japan. Government regulation in (West) Germany was indirect while the government maintained regulatory rules in the United States. Despite these variations, however, the politicoeconomic arrangements did share common features. The arrangements were designed to increase social stability through government spending and/or wealth redistribution for the society as a whole, as well as through governmental and nongovernmental rules and regulations. This stability contributed to the stable development of capitalism by containing the development of Communism from the Left and Fascism from the Right, but not without costs. The maintenance of the redistributive programs increased the size of the government spending, and, therefore, imposed extra-market costs. Also, since the arrangement restricted market competition, it impeded upon the efficient allocation of goods and services, transferring this cost to business firms and consumers. Therefore, as long as the economy was expanding, each country could afford to maintain this system. Yet, since the 1970s, international and domestic economic factors—such as the increase in the price of oil, the development of international economic competition, and the accumulating budget deficit—made it difficult for each country to maintain its arrangement, generating pressure for the reform of the government—the central component of the arrangement—in the advanced industrial countries, including Japan.

Government Reform as Civil Service Reform: Bureaucracy under Stress

Since the major purpose of post–World War II government expansion was to provide goods and services to society, the quality of government operation was not a major concern. Intrigued by the worsening condition of government finances, which involved budget deficits, reformers around the world have kept the management of the bureaucracy, or civil service, under close scrutiny since the late 1970s. Critics of civil service management see its difference from private sector management as problematic. Since private sector firms are exposed to fierce market competition, their managers are driven to utilize managerial flexibility in order to cut the cost of operation, while strengthening the marketability of their products by improving product quality and customer satisfaction. In contrast, government operation in general faces no competition. Whereas a private sector company's business performance can ultimately be measured by its product sales or services, a public sector company usually lacks such clear-cut benchmarks, decreasing the urgency of performance enhancement among civil service managers. Their managers also have little personal incentives to improve operational performance; civil service managers expect to benefit little from better quality of service or improved customer satisfaction. Of course, it is essential for managers to maintain certain levels of quality, because citizens' dissatisfaction with service prompts incumbent elected officials to take action against the managers. However, managers in the public sector expect much less reward from improving their organizational performance than their counterparts in the private sector.

In addition to the lack of incentives, civil service managers face constraints that prevent them from making improvements. Civil service is heavily bounded by rules and precedents, limiting managerial flexibility. This forces civil service managers to improve quality by drastically changing the operation of existing services or introducing new services. Constraints on the improvement of organizational performance are also coupled with those on cost cutting. Since operational costs are predetermined, managers have little incentives to cut costs. Oftentimes, cutting costs actually works against their agency's interests, because by demonstrating that it operates under the estimated budget, an agency undermines its claim to secure or increase budget allocation in future budget-making processes. Also, downsizing the labor force is more difficult in the civil service sector than in the private sector, since unions in the former tend to be more coherently organized than those in the latter.[14]

In Britain, basing their approach on neoliberal ideology, Margaret Thatcher and her Conservative government took on civil service reform from the late 1970s as a part of her effort to roll back the state, which, in her eyes, had become too big and costly to operate. In addition to civil service reform measures such as the privatization of state-owned enterprises, government performance reviews, and introduction of private sector management to the public sector, the Thatcher government embarked on a drastic organizational reform, called the Next Steps initiative, in the late 1980s. The most essential measure of Next Steps was agencification, which separated the operational service–provision function of the government from its executive advisory function. Next Steps created semiautonomous agencies that maintained contract-based business relations with their parent departments and a high degree of internal managerial flexibility. Civil service reform in Britain involved government reorganization that significantly reduced the size of the government bureaucracy.[15]

In the United States, the Clinton administration embarked on a civil service management reform movement in the early 1990s. The movement, whose major slogan was "reinventing government," called for the establishment of a new government that cost less and worked better. Similar to the other civil service reforms discussed above, this reform movement initially proposed reform measures designed to ease excessive rule-orientation, improve customer satisfaction, increase managerial flexibility, and cut down unnecessary government operations, which was consistent with a new dominant idea of public administrations—new public management (NPM). Reflecting the rapid development of information technology in the 1990s, the movement came to include the effective use of information technology in government operation as an important reinvention feature. This movement significantly reduced the size of the civilian federal government labor force and transferred government functions from the federal government to state and local governments. Yet, since the administration faced a Congress controlled by the opposition party, the reform movement did not achieve a drastic enough transformation of the government to be characterized as true government reinvention.[16]

In France, civil service reform has been underdeveloped. As discussed in the next section of this chapter, the French government has taken significant steps toward regulatory reform, including privatization and deregulation, but the bureaucracy's core operation's dedication to social solidarity and egalitarianism—fundamental values of French Republicanism—has been left unchanged. As of 1996, the ratio of civil service employees to total members of the labor force was higher in France than in other major industrialized countries, including Germany, Britain, and the United States, and there was no sign of a major reduction. Furthermore, in the name of state secrecy, a great deal of information on the management of the bureaucracy was protected from public scrutiny. From the late 1980s, prime ministers have made a series of civil service reform attempts to improve the quality of the service, but none of them changed the fundamental format of the bureaucracy. For example, a recent attempt to consolidate and streamline the tax bureaucracy in the early 2000s did not achieve any substantive results.[17]

Civil service reform had been a popular political agenda in (West) Germany since the 1960s, well before it had achieved popularity in other countries, but reform attempts brought about no significant changes in the Weberian hierarchical civil service.[18] NPM, or new steering model, style civil service reform began in Germany's local governments in the early 1990s.[19] With the relocation of the capital to Berlin after the reunification, some functions of the federal government were transferred to local and other peripheral government organizations, and the federal government was downsized. In the late 1990s, changes were made to civil service employment and government accounting to give government management more flexibility.[20] Civil service reform in Germany has been gradual and incremental, lacking a flashy British-style transformation of civil service management.

As exemplified in these instances, civil service reform aimed at reducing costs, increasing managerial flexibility, and improving customer service has been in vogue across the world. Although Japan has been slow in pursuing full-scale civil service reform, these aspects have still been important factors in Japanese government reforms. One of the important goals of the Nakasone reform in the 1980s was the downsizing of the government through the privatization of government corporations. Through its privatization, NTT was given managerial flexibility, though it continued to be under heavy regulatory scrutiny due to its dominance in the market. Reformers took advantage of the public's frustration with labor dispute–laden JNR's notorious customer service by promoting its privatization. The Hashimoto reform in the 1990s fundamentally reformatted the government structure. It reduced the number of government ministries and agencies to ease bureaucratic redundancies and jurisdictional intra-government conflict while increasing the number of political appointees. Influenced by the Next Steps initiative in Britain, the reform also included agencification of government organizations, albeit to a far lesser degree than the agencification in Britain.[21] The Koizumi reform pressed Japan Post and JH to adopt private sector management style, including privatization. Thus, civil service reform has been an important component of government reform in Japan. Civil service reform in Japan has been much slower and much less extensive than in Britain, but is comparable to that experienced in the United States, France, and Germany.

Government Reform as Regulatory Reform

Another important component of contemporary government reform is regulatory reform that changes the role of the government in the economy. Whereas civil service reform changes the organizational format of the government, regulatory reform changes the format of the government's interactions with citizens, especially business actors.[22] Like civil service reform, regulatory reform stormed across the world, especially in advanced industrial countries. As common forces for regulatory change, Steven Vogel identifies "market shifts, the export of U.S. regulation, and macro economic changes."[23] In the contemporary economy, the market rapidly changes as a result of technological developments, particularly in information processing. Since government regulation cannot aptly keep up with market changes, it imposes obsolete regulatory constraints on market activities and obstructs economic development. The inadequacy of government regulation therefore compels political actors to call for regulatory change, especially the reduction of government regulation. As pressure for regulatory change was growing, the U.S. government succeeded in generating a competitive market mechanism through deregulation, and the U.S. model of deregulation has since become an ideological benchmark for regulatory reform, diffused across the world, and accelerated demand for regulatory change. As for macroeconomic change, the pace of economic development slowed down in the 1970s, but demand for government service continued to increase. This constrained government finances and led political actors to explore the reduction of the government's role in the market through regulatory reform.[24] These forces laid the basis for regulatory reform, which included various reform measures, particularly privatization and deregulation.

Because of its direct role in the economy, the government's operation of business—exemplified by the government enterprises in telecommunications, postal service, and electric utilities that exist(ed) in most advanced industrial countries—is likely to be a prime target of regulatory reform. In many cases, government enterprises possess monopoly status and therefore face no competitors. Even if government enterprises are not monopolies, they are likely to have advantages over private sector competitors, such as better tax status, rules targeted to punish their competitors, and their connections with fellow government regulators. Politically, the government operation has been justified because of national security. For example, the maintenance of telecommunications networks is crucial in case of domestic insurgency and external conflict. In the logic of the market economy, government operation has been justified as a solution to prevent the problem of natural monopolies and the inefficient allocation of resources in industries where competitive market mechanisms do not operate properly. However, technological development has made many of the causes of natural monopolies obsolete, such as the traditional role of high launching costs as market entrance barriers, thereby undermining the rationale of the government's operations. In addition to this economic logic, and perhaps more importantly, government leaders have utilized the logic of government finance to rationalize their pursuit of privatization. Since privatization involves the sale of government shares of government enterprises, the government gains revenue. Also, if a government enterprise is experiencing financial difficulties, its privatization excuses the government of costly operations. Either way, privatization eases the financial burden that a government accumulates as a result of macroeconomic change, making it a popular regulatory reform measure. Thus, privatization of government enterprises has become a major tool of government reform.

Government control of market activities is not limited to the government's direct operation of business, however. To ensure social stability, the government imposes strict rules regarding market entrance, operation, and exit on industries closely related to society's basic infrastructure, such as communications, transportation, and public utilities. Essentially, deregulation is simply a regulatory reform measure that abolishes or eases these strict rules. The same economic logic used for the privatization of government enterprises is applicable to strict regulations. Like other government operations, the usage of strict rules has been justified as helping to avoid market failures resulting from the tendency of these industries' structures to prevent competitive market mechanisms from operating. However, technological progress and other economic changes have led to the application of strict rules to certain industries, making the rules a government failure that prohibits the efficient allocations of resources. Though this economic logic has been an important rationale for deregulation, the logic itself was not a driving force behind the enactment of deregulatory measures. Martha Derthick and Paul Quirk articulate the impact of the political dynamics that transformed economic logic into a political reform symbol that promoted deregulation in the United States, the first country to pursue such deregulation.[25] Since deregulation is not a simple application of economic logic, its actual format may not significantly obey traditional economic rules, and deregulation is also often accompanied by reregulation to allow for the development of competition in newly deregulated markets, particularly in the transition period. Deregulation does not simply mean the abolition of regulatory rules; it changes the format of regulation to make market entry and exit easier in heavily regulated industries.

Unlike other advanced industrialized countries, the United States has few state-owned enterprises. Privatization took the form of contracting-out of government operations, and its implication to regulatory reform was therefore rather minimal. However, the United States was the birthplace of the deregulation movement, and deregulation was widespread. The airline and trucking industries were deregulated to introduce competition in the late 1970s, and new air and trucking carriers flooded their respective markets in the 1980s. In telecommunications, the Federal Communications Commission (FCC) began to limit its regulations on basic services in the 1980s, and fierce competition emerged in a long-distance telephone service market formerly dominated by AT&T.[26] The deregulation movement continued to develop in the 1980s. The Glass–Steagall Act of 1933 that separated commercial banking from investment banking was repealed, and the Telecommunications Act of 1996 further liberated the telecommunications market by forcing local telecommunications carriers to allow other carriers access to their networks at a relatively low cost. In the late 1990s, electric utilities were deregulated in California, and price decontrol was implemented. These deregulatory measures invited new investments in these areas and contributed to the prosperity of the United States in the 1990s. However, since these deregulation measures were incomplete due to political pressures, they ultimately brought about the infamous Enron scandal and the IT bubble.[27]

Regulatory reform in Britain was equally drastic and widespread, but more comprehensive, incorporating both privatization and deregulation. In the 1980s, the Thatcher administration privatized British Telecom and liberalized the telecommunications service market, pushing for competition among carriers.[28] In the early 1990s, the government made British Telecom's local networks open to other carriers for interconnection. Similarly, British Airways was privatized and restrictions on entry and prices were eased, leading airline industry liberalization in the European Union (EU).[29] In finance, Britain engaged in the fundamental liberalization of financial activities through the so-called Big Bang and the 1986 Financial Services Act.[30] Also, market deregulation, accompanied by privatization of government corporations, significantly progressed in public utilities.[31] In Britain, regulatory reform, like civil service reform, was thorough, minimizing the service provision function of the state while emphasizing its regulatory functions.

Unlike Britain, France was known for its state intervention in the economy, and the Socialist government in the early 1980s continued this tradition by nationalizing or acquiring the majority of shares of firms in strategic economic sectors—steel, heavy manufacturing, electronics, and the like—crucial for economic development, as well as most financial institutions.[32] Yet, the establishment of the Cabinet by a right-wing coalition that loosely adhered to neoconservative free market ideology in 1986 turned the nationalization trend and privatized major industrial and financial government-owned corporations between 1986 and 1988.[33] The privatization of telecommunications was rather slow. The telecommunications operation organization was established as France Telecom within a government ministry in 1988, which was separated from the ministry in 1991. The government continued to own all France Telecom's shares until it began to sell them in 1997.[34]

With regard to deregulation, the French government recognized early on the importance of flexible financial activities and embarked on financial liberalization in the early 1980s, abolishing major restrictions on financial activities, such as foreign exchange restrictions, interest rate controls, and so on.[35] Deregulation in other areas, however, was slow. France Telecom did not face competition until 1998, when the EU policy forced the French government to liberalize the telecommunications market.[36] Liberalization in electricity and transportation, meanwhile, did not progress, despite the EU's policy for liberalization.[37] Regulatory reform had mixed results in France.

Though not known for drastic regulatory reform, regulatory reform in (West) Germany preceded that in Britain by about two decades. The Adenauer administration began to reduce the government share of major companies, including Volkswagen, in the late 1950s.[38] However, Germany has been slow in privatizing other state-owned enterprises, with the exception of state-owned enterprises in former East Germany, which were denationalized after the unification. Even though reform in the telecommunications regulations was on the political agenda since the mid-1980s, the (partial) privatization did not occur until 1996, when the German government sold off about a quarter shares of Deutsche Telekom, established in the previous year and based on Deutsche Bundespost Telekom.[39] Deutsche Post, which owned Deutsche Postbank, was partially privatized in 1999,[40] but public sector banks—Landesbanken and Sparkassen—operated by Land (state) governments continued to occupy a large share of banking business.[41]

Deregulation also proceeded slowly in Germany. In finance, since restrictions on banking activities had been minimal, making banking deregulation less important, reform was centered around stock market regulatory reform. In order to stimulate the development of various stock-related services, new rules and a new regulatory agency were established after a series of struggles between the federal and state governments in the early 1990s.[42] In telecommunications, as in France, the liberalization of the local telecommunications service market started late in 1998 as a result of EU directives. Similarly, EU policy prompted the progress of deregulation in transport service markets.[43] In the electric utility industry, discussions regarding liberalization at the EU level in the early 1990s prompted negotiations among various stakeholders, such as federal government ministries, local governments, and electric utility companies, and a compromise was reached in the mid-1990s. Competition, therefore, slowly began to develop in the market in the late 1990s.[44]

Regarding regulatory reform, Japan does not lag far behind other advanced industrial countries. Regulatory reform in telecommunications, involving the privatization of government monopolies and the liberalization of the telecommunications service markets began early in the 1980s, roughly concurrent with reforms in Britain and far ahead of those in France and Germany. Although the Japanese government has neither completely broken up NTT nor disposed of its NTT shares, the pace of liberalization is faster in Japan than in France and Germany, where France Telecom or Deutsche Telekom still dominates their respective domestic markets. A great deal of financial liberalization has also been enacted in Japan, dismantling interest rate regulations and abolishing the framework that separated various financial services. Government-operated postal savings continues to occupy a large share of personal banking, often cited as the anomaly of Japanese finance, but its share is comparable to Germany's *Land*-based public banks. In transportation and public utilities, liberalization is slowly and steadily proceeding in Japan, as is the case in France and Germany. Progress in regulatory reform in Japan, therefore, is comparable to that in other advanced industrial countries.

Patterns of Government Reform in the Advanced Industrial Countries

Since the late 1970s, government reform has been in vogue across advanced industrial countries. The general direction of reform is basically the same—the infusion of private sector logic into government activities in civil service reform and the transferring of government activities to the private sector, albeit often accompanied by a new regulatory format. The countries, including Japan, share the same basic direction; however, the pace and extensiveness of reform has varied. Britain (and New Zealand) engaged in systematic government reform. Though often far-reaching, reform in the United States has been less systematic and ad hoc, as exemplified in the big role played by the courts. France, known for its statist tradition, has gone through a fundamental transformation of government activities toward decontrol, but the state maintains control over the economic activities that it deems essential for national welfare. In Germany, no flashy radical reform has been implemented, but reform has proceeded slowly and incrementally. In this section, I identify patterns of government reform and examine its relationship to two institutional aspects of the state—state embeddedness in the economy and the state decision-making structure—through which similar global economic and ideological pressures are filtered. Since the main purpose of the formulation of a typology of government reform using Britain, the United States, France, and Germany is to place Japan's reform in a comparative context, the typology is designed not to develop a comprehensive and precise characterization of each country's political economy, but rather to concisely sketch its essence.

In contemporary government reform in the advanced industrial countries, state actors, such as elected and nonelected government officials in the leadership, play essential roles. Yet, the formulation and implementation of reform is not a simple linear process whereby autonomous state actors transform internally formulated reform policy into authoritative action. On the contrary, since government reform involves changes in various segments of both state and societal organizations, state actors extensively interact with each other and with the societal actors upon whom government reform affects negatively or positively. Therefore, the progress of government reform depends upon the decision-making structure of the state, particularly its fragmentation. Various political institutional factors determine the degree of the structure's fragmentation. Formal macro-institutional arrangements, such as the separation of powers, parliamentary/presidential system, and federalism, are the basis of the decision-making structure, for example, and therefore influence the degree of fragmentation. Yet other factors, such as the strength of party discipline, the internal coherence of the bureaucracy, and the number of veto points, are important as well. Different countries have different sources of fragmentation, but, in general, the degree of fragmentation impacts the coherence of reform results in each country.

The other institutional factor that greatly influences the progress of government reform is the embeddedness of the state in the economy, roughly measured by how deeply and stably the state is integrated into the networks of economic actors. The backbone of the embeddedness is dominant economic ideology. In general, liberal economic ideology deemphasizes the involvement of the state in market activities, whereas nonliberal ideologies, such as the ideologies of statism (France) and social market economics (Germany), are more tolerant of involvement. Even in liberal countries, there exist cooperative (or corrupt) and stable relationships between the government and business.[45] Yet, government–business relations are susceptible to changes in exogenous factors, such as the change of the government party, major adjustments in legal interpretation, and competition among interest groups, making the state less embedded in the economy but more vulnerable to reform forces. In contrast, in nonliberal economies, government and business maintain stable channels of communication and engage in two-way interactions, increasing the relative importance of endogenous interactions and making the state more embedded in the economy. The embeddedness makes the state an integral part of the government reform process, and generally enables the state to at least partially preserve its role in the reform outcome.

Based on these two institutional aspects, we can construct a general typology of the mode of government reform shown in figure 1.1. The British state has a less fragmented decision-making structure. Both of the two dominant political parties have relatively strong party discipline, in which leaders are expected to exercise strong leadership, particularly when the party is in power. Strong party discipline is combined with the virtually unicameral parliamentary system, in which power is concentrated in the prime minister and the cabinet. The bureaucracy is coherently organized but subservient to the political leadership. The centralized government structure also makes it difficult for local interests to resist the prime minister's pursuit of policy initiatives. This decision-making structure provides the executive with a suitable environment for its coherent pursuit of fundamental policy changes, such as government reform.[46] As for the embeddedness of the state in the economy, Britain's long tradition of economic liberalism that deemphasizes the state's role has prevented the state from being integrated into the economic system. The state's involvement in economic activities has been largely macroeconomic, as exemplified by the frequent use of monetary policy to affect economic activities.[47] The state leaves micromanagement to business and labor. With regard to government reform, the low level of embeddedness means that state actors are free from barriers that impede their pursuit of reform. Thus, the British state has a coherent decision-making

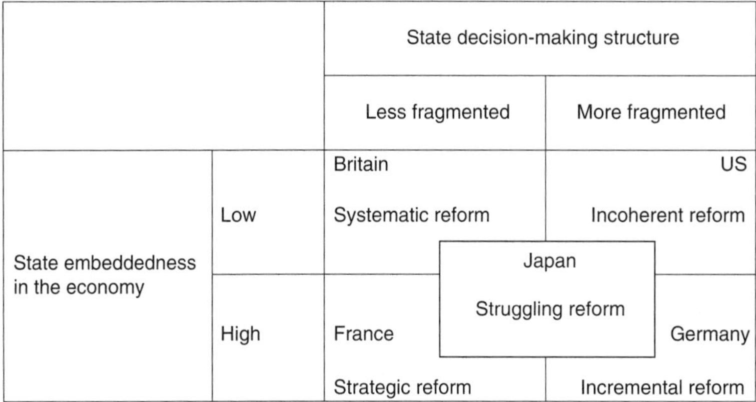

Figure 1.1 Patterns of government reform.

structure and a low level of embeddedness. In this setting, the state enacts coherent and systematic government reforms, as shown in the implementation of the Next Steps initiative, the speedy privatization of government corporations, and the comprehensive deregulations to free up economic activities.

The United States shares a liberal economic tradition with Britain, and the government is therefore expected to play a minimal role in the economy. The government's active involvement in economic activities is mostly macroeconomic; the Federal Reserve controls monetary policy to pursue economic stability and the executive and legislative branches use fiscal policy to stimulate the economy. The government is involved in microeconomic management mainly to correct market failures, such as monopolies, public goods, and externalities, which inhibit the efficient allocation of resources. Although the government provides subsidies and trade protections to specific industries, it does so in an ad hoc manner in response to political pressure. Thus, the state is not deeply embedded in the economy, helping government reform to develop. However, the U.S. state lacks the coherent decision-making structure found in Britain. In the central government, the lack of strong party discipline in both of the two parties complicates the decision-making process, resulting in constant battles both within the legislature and between the legislature and the executive. The strong judiciary provides societal actors with the opportunity to influence the process. Added to these concerns is a system of federalism that leaves individual states significant room to make policy.[48] Within this setting, the government reform movement has to go through complex interactions, and government reform in the United States is incoherent in that it lacks comprehensive systemic change, although it often involves sweeping changes.

The French state is the direct opposite of the U.S. state; the state is deeply embedded in the economy and has a much less fragmented decision-making structure. The French state has a strong and coherent bureaucracy at its core, which is the basis of its embeddedness. During the post–World War II reconstruction period, the bureaucracy played a leading role in promoting economic development, setting up strategic plans for industrial transformation and channeling financial resources to industries and firms deemed essential for economic development. The French state deeply penetrated micro-business management, not only through the provision of advice and incentives, but also through the transfer of personnel, called *pantouflage*. However, state actions were accommodating business interests, developing stable networks between the state and business. The elite core networks served as the center of the decision-making structure, cutting across state and business sectors.[49] Combined with this was the formal government structure, in which strong centripetal forces operated through the dual executive and local governments' dependence on the central government. Thus, the French state has internal and external environments suitable for policy change. Therefore, after the state recognized the problems with its nationalization policy in the early 1980s, it swiftly changed its position to emphasize liberalization, and strategically pursued a policy of liberalization while maintaining state control over essential economic activities.

The German state shares the high degree of embeddedness seen in France, but its mode of embeddedness is different. The basic characterization of the German state is "an enabling state," as compared with the French strong state. The German state has neither the authority nor the resources to allow it to selectively intervene in economic activities. Yet, unlike in Britain or the United States, where the state's importance in economic activities is deemphasized and the state and business form rather ad hoc and often adversarial relationships, the state has been a vital part of economic activities in Germany. The state has been supporting business development by spending on research and development, as well as providing social welfare and contributing to stable labor relations. Furthermore, the state has helped develop and maintain semi-public, self-governing organizations that coordinate and mediate social interests. Thus, the German state is deeply embedded in the economy, but it has an extremely fragmented (or diffused) decision-making structure. The most notable feature of this is cooperative federalism, which gives power to *Länder* (state) governments that also wield influence in decision making at the federal level through their representatives in the upper house: Bundesrat. The electoral system by which representatives are elected to the lower house, Budestag, promotes a multiparty system, and the chancellor is likely to be chosen based upon coalitions among parties, thereby weakening the chancellor's leadership. Furthermore, the government shares power with independent agencies, such as the Bundesbank.[50] Because of the highly business-friendly nature of the German state, it seems likely that government reform supposedly consistent with business interest progresses rapidly and comprehensively. However, this highly fragmented and diffused structure of state decision-making slows down policy formulation and provides multiple veto points. As a result, government reform in Germany is slow and incremental.

Thus, because of the degree of government embeddedness and the state structure, government reform is, in essence, systematic in Britain, strategic in France, incoherent in the United States, and incremental in Germany. Government reform in Japan, however, includes a little bit of each of these features. Japan's reformers tried to comprehensively transform government operations, resulting in Prime Minister Hashimoto's reorganization of the government. Also, government reform in Japan has always included strategic elements. Prime Minister Nakasone called his government reform a comprehensive restructuring of the post–World War II political regime [*Sengo Seiji no Sōkessan*] and emphasized it as a national project. Similarly, Prime Minister Koizumi called his reform a structural reform designed to fundamentally change Japan. Despite political leaders' strong determination to pursue reform, however, the progress of reform varied among different issues, as typified by the different speed of reform in telecommunications and the postal business. These two issues belong to the same ministry's jurisdiction, and are under the heavy influence of the same LDP group. Reforms in these issues have a similar magnitude in terms of its impact on the economy; telecommunications is one of the leading industries while the postal business includes postal savings that absorb a significant portion of personal savings. In spite of the similarities, these two followed very different paths. Telecommunications reform started early in the 1980s and made significant progress, but reform in the postal business advanced very slowly, although it had been under heavy reform pressure (particularly

from commercial banks concerned with the growth of postal savings).
Also, as was found in telecommunications, a big change that involved
various political and business actors was followed by rather incremental change in which reform evolved based upon the interactions
among a narrow range of policy actors. To sum up the nature of government reform, it is a struggling reform in which leaders intend to
pursue comprehensive and strategic reform, and their partial success
results in incoherent reform, accompanied by incremental changes.

This struggling nature of reform politics in Japan derives from its
institutional settings. The Japanese state's decision-making structure
is moderately fragmented. Japan has a parliamentary system of government, seemingly concentrating power in the prime minister, and
the executive branch does not have to face the strong judiciary found
in the United States. Yet, unlike in Britain, the government party lacks
strong party discipline. In the LDP, which has been in power for most
of period since 1955, intraparty faction politics play an important role
and weaken the leadership of the LDP president/prime minister.
Since the mid-1990s, the LDP has been forming a coalition government, and this continues to undermine the LDP leadership. This leadership fragmentation is reflected in the low degree of coordination
within the Japanese bureaucracy, although Japanese bureaucracy
boasts a high degree of autonomy comparable to that of the French
bureaucracy. With regard to the relationship between the central and
local governments, the Japanese state does not have the high degree
of centrism of the British and French states, and local politics are
important, particularly in big prefectures such as Tokyo and Osaka.
Yet, it does not have a formal system of federalism, and the central
government is important in reallocating resources across the nation.
Thus, the Japanese state maintains a decision-making structure that
includes two-way interactions between the center and the periphery.

The Japanese state is deeply embedded in the economy. LDP and
business leaders are in constant communication; political leaders try to
include business interests in policymaking, and business leaders
include the national interest as an important element when they make
recommendations. This is an important part of the embeddedness,
but the more extensive and constant interactions are held between the
bureaucracy and business. In the policy formulation process, representatives from trade associations are included as members of policy
deliberation councils (*shingikai*) and given the opportunity to insert
their interests. Informally, bureaucrats and business leaders constantly
exchange information and form symbiotic relationships. This embeddedness is different from the state-led embeddedness in France in that

the bureaucracy and business are interactive; the bureaucracy's direction toward business activities depends on businesses' cooperation. Yet, this is also different from the society-led embeddedness in Germany in that it is much more segmented, with vertical communications remaining much stronger than horizontal communications, making it very difficult to coordinate across different sets of bureaucracy–business nexus. As characterized by vertical administration (*tatewari gyōsei*), each segment of the state–business nexus is tightly organized, and making policies that span these segments, such as government reform, is therefore very difficult.

The Japanese state has a patterned decision-making structure, and it is deeply embedded in the economy, albeit in a very segmented manner. This is the essence of the institutional characteristics that have forced Japanese government reform to struggle. Particularly for the progress of government reform, the existence of two separate types of state–society networks, with the state deeply embedded in each, is important. One type is the distributive network, consisting of the government bureaucracy and businesses dependent upon government expenditure. Since contemporary government reform seeks to reduce the government's involvement in economic activities and weaken the networks, the members of the distributive networks fight against reform. The developmental networks, however, promote government reform because they believe that the rectification of government excesses in the economy will promote economic development. Contemporary government reform in Japan is a tug of war between these two opposing forces. The state is enmeshed with these two networks, and this is the reason why government reform consistently involves showdowns between reformist and old guard politicians.

Conclusion

The occurrence of government reform is not peculiar to Japan; government reform attempts have occurred in several other major advanced industrial countries, including Britain, the United States, Germany, and France, in addition to Japan. Since the end of World War II, each of the countries developed a similar, if not identical, politicoeconomic arrangement, which prompted each government to play an active role in the economy and allowed it to expand its size. Although this arrangement provided each country with social stability, it also imposed economic costs and constraints on economic activities. Government reforms, including civil service and regulatory reforms, that began in the 1970s and 1980s in these countries were attempts to contain government expansion. In each dimension of government reform, the progress of Japanese reform was not, as some have argued, considerably slower than that in each of the other countries. Although Japan's government reform did struggle, the same is true of reform in each of the other countries. Nonetheless, Japan's government reform had a distinctive pattern of interactions that involved confrontations between reformers and old guard. This stems from the two institutional factors—a diffused but patterned state decision-making structure, and the state's segmented embeddedness in the economy. I further explain the development of the dual state and its current structure in the next chapter to lay the foundation for a case analysis using the concept of the dual state.

Chapter 2

The Politics of the Dual State

As discussed in Chapter 1, Japan's government reform is neither far ahead of nor far behind reforms in other advanced industrial countries. In general, I characterize Japan's government reform as struggling. Reformist leaders' intention to implement comprehensive reform, as found in Britain, was aborted by resistance from bureaucrats and politicians, whereas fundamental reform, such as privatization and deregulation, progressed significantly in certain policy areas. This mode of reaction to reform pressure is explained by the institutional setting, particularly the moderately fragmented decision-making structure and the (high but segmented) embeddedness of the state in the economy. In this chapter, I further examine Japan's government reform in the post–World War II historical context.

The reform movement in Japan surged concurrently with the rise of neoconservative ideology in Britain and the United States, and Japanese reformers sought to achieve the same goal of reducing the size of the government and its role in the economy, leading to resistance among bureaucrats preferring the status quo. Although Japan's reformers shared a similar reform thrust with British and U.S. neoconservative reformers, reform movement was deep rooted in post–World War II politics and political economics in Japan. To demonstrate this, in the first section I identify two fundamental elements—development and distribution—that laid the basis of political stability for countries that suffered from wartime destruction. In the second section, I provide an overview of the LDP government's political trajectory in coping with social instability up until the late 1970s. In the third section, I explain that the dual state, developed through political interactions through the trajectory, is at the core of reform politics. In examining the dynamics of reform, I focus on telecommunications, postal business, and transportation, each of which went through a significant transformation as a result of government reform. Therefore, in the fourth section, I explain each industry's fundamental characteristics and connection to LDP politics, and sum up my argument in the conclusion.

Development and Distribution in Germany, France, and Japan after World War II

As discussed in Chapter 1, government reforms that came into vogue in advanced industrial countries were largely reactions to the government expansion inherent in the politicoeconomic arrangement that developed after the post–World War II period to generate economic and political stability. In the early twentieth century, optimism about the self-regulating market mechanism began to be questioned, and radical solutions to economic problems were implemented, as evidenced by the emergence of militaristic and autocratic governance in Germany and Japan. Although Communists did not seize power in the five advanced industrial countries—the United States, Britain, Germany, France, and Japan—with the exception of East Germany under Soviet occupation, Communist/Socialist movements did persist in the post–World War II period. Furthermore, left-wing radicals were likely to increase their influence, taking advantage of the social confusion following the war. The internal threat of radicalism was combined by the establishment of the Soviet Union, which provided an alternative to capitalism by succeeding in rapid economic development in the early period (though this development did involve Stalinist terror politics). In the early period after World War II, overcoming the potential of radical solutions based on the remains of the Right and the optimism of the Left became the most important issue for the governments of advanced industrial countries.

The proper way in which to establish political stability in the face of the radical solution was also an important issue during the early post–World War II period for West Germany, France, and Japan, each of which had been devastated by the war. For West Germany, the impoverished economy and the establishment of the East German Communist regime posed a threat to political stability. Though France was on the winning side of the war, its political situation was no better; the Fourth Republic established after France's liberation from Nazi Germany was very unstable and eventually collapsed. Similarly, Allied bombing destroyed Japan, and poverty became an important problem as Socialists and Communists, recovering from wartime oppression, began to be active. One of the key ingredients for overcoming the political instability was U.S. commitment to prevent the radical solutions of the Right and Left. The United States provided massive economic aid to these countries to help stabilize them, and developed alliances with them to cope with the development of the Soviet bloc.

However, each of these three countries needed to find ways to establish political stability, and, in this regard, (economic) development and (re-)distribution were important aspects. Development refers to the increase of national wealth, so that citizens have a better living standard, and development sets up the general environment for the maintenance of the capitalist system by eliminating one of the most important elements that helps radical movements to develop, poverty. Because relative deprivation is the source of political stability, development itself cannot generate political stability unless the wealth created by development is distributed among social segments; radicals utilize highly unequal distribution of income as a tool to recruit and mobilize the masses. Even after the states achieved economic recovery from wartime destruction, development and distribution remained important in the political dynamics related to the economy. Political leaders sought economic development, measured not only by growth in Gross Domestic Product (or other economic indicators of the size of a national economy) but also by increases in investment, international trade, and productivity; the leaders were concerned with distributive aspects, such as jobs, taxes, and social security. Development and distribution are important ingredients for the development of political stability and politics in general, but Germany, France, and Japan used different approaches to achieve high economic development and balanced distribution.

The French approach to development and distribution revolved around the state. In the early post–World War II period, France's approach to economic development was highly interventionist. The state's planning commission formulated and implemented a series of plans, each of which identified industries that should lead national economic development and that should therefore be protected from international competition. The state channeled financial resources to these industries through state-controlled financial institutions.[1] Similarly, the system for the distribution of wealth was centered around the state, albeit much less coherently than the system for development. Unlike in the United States, where the provision of social welfare was controversial, the state's role in guaranteeing a civil minimum, or the minimum means of subsistence, to citizens was widely accepted and expected in France.

To contain the growth of the Socialists, conservative parties in power until 1981 courted the rising middle class by supporting the development of a diverse array of social securities, including measures for unemployment, health care, and retirement. However, the actual operation of social security systems progressed in a much more fragmented way. Each social segment set up its own system, and while the state's contribution to each system varied, the state's general commitment to the distributive mechanism through social spending increased over time.[2] The developmental mechanism succeeded in bringing about wealth, which the patchwork distributive mechanism distributed among citizens. Of course, French politics in this period were not without disturbance, as shown by the collapse of the Fourth Republic in 1958 and May 1968 strikes. The system avoided the radical solutions of the Right and Left, however, and even the Socialist regime that took over power from the conservative coalition ended up embracing free market economics after its initial flirtation with Socialist experiments.

The West German approach to development and distribution is often characterized as that of a social market economy. Unlike in France, the state did not dominate economic activities; instead, the state, business, and labor developed consensual relationships in which they were willing to bear short-term costs in order to maintain stability and flexibly cope with changes in the economic environment. Business firms formed industry associations to iron out differences over specific issues, and acted coherently in negotiating with well-organized trade unions. This macro-stability was reinforced by codetermination in companies, in which representatives from labor participated in managerial decision-making. West German companies' reliance on loan financing also formed the basis of this cooperative system. In contrast to the equity financing found in the United States and Britain, in which companies were under heavy pressure from shareholders to maximize short-term profits, in West Germany's loan financing, large commercial banks channeled funding to companies based on long-term perspectives. This long-term stability-oriented arrangement enabled West Germany to achieve a quick recovery from wartime destruction in the 1950s, and brought about prosperity.

Since this mechanism for economic development was sensitive to labor's interests, it distributed wealth and generated the basis for political stability, reinforced by other social mechanisms. Cooperative federalism, in which rich states subsidized poor states, helped to reduce regional economic disparities, and the development of social welfare also led to the wealth being distributed among West Germans.

Germany has a long tradition of social welfare, dating back to Bismarck's days, but post–World War II Germany developed a comprehensive system of social welfare that covered unemployment, health care, and pensions. In the event of an emergency, West Germans would be entitled to generous welfare payments that would enable them to live comfortable lives. Thanks to these distributive mechanisms and political stability, West Germany avoided radical solutions.

Comparatively, Japan's approach to development and distribution was a mixture of the German and French approaches. Japan has separate systems of development and distribution, similar to those seen in France, and the developmental system is organized whereas the distributive system is less organized. However, contrary to the popular belief that the Japanese state engaged in French-style stage-led developmental policy, the Japanese approach to economic development has been based on consensual relationships between state and societal actors. As in the German system, business actors maintain long-term stable relationships, and distributive welfare functions are embedded in the developmental mechanism; business and labor form cooperative relations whereby job security and steady wage growth are ensured to minimize disturbances caused by radical labor movements. The coexistence of development and distribution is special to Japan's competitive export-oriented sectors, and less competitive parochial sectors neither enjoy industrial strength nor maintain company-based distributive arrangements. As a result, these parochial sectors are dependent on government protection and spending for both development and distribution. As shown in the next section, this mixed system developed through political interactions, and served to generate political stability to allow Japan to avoid radical solutions.

The Formation of the Japanese Dual State

Post–World War II Instability: From Fragmentation to Polarization

In the period following the defeat of World War II, Japan was politically and economically unstable. The U.S. occupation forces abolished the Emperor-centered governmental system, and installed a parliamentary system with popular sovereignty. Since parliamentary politics, albeit heavily constrained by the power of the emperor, existed in the prewar period, the systemic transition proceeded without disturbances challenging the legitimacy of U.S. occupation. Since the occupation reform kept the bureaucracy's power intact, bureaucrats engaged in policymaking relatively smoothly under the supervision of the occupation forces, but politics were unstable, and even the conservatives, who would eventually dominate Japanese politics for a very long time, were divided. Along with personal rivalries that persisted through the post–Word War II period, there existed other schisms, such as friction between politicians purged by the occupation forces for their cooperation with the military government and those who were not purged, as well as contention between life-time politicians whose career began before the end of the war and ex-bureaucrat politicians who were recruited after the war. As a result, the Democratic Party was formed by a group dissenting from the Liberal Party—the predominant conservative party—and the Reform party in 1954.[3]

On the other side of the political spectrum, leftists were quickly gaining influence with the end of the war; Socialist and Communist politicians were released from jail or allowed to return from exile when the occupation forces installed freedom of assembly and association. Labor movement gained momentum quickly, and union membership increased significantly, particularly in the government sector. However, the Left was no more coherent than the Right; deep-rooted ideological splits had persisted between the Socialist and Communist parties since the pre–World War II days, and the Socialist Party itself was internally divided between Left and Right wings. Although Socialists won the lower elections in 1947 and formed a coalition government, the Socialist-led government was short-lived. The coalition government included conservatives, and was therefore extremely fragile, but one of the major reasons for the Socialist leaders' weakness was their inability to control the coalition's left-wing faction. After the coalition's electoral defeat in 1949, the two factions intensified their ideological fight, and the Socialist Party split into two camps, Right Socialist and Left Socialist. Parallel to this fragmentation in leftist party politics, labor movement was splitting into three groups, each of which had close relations with either right-wing Socialists, left-wing Socialists, or Communists.[4]

This confusion on both sides of the political spectrum in the early 1950s was resolved in 1955, when, mediated by a business community concerned with the growth of socialist influence, the Liberal and Democratic parties merged to form the LDP after the Right and Left Socialists reunited as the Japan Socialist Party (JSP). This so-called 1955 system, in which the LDP ruled as a government party and faced the JSP as the largest opposition party, continued until 1993, when the LDP's dominance became much weaker and the JSP's influence diminished. In the early period of the 1955 system, the LDP and the

JSP engaged in very confrontational politics. The LDP sought to revise the constitution to make it more nationalistic, pursue rearmament, undermine left-wing union power, and change the electoral system in its favor. The JSP fought back by paralyzing parliamentary politics, and left-wing student organizations held massive demonstrations on the street. This political polarization reached a peak in 1960, when the Japanese government renewed the U.S.–Japan Security Treaty. Although the LDP passed the bill for the renewal, Prime Minister Kishi Nobusuke had to resign due to growing social turmoil, including the surrounding of the Diet by massive demonstrations of students, workers, and citizens.[5]

Though less fragmented than before, neither side of the political spectrum had coherence. Unlike the British Conservative Party, whose party leader exercised strong leadership in party management, the LDP was more like a coalition of factions loosely united against Socialism, and included a great deal of personal rivalries. Similarly, the Left still included a variety of ideologies, ranging from non-Socialist pacifism to pro-Soviet Communism, and lacked the strong organizational structure needed to absorb a wide variety of political and economic preferences and integrate them into a coherent voice, as found in labor in West Germany. Therefore, the polarization of politics developed around a specific issue. At this time, the Japanese public rather vividly remembered hardships during the war, as well as the chaos that followed the end of the war. Therefore, the Left successfully mobilized the public in response to the attempts to reverse the course of the postwar pacifist policy orientation made by some nationalistic conservative leaders who were rehabilitated from the purge that the U.S. occupation forces had imposed for their roles in the military government before the end of the war. The anti-conservative movement was accelerated by economic difficulties that put many of the Japanese into a state of poverty. Therefore, abandoning ideological assertion and shifting political emphasis toward economic development would help the LDP establish dominance in politics by avoiding politically sensitive issues and weakening the Left's base of support. This was exactly the strategy that the LDP took in the following decade.

Economic Development for Stability in the 1960s

Prime Minister Ikeda Hayato, who succeeded Kishi, abandoned an antagonistic approach to politics and took an accommodationist position. Reflecting the shift of the locus of politics and policy from ideology to economy, and recognizing economic growth that would provide wealth and employment as the basis of social and political stability, Ikeda implemented the Income Doubling Plan to stimulate economic development. In contrast to French planning in the same time period, which was formulated by the central planning commission and followed by the French government's direct channeling of funds to heavy industries, the Income Doubling Plan was more like a collection of strategies formulated through interactions between bureaucracies and business organizations in a bottom–up manner as well as confirmations of existing business practices. As its name indicates, the goal of the Plan was to double in real terms the size of the Japanese economy in ten years. While emphasizing private sector economic activities as the fundamental driving force of economic development, the Plan stipulated that the government implement measures to supplement and stabilize private sector economic activities, such as investment in social-overhead capital, the promotion of science and technology, and the creation of a stable business environment that would stimulate productivity growth and prevent excessive competition.[6] The Plan formulated before the establishment of the Ikeda cabinet was more like a statement designed to counter the JSP's approach to economic stabilization through a Socialist approach involving the nationalization of major industries. As many observers have discussed, the actual impact of the Plan on economic development is debatable; economic recovery began to develop preceding the Plan's formulation, and the driving force of economic development did not make substantive adjustments in response to the Plan.

However, the Plan demonstrated that the LDP government officially placed economic development as a political goal to achieve stability, setting aside politically volatile issues such as the revision of the constitution and rearmament. This orientation toward political stability was coupled with the acceleration of activities for economic development. Both government and business recognized the importance of international trade; the successful cultivation of export markets would bring in massive profits, but large-scale penetration into the domestic market by mighty foreign capital would be detrimental to Japanese businesses still in the developmental stage. Since Japan became a member of the General Agreement on Tariffs and Trade in the mid-1950s, the Japanese government needed to significantly liberalize imports and Japanese business needed to enhance its competitiveness. In some important industries, most notably automotives, private sector companies succeeded in achieving competitiveness without much assistance from the government. However, the government, particularly the Ministry of International Trade and

Industry (MITI), actively intervened in private sector activities by encouraging mergers for industrial consolidation, allocating scarce financial resources to firms and industries with high potentials for export growth and promoting technological innovation.[7] Since the MITI's policies were market conforming, these intervention measures were formulated and implemented in interactive ways, and the government and businesses maintained rather symbiotic relationships.

During this period, the Japanese economy achieved rapid development, often called the Japanese miracle, and Japanese business expanded phenomenally. Expansion in the sheer size of the economy provided the Japanese public with wealth. Since economic development was not only an economic goal but also a political one, and firms were both business and social entities, companies shared wealth among their employees, steadily raising workers' pay in accordance with the expansion of their businesses, rather than allocating disproportionately large amounts of wealth to a small number of executives—a practice liable to be attacked from leftist parties. Along with wealth, a large number of Japanese workers, particularly those in big businesses, obtained long-term job security because the expanding economy required companies to retain the labor force. Although labor disputes still continued to occur into the 1960s, economic development and a rather egalitarian distribution of wealth put away the economic causes for labor movements. Left-wing labor movements came to emphasize ideological causes, such as opposition to the revision of the constitution, the abandonment of the U.S.–Japan security alliance in favor of unarmed neutrality, and (re-)granting the right to strike to government workers whose unions formed the core of the left-wing labor movement. Left-wing unions were being marginalized, as was the Left in general.

In addition, the fruits of the economic development were distributed to the lesser-developed segments of society, which were important to the LDP-supporting bloc, through new policy measures, such as crop price controls for farmers, limitations on market competition for noncompetitive small businesses, and government spending on public works in rural areas.[8] Economic expansion and distributive measures taken by government and business not only undermined the basis for the Left, but also fortified the basis for the conservative bloc.

Distributive Welfare Period in the 1970s

Despite the rapid economic development seen in the 1960s, Japanese society was not without turbulence. From the late 1960s through the 1970s, just as in other advanced industrialized countries in the same period, university campuses were flooded with student movements against the Vietnam War, the reextension of the U.S.–Japan security alliance in 1970, the construction of the new Tokyo International Airport in Narita, and so on. Labor disputes also continued to persist, as exemplified by a series of strikes, illegal for government employees, carried out in the national railway and postal unions. Due to their militancy, leftist movements attracted a great deal of public attention, and angered LDP and other conservative politicians. The LDP government tactically coped with leftist movements, refraining from a forceful crackdown to avoid an escalation of activity while continuing to marginalize the movements. By the late 1960s, the Left's threat to LDP power had become less pressing, though Socialists played an important role in preventing the LDP from going back to prewar style nationalist polity as well as in forcing the LDP to make policy adjustments through interactions within the framework of parliamentary politics.

However, other threats to the stability of the LDP and the conservative politicoeconomic arrangement came from other places. One of the most important factors that promoted Japan's rapid economic development was exports, and Japan's success in this area was largely due to the stable international economic environment that the United States provided to its Cold War allies. The economic environment was particularly helpful for Japan; the undervalued yen pushed down the price of Japanese products in the U.S. market, and the low price-level of raw materials, especially oil, eased Japan's dependence upon imports of these materials. However, in the early 1970s, the international environment drastically changed when the United States stopped maintaining the currency exchange rate, resulting in the appreciation of the yen just as the Organization of Petroleum Exporting Countries coordinately raised the crude oil price. As indicated by the fact that each incident was respectively called *doru shokku* (dollar shock) and *oiru shokku* (oil shock) in Japan, they were shocking to the Japanese, who expected a grim future for the Japanese economy.

Combined with this external metamorphosis was the development of Japanese citizens' growing frustration with a system that placed economic development as its primary goal without paying enough attention to social problems caused by the rapid economic development. The lack of environmental regulations for industrial production caused serious environmental problems in industrial areas, which had air pollution from plant and car exhaust and marine pollution due to plant effluent. Despite a dramatic increase in automobile traffic, roads were still underdeveloped, resulting in a rising number of traffic accidents and worsening traffic congestion. Furthermore, although a national health care system covered almost the entire population, social welfare programs, such as systems to support the elderly, childcare facilities, and secondary schools, were severely underdeveloped. These problems were particularly prevalent in large urban areas, and small political parties, such as the Clean Government, Democratic Socialist, and Communist Parties, increased support in these areas. In the 1970s, many of the heads of local governments in urban areas—including governors of Tokyo, Osaka, and Kyoto, and mayors of Yokohama, Nagoya, and Kobe—were non-LDP politicians who emphasized the importance of quality of life, as opposed to economic development and wealth accumulation.[9]

Rapid economic development caused social problems not only in urban areas, but in rural areas as well. In addition to the problems found in urban areas, depopulation was a serious problem in rural areas, due to the massive migration of rural residents seeking employment to the ever-expanding industrial sectors in urban areas. Although agriculture was under government protection, most rural residents lacked the social protection, such as job security, that large industrial corporations provided to urban workers. Since rural areas were the core of the LDP's supporting bloc, the decline in the rural economy posed another serious threat to the LDP's dominance in Japanese politics. The problems, derived from relative stagnation in the rural areas as well as the lack of social welfare, slowly became salient in the mid-1960s. Prime Minister Sato Eisaku, who succeeded Ikeda in 1964, therefore declared social development one of his most important agendas, and sought to increase spending on public works projects.[10]

Although Sato began to emphasize the importance of the distribution of wealth in addition to its creation through economic development, Prime Minister Tanaka Kakuei, who succeeded him in 1972, brought wealth distribution to the forefront of policymaking. To rectify the problems caused by rapid economic development, Tanaka issued the Plan for the Remodeling of the Japanese Archipelago. Just like Ikeda's Income Doubling Plan, Tanaka's plan was a political statement rather than a set of policy programs, and was therefore accompanied by neither specific financial resources nor substantive measures to accomplish a goal. Nonetheless, the Plan shows the shift of the LDP government's policy from development oriented to distribution oriented. One of the Plan's points of emphasis was the development of social overhead capital and social welfare. For this, Tanaka dramatically increased government spending on social welfare programs, such as pensions, childcare allowances, and disability benefits. The other was the redistribution of industries to rural areas, to deal with the economic decline in these areas. Tanaka also dramatically increased government spending on public works, especially in rural areas. He set up plans to expand transportation systems, through the construction of highways, bullet train networks, and bridges over straits that connected islands, using the FILP. Since Tanaka's plan caused inflation and soaring land prices, it was soon discarded, and Tanaka himself lost his position due to corruption charges related to the Lockheed scandal, in 1974. However, Tanaka's spending for stability strategy became the LDP's basic political position, along with its emphasis on economic development through capitalist market economics.[11]

The Structure of the Dual State

Since the LDP has been in power for most of the time since the end of World War II, post–World War II Japanese politics may be regarded as being without conflict and change. One may be tempted to attribute this apparent calmness to Japan's cultural traits, such as a conservative political orientation, consensus-based decision making, and cooperative social interactions, which give priority to stability over change. However, as shown earlier, the LDP (and the conservatives) faced many challenges in World War II Japanese politics, such as the social chaos following the end of the war, the rise of leftist movements in the 1950s, and the socioeconomic changes accompanying the rapid economic development in the late 1960s and the early 1970s. The LDP flexibly handled each challenge by adjusting its policy, as shown both in its abandonment of ideologically charged conservatism in favor of development-oriented pragmatism in the early 1960s and the addition of social welfare and distribution of wealth to its policy platforms in the early 1970s. This flexibility brought about wealth and stability in Japanese society, and enabled the LDP to hold on to power. However, this flexibility was neither based on a coherent grand design nor implemented to transform the entire society, and the politicoeconomic arrangement that developed in the 1970s as a result of the LDP's previous policy adjustments therefore lacked coherence and comprehensiveness. I call this arrangement the dual state, which includes two separate policy networks—the developmental and distributive networks. Each set of networks consists of the LDP, bureaucracy, and business groups, and has distinctive characteristics.

Developmental Networks

Although Japan's economy flourished after World War II, Japan's economic strength has long-standing historical origins. In the mid-nineteenth century, after two and a half centuries of seclusion from international relations, Japan abandoned its feudalistic system of governance and began to transform itself into a modern European-style nation-state. While Japan was surrounded by Western imperial powers that competed for increased influence in East Asia, its own economy and technology were far behind those of Western powers. In order to maintain national autonomy and effectively compete in the international competition in the area, therefore, Japan needed to quickly develop its military and economic power. Emphasizing economic strength as an essential element of national security, the Japanese government actively promoted the development of key industries, such as steel, chemicals, and shipbuilding. Despite its extensive intervention, the Japanese state's policy was market-conforming, in that the purpose of its intervention was not the formation and operation of state-owned enterprise, but rather the assistance of the development of competitive private sector companies. Throughout its involvement in the economy, the state developed close relations with private sector firms, particularly *zaibatsu* (family-run conglomerate) groups. In each *zaibatsu*, a *zaibatsu* bank controlled member companies in various industries, such as steel, chemical, and shipping, and helped their business by channeling funds. The state and business shared an interest in achieving international competitiveness, and created an organizational form of capitalism in which economic actors not only competed in markets, but were also connected in networks of government/ business relations.

Despite Japan's defeat in World War II, which weakened the state bureaucracy's authority and broke up *zaibatsu* conglomerates, the fundamental characteristics of Japanese capitalism persisted. Major Japanese companies formed loosely knit horizontal *keiretsu*, based on *zaibatsu* grouping. In a horizontal *keiretsu* group, a main *keiretsu* bank played a leading, but not exclusive, role in financing member companies to help them engage in long-term management strategies. Similarly, *keiretsu* trading companies played a leading role in marketing products overseas, as well as acquiring raw materials from abroad for fellow member companies, and *keiretsu* member companies cross-shared stocks to defend against hostile takeovers while minimizing share-holders' pressure to maximize short-term profit. In addition to these horizontal *keiretsu* groups, each of which consisted of big

Japanese companies, each major company also formed a vertical *keiretsu* group, consisting of multiple layers of contractors and sub-contractors, which maintained exclusive long-term relations with the major company. Thus, post–World War II Japanese capitalism has operated in a complex web of inter-company relations that generates stable business interactions.

The business environment that emphasized long-term stability effectively enabled Japanese business to catch up with U.S. business in the early post–World War II period. Japanese companies initially succeeded in competing against U.S. companies by taking advantage of low prices, but eventually achieved success by improving product quality and pursuing technological innovations. This catch-up was possible because the long-term associational nature of Japanese business made it very difficult for U.S. business to penetrate into the Japanese market, providing valuable protection to Japanese companies in the infant stage of development. Moreover, Japanese companies, relatively insulated from short-term disturbances, pursued long-term strategies that made their products competitive in the international market. As this competitiveness orientation was held not only by major Japanese companies, but also by their *keiretsu* contractors and subcontractors, the Japanese export sector has become highly competitive, and has brought back wealth to the Japanese society.

The Japanese bureaucracy is an essential component of the developmental networks. Japanese business and bureaucracy have formed a close symbiotic relationship (what Richard Samuels calls "reciprocal consent"), in which business accepts the bureaucracy's jurisdiction while the bureaucracy allows for flexible business operations and refrains from unilateral intervention.[12] Government involvement in the economy is market conforming, in that the government emphasizes the importance of private sector activities for economic development, as opposed to market replacing, whereby a government dominates the operations of major industries. Nonetheless, the Japanese bureaucracy, particularly the MITI, has contributed to economic development by formulating and implementing industrial policies to enhance the competitiveness of Japanese business and upgrade Japanese industry.

Up until the end of the rapid economic development period, when Japanese business, dependent upon government assistance and therefore more susceptible to government instructions than in later periods, lacked the strength and resources to compete in the international market, the bureaucracy channeled low-interest loans to export-oriented industries, assisted high-technology firms to adopt most advanced technologies at a low-cost from the United States and consolidated major industries through the promotion of mergers.[13] After the maturation of the developmental sector, the bureaucracy's role has become less explicit, but the bureaucracy continues to formulate and implement policies for the growth of the Japanese economy, such as organizing joint venture projects for technological development, promoting government reform to reduce government restriction of business activities,[14] and setting up a freer trade environment through multilateral international rule-making.

Although the bureaucracy and business maintain close relationships, their interests may differ, and some businesses defy government policy, such as production cartels that restrict each company's production output in order to collectively deal with reduced demand in the economic downturn. Since involving politicians for mediation increases the uncertainty of outcomes for both sides, the bureaucracy and business work to contain conflict through compromise. However, LDP politicians are occasionally invited to participate in the interaction between them when they cannot solve conflicts. Similarly, politicization is rare in the developmental sector's management–labor relations. In general, companies, particularly big ones, try to secure employment and provided steady salary increases to employees, as well as generous health care and pension benefits. Even when it is necessary to downsize the labor force, companies rarely resort to drastic measures. Instead, by using early retirement with incentives, sending off excess employees to subsidiaries, and reducing the number of new recruits, they gradually downsize the labor force. Since company unions are loyal to the management in the developmental sector, the politicization of labor relations is rare, though not nonexistent, making it hardly necessary for politicians to intervene.

Although LDP politicians rarely intervene in the micromanagement of bureaucracy and business, they are crucial in other stages of policy-making. LDP politicians help bureaucrats maximize their budget allocation, and pass new legislation in the Diet for the promotion of new business and technology or for the improvement of the regulatory environment for the developmental sector. Since economic development is crucial for Japan's national interest, LDP leaders are concerned with the general well-being of the Japanese economy, and are therefore in constant communication with leaders from the bureaucracy and business. In particular, LDP leaders, including the prime minister, regard the condition of government finance as one of the most important issues that influence economic activities, and seek to reduce the budget deficit that has been ballooning since the 1990s.

LDP leaders also take up business leaders' views for the improvement of general business environment, and pursue comprehensive government reform. In the developmental networks, LDP leaders, along with bureaucrats and business leaders, engage in policymaking that is designed to enhance Japan's long-term competitiveness in the international market.

Distributive Networks

While the developmental sector generated a large amount of wealth through international economic activities in Japan, the distributive sector is more parochial, less competitive, and more dependent upon government protection. Although big companies in the developmental sector are major financial contributors to the LDP, and their leaders have close connections with LDP leadership, their employees, mostly urban residents, are not loyal LDP supporters. In contrast, members in the distributive sectors, who tend to reside in rural areas, are reliable LDP supporters who vote consistently for the party, and many of them actively participate in electoral campaign activities for LDP candidates. The distributive networks, which generally consist of parochial uncompetitive economic actors, have developed in conjunction with those of LDP politics. Unlike the developmental networks, which date back to the pre–World War II days, the distributive networks developed mostly after World War II.

In the early period, the distributive networks developed around farmers. In the pre–World War II period, due to a tenant system in which landlords controlled and exploited tenant farmers, most farmers were poor and had little political influence. After the end of the war, the U.S. occupation forces carried out land reforms, and transformed tenant farmers into independent farmers. Since the government procured their main crop, rice, and sold it to consumers, farmers' organizations became active in lobbying for procurement price increases, and developed close connections with the LDP, for whom they provided political support. Farmers' support was crucial for the LDP in balancing out the rise of the power of the Left, whose support was based on urban workers. Although farmers continued to be an integral part of the LDP supporting bloc, their relative importance declined as the number of farmers drastically declined with Japan's economic development. Instead, rural residents in general became crucial supporters for the LDP.

Japan's economic development caused the concentration of industrial facilities around a few industrial centers, particularly Tokyo and

Osaka. This tendency accelerated with the transformation of Japan's industrial structure from heavy-industry manufacturing to knowledge-intensive high technology and service industries. Many manufacturing companies moved their production sites overseas, especially Southeast Asia, to lower operation costs, but left management functions in urban areas. As a result, rural areas have become increasingly dependent upon government spending, particularly on public works. The direct beneficiaries of government spending are construction companies, but government spending benefits rural economies as a whole by infusing funds.[15] Since the main source of government spending is the value created by the developmental sector, government spending includes the (re-)distribution of the wealth to the sector. In addition, government regulations serve as a distributive tool. Restrictions on market entry protect incumbents from new competitors, and formal and informal price control ensures handsome profits. These protective measures impose a social cost that is borne by society as whole, and particularly by the developmental sector.

The distributive sector develops much more cordial relationships with the bureaucracy than the developmental sector. Bureaucracies whose jurisdiction includes distributive sector industries share their interests. Since the distributive sector represents the relatively under-privileged, at least in appearance, the bureaucracy's commitment to this sector modifies the imbalance of wealth distribution, thereby maintaining national unity. The distributive sector's dependence on government spending and regulations furnishes government bureaucracies with jobs in the administration of spending programs and regulatory activities. Also, bureaucrats' operation of government corporations in telecommunications, national railways, and the postal service is an integral part of the distributive mechanism, in that each of them provides infrastructure to rural areas for nationwide universal service. In contrast to the first two, which were privatized in the 1980s, the postal service system has an additional important feature essential to the distributive sector. Its postal savings, which act as the world largest consumer bank, constitute the major source of the FILP that is used for public works projects, and directly contribute to the distributive sector. More importantly, distributive sector companies, for example, construction companies, as well as special government corporations, such as the JH, which is in charge of the construction of nationwide toll roads, hire retired bureaucrats as executives, providing bureaucrats with incentives to serve the interest of the distributive sector. These bureaucracies work hard to maintain the distributive sector.

Along with the bureaucrats, LDP politicians get involved in the operation of distributive networks much more closely than they do in that of the developmental networks. Since LDP politicians are the ultimate decision makers regarding allocation of government funding, both distributive sector bureaucrats and economic actors maintain close connections with LDP politicians, particularly *zoku* (policy tribe) politicians. A *zoku* is a group of LDP politicians, mostly Diet members, organized around a policy area, such as agriculture, construction, and postal business, who exchange information, make decisions, and act in concert at one of LDP's policy committees. Bureaucrats of a ministry in the distributive networks are in constant communication with members of the policy committee who specialize in the ministry's policy area, and they gain assistance in passing Diet bills or competing for budget allocation. Through interactions with bureaucrats, LDP politicians, who lack an equivalent of Congressional staffs working on policymaking in the United States, gain assistance for their policymaking.

LDP's politicians are very important in maintaining the size of government spending and channeling funds to the distributive sector. It is important for each LDP Diet member from rural areas to maintain and increase the amount of government spending to his or her district, so that he or she may emphasize his or her contribution to the local economy in electoral campaigns. Since ideological issues are hardly central campaign issues, and conservative politicians compete with each other in rural areas,[16] LDP Diet members' tangible contributions to local communities, including roads, community centers, and new bullet train stations, give them an edge in elections. This is similar to the pork barrel politics found in the United States and other countries, and is not special to Japanese politics. However, economic activity in Japan is concentrated in Tokyo and a few other metropolitan areas, and rural areas have little potential for economic development, significantly increasing the importance of distributive policy. The big gap between urban and rural areas is symbolic as well as economic in that (young) residents in rural areas look up to Tokyo as the advanced part of Japan. LDP policy has been effectively addressing this gap by institutionalizing the distributive mechanism of government spending to rural areas and keeping the party in power for a long time. Therefore, LDP candidates need to make distributive policy a central issue in elections.

Although LDP politicians' emphasis on distributive policy has general appeal to their constituents, the direct beneficiaries of distributive policy are distributive sector actors. They regard it as being crucial to the maintenance of LDP *zoku* politicians' support for the distributive mechanism in office, and offer active electoral support. In addition to the financial contributions to LDP candidates, particularly by construction and real estate companies, most of them, including postmasters in rural areas, for whom government operation of postal service is essential, actively participate in campaign activities. Since the LDP does not have strong party-based grassroots organizations, and campaign activities are centered around a *kōenkai* (supporting group) that each candidate sets up, financial and personnel electoral support from local distributive networks is crucial for LDP candidates to compete in elections. This prompts LDP *zoku* politicians to work hard for the maintenance of the distributive networks.

The distributive networks work as the core of LDP rule, and developmental sector business leaders find their utilities in balancing out the power of the Left. However, as the threat from the Left was significantly weakened in the 1970s, and economic development became less expansionary, developmental sector leaders began to question government spending and protective regulation for the distributive sector, given that the developmental sector bears the cost of distribution through, for instance, taxation. However, the distributive networks are coherently organized, and the distributive sector, the bureaucracy, and the LDP share common interests. LDP *zoku* politicians and bureaucrats supported by the distributive networks resist reform attempts as an old guard force. Although reformers achieved a great deal of success in government reform, as exemplified in the privatization of NTT, the telecommunications government monopoly, and JNR, the national railway corporation laden with deficits, old guard politicians long withheld drastic reform in national highway construction and postal service—core parts of the distributive networks.

The Basic Structure of Reform Politics in
the Three Policy Areas

Although the dual state, consisting of developmental and distributive networks, had inherent contradictions, each of the two networks was an important component of the LDP support mechanism, and actors from the developmental networks did not engage in fights against the arrangement. In the late 1970s, the neoconservative ideology that emphasized free markets and the minimization of government intervention in the economy became influential in Britain and the United States, and Japan's political and business reform leaders began to question the dual state arrangement. In Japan, as in other advanced industrialized countries, government reform took the form of the privatization of government corporations and the deregulation and liberalization of market activities. In the three key policy areas—telecommunications, postal business, and transportation—reformist politicians and business leaders pursued drastic reforms, including privatization and deregulation. Each of the policy areas had a different relationship with the dual networks. Since some reform measures were designed to abolish or limit the distributive mechanism, bureaucrats and LDP politicians in the distributive networks collaborated to fiercely fight against reform. Other reform measures were the reconfiguration of regulations that were intended to reduce the government's direct commitment to economic activities. In these cases, although they initially resisted reform, bureaucrats competed to retain their power by participating in the reform process, rather than trying to abort it. To highlight the existence of different dynamics in different policy areas, I sketch out the basic structure of reform politics in the three policy areas in the following three sections.

Telecommunications

Since its beginning in 1870, Japan's telecommunications service has been developed and operated by the government, and, until the beginning of the administrative reform movement in the early 1980s, the government's operation had never seriously been challenged.[17] NTT, a government corporation, maintained the government monopoly of telecommunications during the period following the end of World War II. For the development of telecommunications in Japan, NTT actively took measures to expand the telephone service and improve its quality. In 1953, NTT set two major goals: *sugu tsuku* (new subscribers may begin to use their telephone service immediately) and *sugu tsunagaru* (calls are connected quickly). Through the construction of new telephone exchange stations and the aggressive introduction of new technologies, such as switches capable of high-speed high-volume signal transfers, NTT accomplished these two goals by the end of fiscal year 1972. NTT successfully promoted the diffusion of telecommunications service in Japan.[18]

The nationwide installation of telecommunications networks brought about business opportunities for data processing firms. However, by operating its own data processing service, NTT heavily restricted non-NTT firms' use of telecommunications networks in data processing, and demand for the (partial) liberalization of telecommunications service developed in the 1970s. This demand was particularly strengthened by advancements in computer technology. Data processing systems connecting computers created lucrative business opportunities in so-called value added network (VAN) services that dealt with various information processing by using telecommunication networks, but the current regulation prevented non-NTT firms from engaging in VAN services.[19] As telecommunications became enmeshed with data processing and increased its business potential, demand for the deregulation of telecommunications slowly developed, and telecommunications deregulation was therefore incorporated into government reform in the early 1980s.

Although NTT was eventually privatized in 1985, in the early stage of reform, reformers did not have a strong position against government operation of NTT. This was because, unlike the national railways, which accumulated massive deficits, NTT had rather sound management. Furthermore, although NTT maintained a uniform telecommunications system nationwide, the government did not subsidize its operation. In the sense that NTT provided telecommunications service universally in Japan, including sparsely populated rural areas, it was engaged in a distributive activity, and urban users were essentially subsidizing rural users. However, NTT's business was closely connected to developmental networks, especially so-called NTT family firms, including NEC, Fujitsu, and Hitachi. NTT codeveloped telecommunications technologies with the firms and exclusively procured high-tech equipment from them, helping the firms to achieve competitiveness in the international market. Since NTT, as a government corporation, was constantly under the close scrutiny of the Diet, it maintained close connections with LDP politicians in order to avoid disturbances that could arise from political intervention.[20] However, NTT was not particularly dependent on government protection, and had little incentive to resist reform.

When reformers began to consider privatizing NTT, the latter, and its nominal supervisory government agency, the MPT, resisted, preferring the status quo. However, since privatization was going to provide NTT with managerial flexibility and the MPT with the status of a government agency in charge of a leading industry, both organizations ultimately changed their positions and supported privatization. Still, the process was far from a smooth and peaceful one, as NTT, the MPT, and the MITI fiercely fought each other to maximize their influence. The MPT and MITI, for instance, conflicted over the jurisdiction of telecommunications, and the MPT and NTT struggled over the format of telecommunications regulation. In the latter case, the MPT tried to gain policy measures to control NTT operation in the privatization process and to weaken NTT's dominance in the market, while NTT sought to maximize its managerial autonomy and flexibility. Reform in telecommunications began in the Nakasone reform in the early 1980s, and political interactions continued long after the reform.

Postal Business

Just like in the United States, postal business in Japan has been operated by the government, but Japan's postal business operation has been much more intrusive in private sector economic activities. In addition to postal (mail) service, major components of Japan's postal business include postal savings and postal life insurance. Since each of these financial services takes advantage of its status as a government operation and stays out of the stringent regulation of the MOF, each maintains the largest share of its respective financial market, greatly threatening private sector competitors. Therefore, conflict has persisted between the MPT-operated postal business and private sector financial institutions, especially commercial banks, and the MOF, their supervisory agency. As a result, postal business has been a primary target of government reform since the early 1980s.

However, the MPT boasts political might to counterbalance the tide of the reform movement that seeks to contain postal business growth and ultimately privatize its operation. As discussed in the introduction of this book, the MPT maintains the networks of politically active special (*tokutei*) postmasters who provide valuable electoral support to LDP politicians, particularly in rural areas. Based on this, the MPT develops close connections with a group of LDP Diet members who support the government operation of postal business, the so-called *yūsei zoku* (postal tribe). Whenever reformers embarked upon a fundamental reconfiguration of postal business, the MPT mobilized the *yūsei zoku* and prevented or delayed the progress of reform.

Unlike private sector companies, the MPT considers its duty to be the provider of a uniform service nationwide, regardless of profitability, maintaining post offices even in rural areas. To support the nationwide service, it has numerous privileges, including the monopoly of letter delivery service, government guarantees of postal savings and postal life insurance, and tax exemption for post office operation, although, unlike the deficit-laden JNR, the MPT's postal business operation does not receive direct subsidies from the government's budget. In this sense, postal business operation itself is in the distributive networks, but postal business is an integral part of the distributive networks in a more important way. Most of the funds from the postal savings are used for government projects and special government corporations, benefiting distributive networks through the FILP. Therefore, old guard politicians vehemently oppose the fundamental reform of postal business.

Transportation

Along with telecommunications and postal business, transportation, especially national railways, the airline industry, and highway operation, has been one of the major reform agendas. In the reform of national railways, reform progressed around the treatment of JNR, a government corporation. Before its privatization in 1987, JNR was extremely controversial politically, for the following two reasons. Since the provision of railway service throughout Japan was very important for JNR, the corporation had to build and maintain unprofitable railway operations in rural areas. Railway operation was labor intensive, much more so than telecommunications, and JNR was running a large deficit, imposing a heavy financial burden upon the government. Disorderly labor relations exacerbated this financial trouble when left-wing labor unions, an important supporting bloc of the Socialist Party, came into conflict with the management. Therefore, the reform of JNR had two political goals, reducing the government's deficit and breaking an influential labor movement, and reformers achieved this goal through the privatization of JNR.

Although JNR's privatization initially faced resistance from both management and unions, reformers eventually succeeded in privatizing JNR because LDP politicians did not organize opposition to the privatization. The maintenance of (unprofitable) railway service in rural areas was of great concern for LDP Diet members elected from the areas, and to this extent, this was a distributive issue. For these old guard Diet members, the biggest distributive issue regarding the national railways was the construction of new bullet train networks. Since the construction of the new bullet train system was separated from JNR privatization, the old guard politicians did not have a big stake in the privatization issue, leading them to generally support the reform. In the airline industry, deregulation was much less important to distributive politics, and reform was therefore intended to liberalize the market by allowing new entrants, as well as giving incumbent airliners more managerial freedom. Bureaucrats were reluctant to concede their regulatory authority, but, lacking strong support from old guard politicians, deregulation progressed slowly but steadily.

In contrast, the reform (privatization) of the four government corporations for highway systems, that is, JH in charge of the construction and operation of the national highway system, two metropolitan highway corporations, and a highway corporation that operates toll bridges that connect the main island and Shikoku island, was much more controversial, and accompanied by the mobilization of old guard LDP politicians. Reformers questioned whether or not the corporations' inefficient operations took advantage of their monopoly status, but the most fundamental question was the construction of highway networks. Although main routes in and between the two metropolitan areas—Tokyo and Osaka—were profitable, many newly built areas were unprofitable, especially toll bridges connecting the island and Shikoku, a major island southwest of Osaka. The most important issue was the termination of or a cutback on plans for the construction of new routes in the highway system, as these would greatly burden the government financially. This was also the core issue in the distributive networks, both because the cost of the highway system's construction was borne by the (central) government and because LDP politicians regarded the completed construction of planned routes as crucially important. Therefore, old guard politicians vehemently opposed the reform, particularly the transferring of construction to privatized highway corporations, and, according to critics, succeeded in altering the content of the reform.[21]

Conclusion

Japan's government reform developed and progressed concurrently with reform movement in other advanced industrial countries. Similar to other countries, reform movement developed in reaction to the growth of the government since the end of World War II and reformers pursued similar policy measures, such as privatization and deregulation. However, the fundamental dynamics that underlay reform movement were deep-rooted in post–World War II Japanese politics. After taking an ideological stance that heavily emphasized nationalism, in the late 1950s the LDP government became much more pragmatic than ideological, putting economic welfare at the center of government policy. After rapid economic development in the 1960s, the distribution of wealth to underdeveloped rural areas became the core element of the LDP's policy in the 1970s. Through these political interactions, two distinctive networks developed in the Japanese political economy, developmental and distributive networks. Economic actors in the developmental networks pursue the creation of wealth, especially through international business activities, whereas economic actors in the distributive networks are dependent on government spending and protection. As Japan's developmental sector increasingly faced international competition, it became reluctant to bear the burden of maintaining the dual state, prompting reformist LDP leaders to embark on reform. At the same time, since reform measures were expected to undermine the basis of the distributive networks, old guard politicians, whose political support came from the distributive networks, opposed the reform. Interactions involving the developmental-distributive mechanism were intertwined with demand based on neoconservative market-oriented ideology in reforms in telecommunications, postal business, and transportation.

Chapter 3

The Dual State and Government Reforms

After Japan's defeat in World War II, the occupation forces fundamentally changed the structure of the Japanese government. This reformed structure was maintained for about three decades without any major changes. However, beginning in the late 1970s, government reform became one of Japan's central political agendas, and significant reformations of the government have been made since then. The rise of each reform was stimulated by the growth of the neoconservative economic ideology that was downplaying the role of the government in the economy in Britain and the United States. More recent reforms were influenced by the growth of a new management movement that tried to infuse private sector management into public administration. The primary reform measures in Japan, as in other countries, were the privatization of government corporations, the deregulation of market activities, and the reorganization of the government. Despite the fact that reformers used neoconservative logic to carry out reform, the outcomes were determined through interactions in the framework of Japanese politics—the dual state.

In this chapter, I describe the political process of each of the three reforms—Nakasone reform in the early 1980s, Hashimoto reform in the late 1990s, and Koizumi reform in the early 2000s—and demonstrate the relationship between reform and the dual state. I examine each of the three reforms and analyze how LDP politicians, government bureaucrats, and business leaders interacted to promote or resist reform, thereby showing that the interactions between the developmental and distributive networks were the primary determinant of reform outcomes.

The Three Major Government Reforms: Political Process

Nakasone Reform

In the 1970s, the developmental sector faced challenges after its expansion in the 1960s. In the early 1970s, the U.S. government's abandonment of its support for the exchange rate resulted in the appreciation of the yen against the dollar. The drastic increases in oil prices that occurred twice in the decade hit the Japanese economy hard, as it was heavily dependent upon imports of oil and other raw materials for the production of export products. Reflecting the currency appreciation or the price increase in raw materials, Japanese companies were forced to either raise the price of their exports, reducing price competitiveness, or minimize the price increase and compress their profit margin. In addition, Japan's ever-accumulating trade surplus prompted U.S. business and political leaders to act to limit imports from Japan and press Japan to open up to imports. In contrast to the rolling 1960s, the developmental sector began to have grim prospects in the 1970s.

Despite the low growth of the developmental sector, which decreased government revenue, the LDP government continued to engage in massive spending for construction projects, thereby benefiting the distributive sector. As a result, the Japanese government accumulated a budget deficit. LDP leaders and bureaucrats of the MOF were concerned about the deficit, and fiscal austerity became the most important political agenda in the late 1970s. As a part of the solution, LDP and MOF leaders pursued higher taxes, and corporate taxes were raised several times. Business leaders from the developmental sector were unhappy with these tax increases, and began to explore ways to streamline government operations in order to reduce government expenditures.[1] Concurring with business's demand for reform, Prime Minister Suzuki Zenko, who assumed the position in 1980, offered a slogan, "fiscal austerity without tax increase," to solve the deficit issue without imposing the burden of corporate tax increases upon the business community. Similarly, Nakasone Yasuhiro, the director general of the Administrative Management Agency and the leader of a major LDP faction, actively pursued government reform to prove his policy's capability, which was essential to his major goal of becoming a prime minister.

To advance a major administrative reform movement—*Gyōsei Kaikaku* (*Gyōkaku*)—Nakasone established *Rinji Gyōsei Chōsakai* (the Second Provisional Administrative Reform Commission; *Rinchō* hereafter).[2] He recruited Doko Toshio, the honorary chairman of the Keidanren (the Federation of Economic Organizations), a group representing major firms in Japan, as the leader of *Rinchō*, because Doko was capable of mobilizing support for the reform among business leaders.[3] In accepting the position, Doko, refusing to make *Rinchō* a token committee, obtained Prime Minister Suzuki's confirmation that *Rinchō* would be engaged in fiscal reconstruction without a tax increase, that its recommendation would be implemented, that it would discuss reforms with both central and local governments, and that the reform would include the privatization of government corporations.[4] In March 1981, Doko started *Rinchō* with nine members, including business leaders, labor leaders, a retired bureaucrat, and an academic.[5]

Backed by support from business leaders, particularly in the developmental networks, and the general public, Doko consistently pressed Prime Minister Suzuki to pursue the reform. When he felt Suzuki was backing away from their promise of "fiscal austerity without a tax increase" by increasing government spending or taxes, he threatened to resign from his position, thereby preventing the LDP from overtly opposing the *Rinchō* reform.[6] Strong support for *Rinchō* made it difficult for bureaucrats to openly resist discussion of the government reform, and *Rinchō* quickly put together the first report, submitting it to Prime Minister Suzuki in July 1981. The report not only discussed measures to reduce government spending, but also indicated *Rinchō*'s intention to improve the operation of government corporations, such as JNR and NTT, suggesting privatization as a possible reform measure.[7] The release of *Rinchō*'s first report signaled the beginning of a full-scale movement for government reform that emphasized reduction in the size and influence of the government in the economy, a neoconservative agenda that was concurrently in vogue in the United States under the Reagan administration, and in the United Kingdom under the leadership of Prime Minister Margaret Thatcher.

Following the first report, various sections of *Rinchō* began to discuss concrete measures in September, particularly the privatization of the government businesses. Their primary target was JNR. JNR, because of its inability to contain left-wing labor unions and its maintenance of unprofitable train operation in rural areas, was incapable of rationalizing its operations, and had accumulated a huge deficit that imposed a significant financial burden upon the government.[8] JNR was also unpopular among the public for its low service level, making the railroad an easy target for reformers. Similarly, NTT had had some scandals involving financial wrongdoing, but the level of public criticism against NTT was much lower than that against the JNR. NTT had more stable labor relations than the JNR and was free of financial difficulties, but *Rinchō*, through communication with NTT president Shinto Hisashi, a protégé of Doko and a former president of a shipbuilding company who assumed the position in 1981, noticed the possibility of NTT becoming another badly managed government corporation.[9]

In May 1982, *Rinchō* released a preliminary report and made public its intentions to privatize the national railroad and NTT. In July 1982, *Rinchō* released its third comprehensive report and submitted it to Prime Minister Suzuki. Based on its fourth section's preliminary report, it formally recommended the privatization of NTT. After the release of *Rinchō*'s third report, Prime Minister Suzuki quickly worked for the implementation of its recommendations, and brokered a Cabinet agreement that outlined the pursuit of the administrative reform in September 1982. However, in the same month, it became clear that the attainment of fiscal austerity, Suzuki's political goal, was impossible, and that it was necessary to issue bonds to pay for the redemption of matured government bonds. Failing to keep his promise and finding his support in the LDP weathering, Suzuki decided to resign from his position in October. In the primary elections to choose its president by LDP members, Nakasone won 57 percent of votes, leading the other candidates to drop out. As a result, Nakasone became prime minister in the same month.[10] Since Nakasone had been supportive of *Rinchō* and administrative reform, discussion for the privatization of NTT and JNR continued to develop.

By the time the *Rinchō* released its third report, both the MPT and NTT—the two most import political actors related to NTT privatization—were in favor of the privatization of NTT.[11] Since NTT would lose its control over telecommunications as a government agency through privatization, the MPT expected to take over NTT's regulatory functions and establish strong authority over telecommunications, an industry that would stimulate economic development. Although NTT would lose its monopoly, it would be freed from detailed control by the Diet, and would gain managerial autonomy. However, the MPT and NTT disagreed over how best to privatize the latter. To enhance its regulatory power and to promote competition after privatization, the MPT sought to gain detailed control over NTT's business while exploring ways to reduce its monopoly power, including breaking up NTT. NTT, however, tried to minimize the MPT's control, in order to enhance managerial flexibility. At the same time, it sought to preserve its business format as much as possible, in order to effectively compete against the new telecommunications carriers that would be allowed to operate after NTT's privatization. Since the MPT and NTT disagreed over the proper format of privatization, LDP leaders, particularly Hashimoto Ryutaro, the chair of the LDP's policymaking organ, the Policy Affairs Research Council (PARC), mediated the conflict between the MPT and NTT. As a result of the mediation, the bill for NTT's privatization eventually passed the Diet in December 1984, and NTT began to operate as a private sector company on April 1, 1985.[12]

Although the interaction between the MPT and NTT was at the center of the reform politics of telecommunications, other political actors got involved in the reform process as well. The privatization of NTT ended its monopoly of the telecommunications market, allowing new entrants. Since many of prospective new entrants were high-tech manufacturers, the MITI intervened in the reform process to minimize the regulation of the MPT so that new entrants would be free to operate. This strategy served the MITI's own interests as well. Since (tele)communications were merged with computer networks, the MITI was trying to expand its jurisdiction into telecommunications. Also, the MOF was particularly concerned with the treatment of NTT stocks, which would eventually be sold on the market. The MOF wanted to use the revenue from the sales of NTT stock solely for the reduction of the government deficit, colliding with the MPT's interest in using the revenue for the promotion of telecommunications. The MPT, MITI, and MOF fought fiercely, mobilizing *zoku* politicians and lobbying LDP leaders, particularly Hashimoto.

As for JNR privatization, even though the *Rinchō* report specifically presented the privatization of JNR as a reform measure, there was no consensus over how to proceed with the reform of the JNR. It was unclear if JNR was going to be privatized, because both mainstream JNR executives and major JNR labor unions opposed privatization; further, the LDP and the Ministry of Transport (MOT) did not have a clear stance. As a result, extensive negotiations continued among JNR, the LDP, business leaders, and the MOT. Since Nakasone strongly supported the implementation of the *Rinchō* report, and most political actors agreed that a fundamental reform was necessary, a movement for reform slowly developed. The primary actor that formulated concrete plans for the JNR reform was the JNR Reconstruction Administrative Committee. The Committee was established in June 1983 as an advisory committee for the prime minister, and consisted of a business leader, an ex-MOT bureaucrat, and academics. Although the majority of JNR executives were opposed to privatization, Committee members extensively lobbied LDP leaders and MOT bureaucrats. By the time the Committee presented its final report to Prime Minister Nakasone in July 1985, the LDP and MOT had agreed to pursue the privatization of JNR. Since privatization involved complex political issues, such as the treatment of the massive JNR deficit, the establishment of regional carriers, and the reduction of labor force, interactions among political actors continued for a long time, but bills for the privatization of JNR eventually passed the Diet in December 1986. JNR was privatized as JR carriers, six regional passenger carriers and a freight carrier, along with affiliates. JR started to operate in April 1987.[13]

The major accomplishment of Nakasone reform was the privatization of NTT and JNR.[14] Neither of the two organizations was small or weak; each had some 300,000 employees and substantial political clout. Furthermore, each organization was regarded as an important government operation among the public and in the government, and each maintained close connections with major political parties—the LDP and the Japan Socialist Party—and the bureaucracy. The strong pursuit of reform by *Rinchō*, whose core members were reform-minded business leaders from the developmental sector, made the privatization of each large, powerful government corporation possible; Prime Minister Nakasone provided valuable background support for *Rinchō*. Despite this accomplishment, however, the reform could not cut into the core of the distributive mechanism. *Rinchō* recognized problems associated with the PSF, the FILP, and special government corporations, and discussed ways to solve the problems. However, *Rinchō* could not come up with concrete plans, leaving subsequent government reform movements to tackle the problems.

Hashimoto Reform

The government reform movement led by business leaders continued after Nakasone's reform. *Rinchō*'s function, however, was taken over by the Advisory Council for the Promotion of Administrative Reform (*Gyōkakushin*). Similar to *Rinchō*, *Gyōkakushin* consisted of business leaders, academics, labor union representatives, and retired bureaucrats, and had three major sessions between 1983 and 1994. In the third session, which began in 1990, *Gyōkakushin* discussed the role of the government in the economy and vertical administration (*tatewari gyōsei*) as major topics. In the discussion of the role of the government, the PSF became a key issue, along with the reform of the FILP and special government corporations. In 1993, *Gyōkakushin* issued several reports and called for the discussion of fundamental governmental reform. Unlike *Rinchō*, *Gyōkakushin* could not come up with concrete plans for government reform, because bureaucrats resisted the formulation of reform plans through lobbying *Gyōkakushin* members; further, LDP leaders, including Prime Minister Miyazawa Kiichi, neither provided strong support for nor followed up on *Gyōkakushin*'s recommendations.[15]

However, a major political event that changed the political environment surrounding administrative reform movement occurred in August 1993. Due to the LDP split, the party lost its power for the first time since 1955, and a coalition government was established. The new prime minister was Hosokawa Morihiro, who had been a chair of a section of *Gyōkakushin*. Hosokawa's government emphasized government reform as the most important issue. The non-LDP coalition government was short-lived, however; it ended in June 1994, when the LDP come back to power in coalition with its former archenemy the Social Democratic Party (SDP)[16] and reformist Sakigake (harbinger). The new coalition government, headed by Socialist Murayama Tomiichi, established the Administrative Reform Committee (*Gyōsei Kaikaku Iinkai*) to succeed *Gyōkakushin* as an organization to deliberate reform measures in December 1994.

After working on deregulation and government information disclosure as reform agendas, the Committee began to discuss the reduction of the role of the government in 1996, focusing on the reform of the PSF as the central issue. In December 1996, the Committee issued a report on the division of labor between government and private sectors. The report emphasized as a basic principle that those government services that the private sector was able to offer should be transferred to private sector operation, and that benchmarks should be established to evaluate government services. It laid the basis of further government reform in the reduction of the size of government services, to which the PSF was essential, both as a government-run financial service and as the source of the FILP that enabled major government services to operate.[17]

In the same period, public trust in government bureaucracy declined, due to a series of events, including the following, that centered on the bureaucracy. When a major earthquake occurred in the Kobe area in 1995, the government was not able to effectively engage in rescue operations. Both bureaucratic red tape[18] and vertical administration[19] deterred the timely implementation of comprehensive recovery measures. Following the earthquake, public criticism developed against the

MITI take over the MOF's banking regulation authority in the formulation of the report, the MITI chose instead to ally with the MOF, and lobbied the ARC to take over the MPT's authority over telecommunications, which was becoming an industry crucial to economic development, due to the development of the Internet. The MITI's lobbying paid off, and the report proposed to remove authority from the MPT and incorporate it into the MITI's jurisdiction. The report proposed to transform the MITI into a ministry that oversaw economic development.

Table 3.1 Government structure proposed in the Administrative Reform Council's interim report

Existing	Proposed in the interim report
Cabinet	Cabinet
Cabinet Secretariat	Cabinet Secretariat
Prime Minister's Office	Cabinet Office
Management and Coordination Agency	
Defence Agency	
Economic Planning Agency	
Environment Agency	
National Land Agency	Ministry of General Affairs
Science and Technology Agency	Telecommunications and Broadcasting
Etc.	Commission
	Postal Service Agency
Ministry of Justice	Etc.
Ministry of Foreign Affairs	
Ministry of Finance	Ministry of Defence
Ministry of International Trade and	Ministry of Justice
Industry	Ministry of Foreign Affairs
Ministry of Posts and	Ministry of Finance
Telecommunications	Ministry of Industry
Ministry of Transportation	Ministry of Land Development
Ministry of Construction	Ministry of Land Maintenance
Ministry of Agriculture, Forestry and	Ministry of Environmental Safety
Fisheries	Ministry of Employment and Welfare
Ministry of Labor	Ministry of Education and Science
Ministry of Health and Welfare	
Ministry of Education	
Ministry of Home Affairs	

Source: Yoko Kaneko, *Government Reform in Japan*, paper presented at the First Specialized International Conference of International Institute of Administrative Sciences, July 1999, London, U.K., 7; Gyōsei Kaikaku Kaigi Jimukyoku OB-Kai, *21 Seiki no Nippon no gyōsei* [Japan's Public Administration in the Twenty-First Century] (Tokyo: Gyōsei Kanri Kenkyū Sentā, 1998) 562–64.

In contrast, the report also suggested the break-up and consolidation of many ministries that were closely connected to the distributive mechanism. Its recommendations were particularly devastating to the MPT. The report proposed that postal businesses be separated into three entities—the postal service, the postal savings, and the postal life insurance systems. Although it supported government operation of the postal service, it proposed the privatization of the postal life insurance as soon as possible, and called for the beginning of the discussion and preparation for the future privatization of the postal savings. The report also treated the MPT harshly with regard to its telecommunications policymaking, separating the MPT's regulation and promotion of telecommunications. As described above, the telecommunications promotional function was to be incorporated into the MITI, whereas the regulatory function would be taken up by an FCC-style committee in charge of telecommunications and broadcasting, which would be attached to the proposed Ministry of General Affairs, an incorporation of the Ministry of Home Affairs and the Administrative Management Agency.[24] Similarly, the report was shocking to the Ministry of Construction. Its River Bureau was to be absorbed by the Ministry of Agriculture as the Ministry of Land Maintenance, and the other bureaus were to be incorporated into the Ministry of Land Development. The report sought to rationalize the governance mechanism of the distributive sector by eliminating redundancies as well as downsizing.[25]

Since the ARC released the report without consulting the LDP, bureaucrats from the ministries closely connected with the distributive networks lobbied LDP Diet members. In opposing the ARC's plan, the MPT emphasized the importance of the government operation of the postal business. Since the privatization seemed to weaken the *tokutei* postmasters who provided electoral support for LDP politicians in rural areas, many LDP politicians sided with the MPT in opposing the ARC's plans. At an LDP meeting attended by about 120 *yūsei zoku* Diet members in late August, many attendants expressed their displeasure with the ARC's initiative in administrative reforms, calling for the LDP to regain control over reform decisions.[26] Displeasure with the ARC initiative was shared by the LDP members who were concerned with other policy areas. In particular, construction-related *zoku* members began to criticize the ARC.[27] At an LDP meeting on administrative reform in early September, although Prime Minister Hashimoto, along with former prime ministers, maintained his support for the plans articulated in the ARC's interim report, many LDP members openly criticized the ARC.[28]

Prime Minister Hashimoto was determined to pursue the administrative reform, but, vulnerable to pressure from major LDP factions, he could not maintain strong control over LDP members. This weakness came to the fore when he shuffled cabinet members in September. It was customary to appoint new faces to cabinet positions in accordance with the balance of power among LDP factions. Hashimoto wanted to retain Muto Kabun as the secretary of the Management and Coordination Agency because of his commitment to the ARC-based administrative reform movement. However, one of the major factions demanded the appointment of Sato Koko, the head of the LDP committee on administrative reform, as the secretary. Bowing to pressure from the LDP factions, Hashimoto drastically changed the composition of the cabinet. Sato became the secretary and Muto succeeded Sato's position, the director of the LDP committee on the administrative reform. This switch itself imposed discontinuity on the ARC's pursuit of administrative reforms.[29] Moreover, Sato's appointment was problematic because he had been convicted of bribery in the infamous Lockheed scandal in the early 1970s. Public outrage followed his appointment. Sato had to resign shortly after his appointment and was replaced by Ozato Sadatoshi, who was not known for commitment to government reform but was deeply involved in the promotion of public works.[30] Thus, the ARC-based administrative reform began to lose momentum, along with Hashimoto's leadership.

In concert with LDP Diet members, bureaucrats intensified the fight against the ARC's plan. MPT maximized its leverage—*tokutei* postmasters—to try to overturn the reform plans set by the ARC. In some local areas, including Prime Minister Hashimoto's constituency in Okayama prefecture, *tokutei* postmasters, in protest against the plans, kept the collection of LDP membership fees and LDP member recruitment activities on hold.[31] In addition, the *tokutei* postmasters' association postponed the beginning of the unofficial campaign for the House of Councilor (HC) elections scheduled to be held the following summer. Along with the public display of displeasure, the association submitted a petition to the LDP association of *yūsei zoku* Diet members, demanding that MPT's postal business and telecommunications policymaking functions not be separated and that postal businesses continue to be under government operation.[32] Due to the rise of the anti-ARC movement, most LDP members began to feel that at least some rectifications of the government reorganization plan set by the ARC were necessary.

Despite the growing frustration among LDP Diet members, Hashimoto did not quickly concede. In particular, he was persistent about reducing the number of government ministries. In addition, Hashimoto's postal service reform was supported by reformist LDP politicians. Among the reformers, Minister of Health and Welfare Koizumi Junichiro was most vocal about the postal business reform. When it was becoming clear in the LDP that postal businesses would continue to be under government operation, Koizumi publicly criticized the idea, and threatened to resign in protest if the LDP maintained the current operational format of postal businesses. Rejecting the status quo, Koizumi called for the abolition of the PSF's role as the source of the FILP and the liberalization of the postal delivery service market. Koizumi's reform proposal, particularly the abolition of the transfer of funds from the MPT to the MOF, was a part of Hashimoto's reform plans. Arguing that the FILP kept inefficient and unnecessary government-affiliated corporations alive, Hashimoto proposed the termination of the flow of funds from the PSF to the FILP.[33] Hashimoto and reformers remained persistent about these aspects of postal service reform, even though they became flexible about abandoning the radical reform plans contained in the ARC interim report.

The plan to reorganize the MPT that Hashimoto finalized in mid-November among the LDP and later included in the ARC's final report, issued in December 1997, was mostly consistent with the MPT's preferences, reflecting the power of *yūsei zoku* politicians, while incorporating reformers' proposals to some extent. Ruling out the separation of the three postal businesses and the partial privatization that the ARC's interim report had proposed, the final plan confirmed the continued combined government operation of postal businesses, and proposed the establishment of a government corporation in charge of the businesses within five years. The employees of the corporation would continue to retain the status of government officials, unlike those of NTT when it was a government corporation, and the corporation would not be required to go through annual legislative approval and adopt private sector firms' management style and accounting methods. Since the new postal business corporation would operate more like a private sector company, its establishment would make it easy to privatize postal business. Therefore, both the LDP's agreement and the ARC's final report stipulated that the further revision of postal business operation not be done. At the same time, however, the reorganization plan, reflecting reformers' preferences, confirmed the abolition of the transfer of funds from the PSF to the FILP, and required the MPT to begin preparations for the liberalization of the postal delivery service market by allowing private sector carriers to operate.[34] However, it seemed at the time that the

MPT gained too much and that reformers gained too little; both the proposed establishment of the postal business corporation and the liberalization of the postal delivery service later gave reformers the opportunity to try to further postal business reform when Koizumi became prime minister in 2001, as discussed in the following section.[35]

Similarly, the Ministry of Construction avoided being broken up. Instead, the ministry as a whole was determined to be merged with the MOT, along with two small land-related agencies. Other controversial issues, such as the separation of the regulatory function of the financial market from MOF and the upgrade of the Defence Agency into the Ministry of Defence, were eventually settled, and *Chuō Shōchōtō Kaikaku Kihon Hō* (The Basic Law for the Reform of Central Government Organizations) passed the Diet in June 1998.[36] The new government format, as shown in table 3.2, took effect in January 2001. The Hashimoto reform was remarkable in that it fundamentally

Table 3.2   The structure of old and new government ministries and major agencies

Old system	New system
Cabinet	Cabinet
Cabinet Secretariat	Cabinet Secretariat
Prime Minister's Office	Cabinet Office
Management and Coordination Agency	National Public Safety Commission
Defence Agency	Defence Agency
Economic Planning Agency	Ministry of Public Management, Home
Environment Agency	Affairs, Posts and Telecommunications
National Land Agency	Postal Service Agency
Science and Technology Agency Etc.	Fair Trade Commission
Ministry of Justice	Ministry of Justice
Ministry of Foreign Affairs	Ministry of Foreign Affairs
Ministry of Finance	Ministry of Finance
Ministry of International Trade and Industry	Ministry of Economy, Trade and Industry
Ministry of Posts and Telecommunications	Ministry of Education, Culture, Sports, Science and Technology
Ministry of Transportation	Ministry of Land Infrastructure and Transport
Ministry of Construction	Ministry of Agriculture, Forestry and Fisheries
Ministry of Agriculture, Forestry and Fisheries	Ministry of Health, Labour and Welfare
Ministry of Labor	Ministry of Environment
Ministry of Health and Welfare	
Ministry of Education	
Ministry of Home Affairs	

Source: Kaneko, *Government Reform in Japan*, 7; Prime Minister's homepage, http://www.kantei.go.jp/foreign/constitution_and_government_of_japan/charts_e.html.

changed the format of the Japanese government. While reducing the number of ministries, it expanded the organ supporting the prime minister's leadership. These organs became very important when Koizumi, as prime minister, pursued government reform. However, the reform stopped short of changing the distributive mechanism, and this fight had to be taken up by Koizumi, as discussed in the next section.

Koizumi Reform

Although Prime Minister Hashimoto strongly pursued government reform, his power base within the party was not particularly stable. Therefore, after the LDP lost the House of Councilors elections in 1998, primary because of Hashimoto's unpopular decision to raise the tax rate of the value added national consumption tax from three to five percent, Hashimoto resigned, and was succeeded by Obuchi Keizo, an influential member of *yūsei zoku* and therefore not an ardent reformer. Obuchi became suddenly ill in April 2000 (and later died, in May 2000), and Mori Yoshiro became prime minister. Although Mori was not known as a *zoku* member, he was not a reformer, either. No major government reform attempt developed under these two prime ministers. However, the situation changed completely in April 2001, when Koizumi, who had placed the privatization of postal business as the central reform issue, became prime minister after extremely low levels of popularity led to Mori's resignation. Koizumi's slogan was "no structural reform, no economic recovery" (*kōzō kaikaku nakushite keiki kaifuku nashi*), and he argued that government reform was essential for overcoming the economic difficulties that Japan had been facing. Quite naturally for Koizumi, he placed postal businesses as his number one target of government reform.

Since the public was frustrated at the government's inability to effectively deal with economic problems and unhappy with seemingly business-as-usual LDP politics, they enthusiastically supported Koizumi, who was openly critical of the LDP's old style politics' resistance to drastic reforms. To the relief of the Ministry of Public Management, Home Affairs, Posts, and Telecommunications (MPHPT), into which the MPT was incorporated, and *yūsei zoku* members,[37] as a result of the Hashimoto reform, which had targeted the establishment of a government corporation to operate postal businesses—Japan Post, the operation of postal businesses was in the transition phase. Besides the no-privatization clause in the government reorganization law, *yūsei zoku* politicians maintained that it was premature to discuss the privatization without knowing the fate of Japan Post.[38] Moreover, since Koizumi, as a Hashimoto cabinet member, was responsible for this arrangement, it was difficult for him to ignore this arrangement and jump to the privatization of postal businesses. Consequently, Koizumi set the privatization of postal businesses as a long-term goal that would be discussed after the establishment of Japan Post.[39]

Koizumi sought to develop the discussion over the privatization of postal businesses at the Advisory Council to Consider the Modalities of the Three Postal Businesses, which he established in May 2001. The Council was headed by a business critic who was an ardent supporter of the privatization of postal businesses, and its members included economists with similar positions. Koizumi had reportedly intended to develop concrete plans to privatize postal businesses at the Council and make them public with the passage of the bills for the establishment of Japan Post sometime in June 2002. However, moderate members of the Council were cautious about formulating definite privatization plans without knowing how Japan Post was going to operate.[40] When the Council issued its final report in September 2002, it did not specify privatization as the only future course of action for Japan Post. Instead, the report conditionally presented three ways of transforming Japan Post.[41] Although both commercial banks and life insurers welcomed the report, it did not put forth forces for the privatization of postal businesses.

Although Koizumi was not able to move forward with the privatization of postal businesses, his prime ministerial position enabled him to intervene in the legislative process of the bills for the establishment of Japan Post. As discussed earlier, the major final provisions regarding postal businesses in the Hashimoto administrative reform were the establishment of Japan Post and the liberalization of the postal service market. The latter became an issue of contention in the legislative process between Koizumi (the reformer) and *yūsei zoku* politicians (the old guard), while the more important postal savings and postal life insurance were virtually untouched.[42] Placing the establishment of Japan Post as the first step toward privatization, Koizumi demanded the complete liberalization of the postal service market. *yūsei zoku* politicians regarded the government monopoly in the market as crucial for the maintenance of the postal networks, particularly in rural areas, and opposed even partial liberalization.

For the MPT/MPHPT, it was important to limit the liberalization of the postal service market. In the package delivery market, the postal service faced fierce competition from private sector carriers, particularly Yamato Transport, and the MPT/MPHPT found it difficult to generate a profit. In the letter delivery service market, however, only the postal service was allowed to operate, and the MPT/MPHPT therefore succeeded in making a profit, mainly from direct mail, by which companies sent huge numbers of letters to potential customers. When the MPT/MPHPT was preparing the liberalization of the postal service market before Koizumi's ascension to power, it planned to liberalize the market only for the delivery of letters beyond a certain weight, or for a high-speed delivery service that would incur extra charges, citing common restrictions on entrance into the postal service market in major countries, such as the United States, Germany, and France.[43] However, Koizumi insisted on unlimited liberalization, and instructed the MPHPT minister to formulate a plan for unlimited liberalization. As a result, the MPHPT worked to develop a plan to allow new entrants in all kinds of letter delivery, but the plan would have imposed certain conditions at the same time, such as nationwide coverage, to prevent new entrants from concentrating on business in lucrative urban areas.[44]

In March 2002, the MPHPT came up with a draft of the bill to allow new entrants into the letter delivery service market—*Shinsho Bin Hōan* (the Letter Delivery Service bill, the LDS bill, hereafter)—along with the bill to establish Japan Post. According to this draft, the MPHPT would allow private sector carriers to handle the delivery of letters with a weight of 250 grams or less.[45] However, the draft stipulated strict conditions for the carriers including the following three. First, the MPHPT would regulate the activities of the carriers. Second, each of the carriers would have to place a mailbox at each locality, and a total of 99,000 nationwide. Third and finally, it would have to deliver letters in a couple of days at a flat rate. Yamato Transport, the largest carrier of package delivery that had showed interest in entering the market, immediately questioned the necessity of maintaining such a large number of mailboxes.[46] Although Koizumi pressed the MPHPT to allow the carriers to accept letters at "convenience stores," such as Lawson's, Seven Eleven, and Am Pm, Yamato Transport officially dropped its plans to operate letter delivery in late April, to the dismay of Koizumi. Yamato Transport reasoned that the market would be regulated by the MPHPT, with a close connection to Japan Post, and that it would not be able to engage in free business activities.[47]

More intensive opposition to the LDS bill came from *yūsei* LDP politicians. When the director general of the MPHPT's Postal

Services Policy and Planning Bureau presented the draft of the LDS bill at a meeting of the LDP's General Affairs committee, which was in charge of policy issues related the postal businesses, its members—*yūsei zoku* Diet members—criticized the MPHPT for formulating a draft that included the liberalization of the postal service market, and refused to endorse the bill.[48] Due to the committee's refusal to approve the LDS bills and the bills to establish Japan Post (the Japan Post bills, hereafter), the LDP did not approve the bills. Since it was customary for the Cabinet to send the bills after getting the approval of the LDP to cut down on intra-LDP negotiations in the Diet, the bills were stalled. As Koizumi had made it public that these bills were of primary importance, he sent the bills to the Diet without LDP approval in late April 2002.[49]

Even after the submission of the bills to the Diet, however, disputes between Koizumi and the members, all of whom were from the LDP, continued. Whereas Koizumi continued to insist on passing the bills without any amendment, *yūsei zoku* Diet members demanded the inclusion of measures in the LDS bill to make it more difficult for private sector carriers to enter into the letter delivery service market. Although most of the *zoku* members were stubborn, their leaders showed some sign of flexibility. In fact, the passage of the bills, particularly the Japan Post bills, was essential for the continued operation of postal businesses. Since Japan Post was scheduled to start in April 2003, the bills' failure to pass in the current Diet session would make Japan Post devoid of any legal justification to operate postal businesses, resulting in chaos. To prevent this, the leader of the *yūsei zoku* Diet members, Nonaka Hiromu, undertook a mediating role. Since the *zoku* members were likely to accept the deal that Nonaka was going to broker with Koizumi, the standoff seemed to end soon. However, Koizumi was unwilling to make any compromises. To the contrary, in giving an account of the postal service–related bills at a floor session of the HR in mid-May 2002, Koizumi made it clear that these bills were the first step toward the privatization of postal businesses, and emphasized that the aforementioned Advisory Council to Consider the Modalities of the Three Postal Businesses would formulate concrete plans for the privatization. This statement infuriated Nonaka, who gave up his mediation attempt.[50]

With the lack of any substantive activity to mediate between the two opposing blocs, the conflict continued to escalate within the LDP. Knowing that Yamato Transport was not going to enter into the letter delivery service market, and that the proposed liberalization of the market would not be making any substantive impact, Koizumi adjusted his strategy, ordering the MPHPT to narrow down the definition of letter delivery services whose operators would have to meet stringent requirements specified in the LDS bill. In particular, Koizumi demanded that the MPHPT exclude the delivery of direct mail from the application of regulation for letter delivery service. Since direct mail was an important source of postal service revenue, this could have potentially had a devastating effect. Koizumi thought that more fierce competition would force Japan Post to look for more managerial freedom and eventually seek privatization. Obviously, *yūsei zoku* Diet members vehemently opposed Koizumi's attempt, as the attempt would make it difficult for Japan Post to maintain operation in the rural areas whose interests they represented.[51]

Without any sign of a breakthrough, the deadlock continued, and it was increasingly likely that the bills would be scrapped with the end of the Diet session. Toward the end of June, Nonaka got back into mediation, and persuaded *yūsei zoku* Diet members to accept the liberalization of the postal service market. Senior LDP members who were relatively neutral to this issue, including PARC Chair Aso Taro, became active in solving the dispute.[52] Since Aso emphasized in his meeting with Koizumi on July 1 that the bills would, in the absence of amendments, be abandoned, Koizumi agreed to amend the Japan Post bills, while insisting on the passage of the LDS bill without amendment.[53] As a result, both sides agreed to pass the LDS bill and liberalize, albeit with strict conditions, the postal service market. As for the liberalization of direct mail delivery that Koizumi wanted, it was agreed that some direct mail would be excluded from the application of tough letter delivery service regulation. In return for these concessions to Koizumi, *yūsei zoku* Diet members succeeded in making the following three amendments to the Japan Post bills. First, the bill would specifically state that Japan Post would maintain post offices all over Japan, so that Japan Post would not eliminate *tokutei* post offices in unprofitable rural areas. Second, the amount of payment that Japan Post, as a corporation, would make to the general government revenue wound be reduced. Third and finally, Japan Post would be allowed to establish subsidiaries, to add flexibility to its management.[54] The bills passed the Diet on July 24, 2002, and Japan Post was established in April 2003.[55]

During the LDP presidential elections in September 2003, Koizumi promised that, if reelected, he would privatize Japan Post in April 2007. Koizumi beat out other candidates who were reluctant to pursue the privatization. After winning the LDP presidential elections that enabled him to continue to be prime minister, Koizumi instructed his cabinet members to begin the deliberation of Japan Post privatization. Minister of State for Economic and Fiscal Policy Takenaka Heizo—who was in charge of the deliberation—set up the five principles for privatization that defined basic strategy for the privatization. The first two principles—shifting of funds (from postal savings and postal life insurance) to the private sector and privatization as a part of comprehensive government reform—were based on reformist ideas. However, the other three—maintaining convenient service to citizens, utilizing Japan Post's existing nationwide networks, and consideration of employment of Japan Post's workforce—seemed more like concessions to *yūsei zoku* politicians who argued that privatization would result in the abolition of post offices in rural areas and the downsizing of Japan Post workforce.[56] These concessions greatly watered down the privatization reform, but policymaking for Japan Post privatization proceeded based on the five principles.

During the same period, Koizumi, as the leader of the LDP, led the HR election campaign in October and November 2003. In the HR campaigns, both the LDP and the Democratic Party of Japan (DPJ) set an election manifesto to clarify their positions on major policy issues. Koizumi put Japan Post privatization as one of the central issues in the LDP manifesto, overcoming resistance from *yūsei zoku* and other old guard politicians.[57] Koizumi's popularity among the public helped the LDP win the majority of HR seats, but its margin over opposition parties was so slim that the LDP continued to maintain coalition with the Clean Government Party (CGP). Nonetheless, Koizumi regarded the LDP "victory" as the public's approval of his pursuit of Japan Post privatization, and accelerated privatization policymaking.

The discussion to formulate plans for Japan Post privatization was held at the Council on Economic and Fiscal Policy, an organization within the prime minister's office, allowing them to keep LDP *yūsei zoku* politicians out. In August 2004, the Council issued the basic plan for Japan Post privatization. According to the plan, Japan Post would be abolished in April 2007, and broken up into a shareholding company and four companies for postal service, postal savings, postal life insurance, and post office service networks. The plan set a 10-year transition period during which the postal savings and postal life insurance companies would be completely privatized and freed from government control, however, the government would continue to have some influence over the other three organizations.[58] Many LDP politicians opposed the plan, arguing that the plan did not ensure post offices in rural areas, whose *tokutei* postmasters were major LDP supporters, to operate after privatization and break-up. However, Koizumi ignored opposition from the LDP and adopted the privatization plan at a Cabinet meeting without consent from the LDP in September although it was customary to gain approval from the LDP beforehand.[59]

Following the cabinet decision, Koizumi reshuffled the cabinet and LDP leadership. To foster consensus to promote Japan Post privatization, Koizumi appointed politicians supportive of privatization to LDP leadership positions, mostly ignoring seniority and influence of major factions. One of the most important cabinet appointments was to create the position of Minister of State for Privatization of the Postal Services and assigned to this position was Takenaka, who also continued to serve his current position.[60] While Takenaka and his staff worked on the details of the bills to privatize Japan Post, pro-privatization LDP politicians negotiated with LDP members, many of whom were still opposed to the privatization. Since Koizumi was adamant about privatizing Japan Post, LDP members could not fundamentally change the content of the privatization bills. When Koizumi decided on an outline of the privatization bills in April 2005, while sticking to the break-up and privatization of Japan Post contained in the cabinet decision, some concessions, such as allowing cross-sharing among privatized postal companies and setting up a ¥1 trillion universal service fund to help postal savings and life insurance companies to provide service to rural areas, were made to LDP members.[61] Since many LDP members were not satisfied with the bills, the LDP leadership further negotiated with the Koizumi administration, but few other concessions were made when they finally reached an agreement in late April.

Even after Koizumi sent Japan Post privatization bills to the HR, a significant number of LDP HR members were against the bills. Since all opposition parties, including the DPJ, also tried to abort the bills, it seemed very unlikely that the bills would pass the HR. Nonetheless, Koizumi did not soften his stance. While refusing to make amendments to the bills, Koizumi threatened to dissolve the HR and call a general election even though more than 2 years out of a 4-year term were left. Many LDP did not want to go through another election so early, and thought that should elections be called, LDP might be broken up and lose its power. Concerned with the development of a serious schism within the party, the LDP leadership actively mediated between the Koizumi administration and party members. Nearing the voting on Japan Post privatization bills in the HR, the LDP leadership persuaded Koizumi to make some amendments to the bills. The amendments stipulated that the shareholding company be allowed to (continue to) hold shareholder voting rights over the postal bank and postal life insurance companies, that the size of the universal fund may be bigger than ¥1 trillion, that post offices deal with savings and postal life insurance, and that the privatization plan would be revised every three years.[62] As a result of this compromise, the majority of LDP HR members agreed to support the bills.

Still, about 50 LDP HR members were reported to be against the bills. Since 46 defections from the LDP would defeat the bills, the LDP leadership scrambled to reduce the number of defections, emphasizing that the defeat of the bills would definitely lead Koizumi to dissolve the HR, that defectors would be punished in accordance with LDP party rules, and that the LDP would not offer endorsements in the election. Uncompromising hard core *yūsei zoku* politicians held a series of meetings to maintain a united front, while *tokutei* postmasters continued to press LDP HR members to reject the bills. The fate of the bills was uncertain, but Koizumi insisted that the Japan Post bills be passed during the current session of the Diet scheduled to end in August, which could not be extended because the session had already been extended once. Koizumi went ahead and had the HR vote on the bills on July 5, 2005. Although the bills passed the HR and they were sent to the HC, the victory margin was a mere 5 votes since 37 LDP members voted against the bills whereas another 14 abstained.[63]

The slim margin revitalized hard core *yūsei zoku* politicians, who set out to defeat the bills at the HC, adopting a new strategy called Operation Stealth. During the battle at the HR, they demonstrated their strength by making public those who opposed the bills. This showed the LDP leadership whom they should talk to and persuade not to defect.[64] Learned from this experience, *yūsei zoku* politicians did not disclose which HC members, except those core defectors, were likely to vote against the bills, leaving many LDP HC members not to clarify their position. They kept the possible defectors off the "radar" of the LDP leadership, just like Stealth Fighters undetectable by the enemy radar. Since the LDP–CGP coalition had a very slim margin in the HC, only 18 LDP defections would abort the bill. However, Koizumi was adamant about passing the bill in the current session and refused to consider carrying it over to the next session. He reiterated that if the bills were defeated at the HC, he would dissolve the HR.[65] To appease the opponents, LDP leaders in the HC won more concessions, which made it possible for Japan Post privatization plan to be revised in the future. The leaders suggested that the opponents would be able to discuss the privatization even after the passage of the bills. These measures did not lead many of the opponents to change their positions, and the bills were defeated on August 8 by 125 to 108 in the HC, with 22 LDP members casting no votes. On the same day, as promised, Koizumi quickly dissolved the HR.

In preparing for the HR elections scheduled to be held on September 11, 2005, Koizumi wielded very strong leadership. Koizumi and the LDP leadership not only removed the LDP dissenters who voted against the Japan Post privatization bills from the LDP candidate list but also nominated an LDP candidate against each dissenter in his or her district. While strengthening his reformist image through the uncompromising stance toward the old guard, he criticized the DPJ for opposing postal privatization because of its connections with postal labor unions, and portrayed the DPJ as a party against reforms. Koizumi's strategy turned out to be very effective and the LDP won a decisive victory. By wining urban and suburban districts, the stronghold of opposition parties, the LDP won 296 seats out of 480. Following this victory, Koizumi quickly resubmitted the postal privatization bills to the Diet. This time, not only LDP and CGP Diet members but also some of the dissenters both in the HR and HC cast their votes for Japan Post privatization. The bills passed the Diet swiftly in October 2005, scheduling the privatization of Japan Post in October 2007, six months after the original date. Although Koizumi achieved his goal of Japan Post privatization, this privatization involved a long, painstaking process and required a great deal of strong political leadership. Old guard politicians held off reform for a long time. Also, it must be added that there will be a ten-year transition period and that the real impact of the privatization is still too early to be assessed.

Along with the postal business reform, Koizumi targeted the reform of special government corporations (*tokushu hōjin*), which symbolized the inefficiency of the Japanese government. Each special government corporation maintained close relations with a government ministry—which sent its retired bureaucrats to the corporation as executives—and, therefore, its management was not exposed to scrutiny while enjoying privileged status and facing no private sector competitors. Since special government corporations had access to funds, particularly from the FILP, they spent an enormous amount of money on costly projects that did not seem to serve the public interest. Special government corporations were not only a symbol of the wasting of resources by the government, but also a potential source of financial disaster that would need to be solved by tax money. Many special government corporations ran deficits, although they concealed the severity of the problem by using special accounting methods. Therefore, many LDP leaders recognized that reforming special government corporations was necessary, and had begun to work on reform plans before Koizumi became prime minister. The leaders sought to improve the corporations' operation through gradual improvement in management, but Koizumi went further, arguing that drastic change, including privatization, was necessary.

Among special government corporations, Koizumi targeted public highway corporations (PHCs)—JH, the Metropolitan Expressway Public Corporation, the Hanshin Expressway Public Corporation, and the Honshu-Shikoku Bridge Authority. Each of the PHCs used an enormous amount of FILP funds to construct nationwide highways, regardless of profitability, and the PHCs as a whole had accumulated an estimated ¥40 trillion debt. Due to the accumulating deficits, the Honshu-Shikoku Bridge Authority, which constructed and operated three bridges between the main island and Shikoku, a big island in western Japan, needed the government to inject funds to pay for the debt. Although major highways in and between the two metropolitan areas, Tokyo and Osaka, generated profits, the revenue was used for the construction of new highways in rural areas, and it was feared that the JH might not be able to pay back its large debt, which would heavily constrain government finances. Each of these PHCs had former bureaucrats, particularly from the MLIT, as executives, and its management lacked transparency. Koizumi singled out the PHCs as the major target of his special government corporation reform.

For Koizumi, privatization was the only way to reform the PHCs, because it would infuse managerial discipline to the corporations and enable them to pay back their debts while preventing them from constructing unprofitable routes. However, MLIT was reluctant to drastically change the PHC's operation, because it would make it impossible to further construct highways. Similarly, LDP old guard politicians, particularly *dōro zoku*, a group of LDP Diet members who were concerned with transportation policy, vehemently opposed a fundamental change of the PHCs, because they thought it essential to finish constructing planned national highway networks of 9,342 kilometers, of which 2,383 kilometers was still to be built. For *dōro zoku* politicians, the construction of the 2,383 kilometers was the essential issue, because it would benefit their rural constituents as well as local construction companies. Both the MLIT and LDP's *dōro zoku* tried to delay Koizumi's PHC reform.

Nonetheless, Koizumi was determined to pursue the reform. In November 2001, he officially declared that he would embark upon the privatization of the PHCs with the revision of the plan to construct the national highway networks of 9,342 kilometers, and that the government would stop allocating a budget of roughly ¥300 billion yen to JH from the next fiscal year.[66] In June 2002, to formulate an action plan for PHC's privatization, Koizumi created the Dōro Kōdan Mineika Suishin Iinkai (the Committee for the Promotion of the Privatization of Public Highway Corporations). The Committee was headed by a former president of Japan's largest steel manufacturer. The members included the chairman of JR West, who actively supported JR's privatization, academics knowledgeable of transportation and public administration, and a writer who extensively criticized the inefficiency of government operation, including PHCs. Koizumi appointed the writer despite intense opposition from LDP *dōro zoku* politicians, who thought he was too radical.[67] At this stage of the PHC reform, Koizumi showed his direct commitment to reform.

Backed by Koizumi's support, the Committee extensively examined PHC operations, overcoming resistance from the MLIT and JH, which begrudged accounting and other information regarding PHC operations. However, as the members put together a final report, upon which Koizumi was expected to formulate PHC privatization plans, disagreements became clear among them. The Committee chair and another member were willing to compromise with LDP *dōro zoku* and the MLIT, and endorsed a plan that would allow a privatized JH to continue to build highways, claiming that an extreme reform plan would not attract support from the LDP. In contrast, the rest of the Committee members insisted that the reform plan must prevent the privatized JH from constructing further unprofitable highways. Facing opposition from the majority of the members, the chair resigned, and the reformist members drew up the final report. According to the report, the new arrangement would create a division between a highway system holding organization and five privatized highway operating companies. The holding organization would lease highway facilities to the operating companies, and repay the debt—which it would take over from the PHCs—by using lease revenues. The operating companies would purchase the facilities from the organizations in about ten years. In general, this plan's main purpose was the rationalization of highway operation and the repayment of debt, while making it impossible for the LDP to force the companies to build new highways.[68] With the release of the report, Koizumi set PHC reform as an important political agenda. He emphasized the reform in the LDP presidential election and the HR elections in fall 2003.

Although the MLIT was uncooperative with the Committee, it did not openly criticize Committee discussion during the deliberation process. Whereas LDP *dōro zoku* vehemently opposed the final report, and questioned its legitimacy because it was made after the resignation of the Committee chair, MLIT did not express its view on the report. However, since the MLIT, as a government ministry in charge of road construction and maintenance, was the primary formulator of Diet bills for PHC privatization, the MLIT became the most influential actor in the PHC reform. For the MLIT, PHC privatization was not necessarily undesirable, since the MLIT and PHCs, especially JH, had tense relations. Many JH executives, including the president, were retired bureaucrats from the Ministry of Construction, the MLIT's predecessor, but JH still tried to maximize its autonomy, often colliding with the MLIT. The dismissal of JH president Fujii Haruho, a former Vice Construction Minister, from the top position in October 2003, did not decrease the MLIT's influence over the reform process.[69] On the contrary, the decline of JH's influence gave the MLIT the flexibility to deal with the reform; the MLIT explored the construction of certain highways directly via the government that JH once opposed.

For the MLIT and LDP *dōro zoku* old guard politicians, the format of PHCs was of secondary concern. For them, the most important issue was the continued construction of national highway networks. For this purpose, the MLIT and LDP were willing to compromise with Koizumi and reformers. After extensive negotiations among them, an agreement was reached in December 2003. Following the reform committee's final report, the agreement stipulated that PHCs would be reorganized into a highway network holding company that would lease highway facilities to six highway operating companies. However, unlike the final report, the agreement did not include a mechanism that would prevent the construction of (unprofitable) highway routes, although the agreement included the reduction of government expenditures on highway construction. Under government guidance and support, the highway operation companies would continue to build new highways; their bonds for highway construction would have government guarantees, and their debt resulting from the construction would be taken over by the highway holding company.[70]

Three of the PHC privatization committee members harshly criticized the final agreement because it would neither stop the construction of unprofitable highway routes, whose cost would eventually have to be borne by the government, nor infuse privatized highway operation companies with management based on market principles. These members resigned in protest. However, Koizumi and two of the reform committee members emphasized the cost-cut and the PHC privatization as a success while old guard LDP politicians were satisfied with a result that would allow them to push for the continued construction of highway networks that would benefit their constituents and financial supporters, namely construction companies. Therefore, after the agreement, the PHC privatization process proceeded without any disturbance. The bills for the privatization of the PHCs passed the Diet in June, 2004, and the PHCs were privatized in October 2005.

Conclusion

The political process of government reform since the early 1980s is distinctive among LDP political instances in which behind-the-scenes maneuvering was used to handle conflicts. Each of the three major government reforms—Nakasone, Hashimoto, and Koizumi—involved dynamic political interactions and a great deal of disputes among the LDP politicians and government bureaucrats. Each of them was different from business-as-usual LDP politics in that they achieved major changes in government structure, such as the privatization of major government corporations, deregulation, and government reorganization. However, it would be an exaggeration to portray each reform as the prime minister and his reformers' success story. In fact, the prime minister was very important in bringing in government reform as a primary political agenda; reformist business leaders and academics at advisory councils—who were from the developmental networks or who regarded government reform as a crucial measure for the development of the Japanese economy—played an important role in formulating concrete reform plans. In this sense, reformers were able to set a general direction for the initial stage of each reform.

However, as each reform progressed, prime ministers and reformers faced substantial resistance from bureaucrats and LDP old guard politicians. Neither bureaucrats nor old guard politicians tried to totally abort the reform. Instead, they worked to adjust the direction of reform. Bureaucrats, as primary bill writers, tried to preserve their influence. Moreover, as typified in the relationship between the MPT and NTT in telecommunications reform, the privatization of a government corporation often shifted regulatory and policy-planning authority from a corporation to a ministry, and bureaucrats were therefore sometimes able to enhance their authority. As for the old guard politicians, they were willing to allow reformers to declare victory. However, they succeeded in minimizing the impact of the reform on the distributive networks, as exemplified by the privatization of public highway corporations; Koizumi succeeded in privatizing them, but failed to stop the construction of national highway networks, due to resistance from old guard politicians and bureaucrats.

Thus, government reforms were closely related to Japan's dual state, consisting of developmental and distributive networks. The outcome of each reform was determined by the interaction between the two networks. Those reform measures that did not threaten the well-being of the distributive networks, such as the privatization of NTT and JNR, faced less resistance from old guard politicians and bureaucrats than those that were closely connected with the distributive networks, such as the privatization of postal businesses, government reorganization, and the privatization of public highway corporations.

Chapter 4

Postal Business: Old Guard Politics Die Hard

Introduction

Since the early 1980s, three major government reforms—Nakasone, Hashimoto, and Koizumi—sought to reduce the government's role in the economy, and make government operation more efficient. In each reform, various political actors, including LDP leaders, LDP *zoku* members, bureaucrats, and business leaders, battled around reform measures. Although none of the reforms was a complete success, each reform resulted in significant changes in government operation, exemplified by Nakasone's privatization of NTT and JNR, Hashimoto's reorganization of the government, and Koizumi's privatization of JH. In each of these reform periods, the prime minister and reformist politicians set reform as a paramount agenda and invested resources for reform, leading the old guard bloc to become active in aborting or minimizing the progress of reform. This tug of war generated showdowns and resulted in compromise that watered down reform measures. However, political interactions were not limited to the reform period but developed on the basis of continuous interactions in the nonreform period between reformers and old guard in each policy area. Although the magnitude of political interactions was smaller in nonreform periods, policy evolved slowly but significantly. In this chapter and the next, I analyze interactions between reformers and old guard political actors in specific policy areas, namely postal business and transportation, each of which is central to the distributive networks.

In this chapter, I focus on old guard politics in the postal business, particularly the politics of the postal saving fund (PSF), the world's largest bank that provides a vast amount of funds to Japan's distributive networks. In the following section, after briefly describing the historical background of the PSF, I discuss the PSF's importance to the distributive networks. In the third section, I analyze the interaction between reformers and old guard political actors in the reform of taxation on interest income where the treatment of tax exemption of PSF accounts became a key issue. In the fourth section, I discuss reform politics that developed with the progress in the liberalization of the Japanese financial market. In the fifth section, I provide an overview of the other two components of the postal business, postal life insurance and postal service, followed by the conclusion. Through these analyses, I demonstrate that the old guard bloc interacts with various levels and skillfully preserves or even enhances the strength of the postal business.

The Postal Savings Fund and the Politics of the Distributive Networks

The Japanese government established the PSF in 1875, and the Ministry of Communications, the antecedent of the MPT, was given operation authority in 1885. The government initially used the PSF to encourage citizens, who were used to feudalistic economic transactions and unfamiliar with capitalism, to save money. Since the PSF quickly expanded, the government regarded the PSF as a valuable source of government finance and in 1941 introduced the *teigatku* (fixed rate long-term) account, the PSF's most popular account, to raise wartime military funds. It must be noted that the introduction of *teigaku* has had a long-lasting impact because it has been a very popular personal financial service. Its maturity period is ten years with a fixed interest rate higher than commercial banks' fixed deposit.[1] Depositors were able to withdraw funds without being penalized after six months (or one year before 1948) unlike commercial banks' fixed-term accounts whose depositors have to pay a fee for early withdrawal. Thus, *teigaku* is very attractive to depositors because of its (government-ensured) security, high yield, and flexibility.[2] *Teigaku* is a driving force of the expansion of the PSF and it is the source of dispute between the MPT and commercial banks who regard *teigaku* as having an unfair advantage.

After World War II, *Yūbin Chokin Hō* (the Postal Savings Law) was established in 1947. Several revisions made in the decade following the law's establishment, defined the basic characteristics of the PSF, such as the warranty of principal as well as interest by the government, the maximum amount per depositor, and three types of PSF accounts—*tsūjō* (ordinary), *tsumitate* (installment), and *teigaku* savings.[3] The laws related to the PSF were further revised in 1963 so that the MPT was able to change PSF interest rates after deliberation at its Postal Council without going through time-consuming legislative processes. This enabled the MPT to keep PSF interest rates higher than that of commercial banks. By utilizing these advantages, the MPT continued to expand the PSF through the postwar reconstruction and rapid development periods.

The PSF has been a crucial element of the distributive networks. As described in figure 4.1, the PSF is a source of the FILP. The deposits that post offices collect are lent to the Investment Fund Account operated by the MOF, and the MOF lends money to government-related projects through the FILP. Although the FILP was used to stimulate industrial development, most of the funds are used for (construction) projects to stimulate regional economic development. As discussed in chapter 5, vast amounts of funds for the construction of railways and highways in the rural area came from the FILP. Also, the FILP money goes to special government corporations (*tokushu hōjin*), among which JH is the biggest, in charge of allocating funds to rural projects.

Similar to the mechanism where the FILP channels funds to rural areas and benefits LDP supporters, especially construction companies, the PSF itself works as a distributive mechanism that benefits *tokutei* (special) post offices. Of 24,000 post offices in Japan, about 18,400 are *tokutei* post offices. Historically, the Japanese government appointed locally influential and wealthy persons, particularly in rural areas, as postmasters of *tokutei* post offices in order to develop a postal system in the late nineteenth century. The position of the *tokutei* postmaster has been transferred by inheritance, and *tokutei* postmasters have been the center of social activities in rural areas.[4] For *tokutei* postmasters, the government operation of postal business is crucial because the *tokutei* post office system would not be viable if postal business were operated as a cost-conscious private sector business; maintaining a vast number of *tokutei* post offices in sparsely populated rural areas would be too costly for a private sector business. *Tokutei* postmasters are particularly concerned with the PSF because of three reasons: the PSF is the key component of postal business in Japan and operational profit to be distributed to postmasters mainly derives from the PSF (and postal life insurance, to a lesser extent); second, most post offices are not an essential part of postal delivery service and their main business is to handle the PSF; third and finally, since the MPT

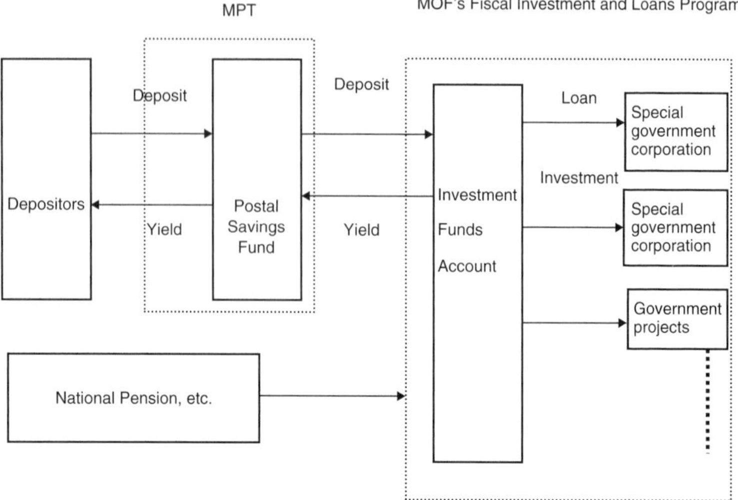

Figure 4.1   The Postal Savings Fund and the Fiscal Investment and Loans Program. *Source*: Compiled by the author.

provided bonuses to postmasters for succeeding in retaining existing PSF depositors and attracting new depositors, *tokutei* postmasters have a short-term monetary incentive to expand the PSF.

Tokutei postmasters have been politically active for the maintenance of the government operation of the PSF and other postal businesses. After World War II, *tokutei* postmasters were organized as a supporting bloc for the LDP. When Tanaka Kakuei was the MPT minister in the late 1950s, he expanded the *tokutei* post office system and developed organizational cohesion among *tokutei* postmasters.[5] In Diet elections, *tokutei* postmasters actively campaign for LDP candidates behind the scenes. Since current postmasters and their employees are civil servants, they are prohibited from participating in political activities. As a result, their family members and former postmasters act in public as proxy. They have a national organization, named *Taiju*, which is the biggest LDP supporting organization with about 230,000 members. Their overall ability to mobilize voters is shown by the results of the HC elections. Since the HC elections include a nationwide district, election results show the strength of the nationwide organization. In the 1980 HC elections, Osada Yuji, a former MPT administrative vice minister, was a candidate in the nationwide district, and attracted over one million votes.[6] In the 2001 HC elections, Koso Kenji, a former director of a regional Postal Administration Office, gained about 480,000 votes. There is a decrease in the number of votes obtained by the MPT candidate; *tokutei* postmasters' strength has somewhat weakened, but Koso's vote was the second highest in the LDP, and their political strength is still substantial.[7]

For MPT bureaucrats, the financial health of the PSF and other postal businesses is crucial and its deterioration would make them vulnerable to criticism from the public and politicians. MPT bureaucrats sought to protect the advantages given to the PSF, using the political might of *tokutei* postmasters. In influencing the policymaking process, MPT bureaucrats maintained close relations with *yūsei zoku* (postal policy tribe) politicians, for whom *tokutei* postmasters provide valuable electoral support in their (rural) districts. In the annual budget making process, *yūsei zoku* politicians press the stingy MOF to increase budget allocation to the MPT. In the reform period, as shown in their activities against Koizumi's reform, *yūsei zoku* politicians act as old guards. In other times whenever the PSF's privilege was threatened, *yūsei zoku* politicians actively defended the advantages of the PSF. Their strong connection to *yūsei zoku* politicians put MPT bureaucrats in an advantageous position in bargaining even when *yūsei zoku* politicians were not mobilized because MOF bureaucrats, MPT bureaucrats' counterpart in negotiations related in PSF reform, had to consider the possible impact of politicization.

Criticism of the MPT's operation of the PSF comes from commercial banks whose business has been threatened by the success of the PSF. The PSF has consistently maintained one-third of the total personal savings, and its deposit dwarfs Japanese private sector megabanks. Commercial banks were particularly frustrated with numerous privileges given to the PSF, such as a higher interest rate, lax tax scrutiny, and lack of urgency for profit making. Since the early days of the post–World War II period, commercial banks have been arguing that the PSF be supplementary to private sector financial institutions.[8] Unlike the MPT, commercial banks lacked strong grassroots political organizations to support LDP candidates in their districts, and the size of the *ginkō zoku* (banking policy tribe)[9] was very small. However, commercial banks have been major financial contributors to the LDP and LDP leaders could not ignore them. Therefore, the MOF, particularly its Banking Bureau, which is the regulator of banking and the protector of banks' interest, works for commercial banks in the policymaking process, continuously rejecting the MPT's repeated request for the introduction of new measures for PSF operation.

Since the MPT's political might was balanced by the MOF's position to approve changes in PSF operation, neither side had generally been successful in radically changing the existing format. Whereas the MOF and commercial banks could not weaken PSF operation, the MPT failed to acquire new measures to strengthen the operation. The momentum to break the equilibrium mainly came from policy development external to the interaction between the two ministries. As shown below, LDP leaders' commitment to tax reform compelled the MPT to eventually accept taxation on PSF accounts, and the U.S.–Japan agreement on the liberalization of the Japanese market led the MPT to make PSF interest rates comparable to that of commercial banks; the MPT gained invaluable concessions from the MOF in each case.

Postal Savings and Tax Reform

In the early 1970s, Japan's post–World War II rapid economic development came to an end, due to radical devaluations of the dollar and dramatic increase in crude oil price. To stimulate the economy in the low growth period, the Japanese government expanded, particularly in public works projects including road construction, as shown in Chapter 5. As a result, the government's balance sheet rapidly deteriorated, and regaining fiscal authority became a political agenda for LDP leaders and MOF bureaucrats in the late 1970s. The MOF and reformers reduced spending through the administrative reform, and they sought to raise government revenue by reforming the tax system. Although taxation on wage income was the most important, changes in taxation on interest income were expected to have significant impact on government revenue, particularly due to the high savings rate of the Japanese. Although the PSF absorbed about one-third of the entire Japanese savings, its accounts were exempt from taxation and suspect of being used for tax evasion. Therefore, taxation on PSF accounts was one of the central issues in (interest income) tax reform.

Green Card Controversy

As a part of tax reform, the MOF planned to raise tax revenue from interest income through the introduction of a system that would monitor the use of tax exemptions. Until 1987, there were various tax exemptions on interest income. Two of the major tax exemptions were given to deposits in commercial banks and the PSF to stimulate savings by citizens. Tax exemption for bank accounts was called *maruyū* among the public. *Maruyū* began in 1963 and exempted each individual's interest income from up to the total of ¥300,000 of bank deposits. The limit on *maruyū* tax exemption was eventually raised to ¥3 million per person in 1974. Similarly, interest income from PSF accounts is exempt from taxation, although each individual was allowed to deposit up to ¥3 million as the principal.[10]

This tax exemption arrangement was liable to abuse both at commercial banks and post offices. Unlike in the United States where tax authorities can detect the flow of funds based on Social Security Numbers, there was no comprehensive system to screen individual deposits in Japan. It was possible for depositors to evade taxation by illegally holding multiple accounts, using fake names. In order to prevent this tax evasion, the MOF frequently did on-the-spot investigations of the branches of commercial banks without official warning, and penalized them when they found the illegal use of the *maruyū* exemptions. Through these investigations, the MOF had rather strict control over deposits at commercial banks, but it did not have any authority over the PSF to exercise surveillance because the PSF came under the MPT's jurisdiction and was off limits to the MOF. Despite the MPT's denial, commercial banks suspected that the MPT did not strictly observe the deposit limit by allowing depositors to open multiple accounts, that this lax enforcement lured citizens to the PSF.

Thus, *maruyū* and PSF tax exemptions themselves reduced government revenue, but their abuse hurt the deficit-laden Japanese government even more. To solve this problem, in December 1979, the Government Tax System Research Council (GTSRC), the MOF's policy deliberation body in tax policy, proposed the establishment of the Green Card system to deter tax evasion. In this system, the government would issue each Japanese citizen an ID card, and he or she would have to present it when opening an account at banks. By using this system the MOF tried to prevent depositors from opening multiple accounts and abusing tax exemptions. Based upon this proposal, the LDP sent a bill to the Diet to establish the Green Card system, and passed it without any major dispute in March 1980. The Green Card system was scheduled to start on January 1, 1984.[11]

Since the impact of this system was not clear when it was introduced in 1980 and the MPT's official position regarding tax exemption abuse was that there had been no illegal use of the PSF accounts, the MPT did not oppose the new system although they suspected that the Green Card was an attempt by the MOF to intrude into the MPT's autonomous management of the PSF.[12] Commercial banks initially welcomed the passage of the Green Card bill because they thought this system would deter suspected tax evasion at the PSF. Contrary to the wishful thinking of commercial banks, the planned introduction of the Green Card system actually gave a big boost to the PSF at the expense of commercial banks; the expected enactment of the Green Card system caused a massive transfer of funds from bank accounts to the PSF in 1980.

When the bill passed in the Diet, it did not specify how the new system would be implemented other than its enactment in 1984, leaving the MOF to determine specifics. The public somehow believed that post offices would check the Green Card only for those deposits made after January 1, 1984, and that banks would have to check those deposits made before then. Those depositors who illegally had multiple tax-exempt accounts moved their funds from banks to the PSF's *teigaku* deposit, which had the maturation period of ten years and would enable the tax evaders to avoid the surveillance based upon the Green Card system for ten years.[13] Due to this massive transfer, commercial banks began to lobby with pro-bank LDP politicians, calling for parity between banks and the PSF in the application of the Green Card system. The LDP leaders could not ignore this legitimate argument made by one of the biggest providers of funding for the party, and this pro-bank campaign gained momentum within the LDP. Consequently, the MPT agreed to check the Green Card of the PSF customers who had opened an account before January 1980 when they made a withdrawal.[14]

Ironically, this politicization turned the tide against the MOF and reformers. The new agreement would enable the MOF to exercise ex post-scrutiny of PSF accounts opened before the establishment of the Green Card system and to increase influence over the MPT's PSF operation. Threatened by the MOF's possible intrusion into the MPT's autonomy of PSF operation, the MPT mobilized *yūsei zoku* politicians, then headed by Kenemaru Shin, one of the LDP bosses, and embarked on a campaign against this Green Card system in April 1981.[15] The MPT's opposition movement quickly gained momentum and in April 1982, about 300 LDP Diet members, about three-fourth of total members, signed a petition and demanded the reconsideration of the enactment of the Green Card system.[16] Unfortunately for the MOF and reformers, banks withdrew their support for the system because depositors began to shift their funds from bank accounts to not only PSF accounts but also other financial commodities such as stocks, bonds, and foreign accounts, which would not be affected by the system. Also, opposition parties were against this system, because they thought that it would infringe upon privacy.[17]

Since the MOF drafted the system, it did not want to withdraw its implementation and hurt its reputation. Therefore, the MOF relegated the treatment of the Green Card system to LDP's Tax System Research Council (LTSRC),[18] chaired by Yamanaka Sadanori.[19] Given this development, Yamanaka coordinated efforts within the LDP to suspend the system. In 1983, a year before its enactment, the Diet voted to postpone the establishment of the system for three years. In the following year, the Diet passed the bill that officially abandoned the Green Card system.[20] Thus, the MPT successfully aborted the MOF's reform measure to strictly enforce tax exemption rules to PSF accounts that would have made it nearly impossible for citizens to open multiple PSF accounts to evade taxation on their interest income.

Taxation on Interest Income

Despite the Green Card fiasco, the MOF continued to pursue reform of taxation on interest income because the loss of tax revenue from tax evasion was too large to ignore. According to the MOF's calculation, legitimate and illegitimate uses of *maruyū* tax exemptions for bank accounts cost the MOF ¥302 billion in tax revenue in the fiscal year 1982 alone. The MOF suspected abuses were still prevalent because the number of tax exempt accounts was far higher than the entire Japanese population (about 100 million) at the PSF and commercial banks—the PSF had 318 million accounts whereas the total of *maruyū* accounts at banks was 220 million.[21] The Green Card system would have solved the problem, but since the MOF failed to enact the system, it needed to come up with an alternative measure, including the abolishment of the tax exemptions without which some estimated that tax revenue would be increased by ¥1 trillion.[22] The MOF and the GTSRC began to discuss alternatives in spring 1984 and issued a preliminary report in September 1984. Although the GTSRC's position was still vague, it emphasized the necessity to revise the system and requested the MOF to formulate concrete plans.[23]

Thus, the MOF renewed its attempt for income tax reform but the MPT continued to oppose the reform of taxation on interest income, arguing that the expansion of tax exemption on interest income was necessary to encourage savings given Japan's rapid progress toward an aging society.[24] Nonetheless, the political environment related to taxation on the PSF was gradually changing. LDP leaders were increasingly concerned with deteriorating government finance. Recognizing the inevitability of the reform of the tax system, they explored the possibility of imposing taxes on PSF and bank accounts.[25] Backed by support from LDP leadership, the MOF continued to discuss interest income tax reform at the GTSRC in collaboration with LDP's deliberation council for government finance. Eventually, the MOF formulated a reform plan whose central measure was to impose low-rate tax on interest income from PSF and bank accounts (5–10 percent), and proceeded with legislation. Yet, the MPT opposed this plan and mobilized LDP *yūsei zoku*.[26]

Due to the growing opposition toward the MOF, LDP leaders dropped the plan to introduce low-rate taxation on interest income from PSF and bank accounts. The LTSRC instead chose to support another plan that would tighten control over the limit of tax exemption for interest income from PSF and bank accounts. The LTSRC made other proposals including the requirement of the presentation of public documents to confirm the depositor's identity, the obligation for the MPT to withhold tax on income from illegal use of tax exemptions for PSF accounts, and the possible introduction of audit of PSF accounts. Although the LTSRC deferred to the MOF and MPT to set details, it set a general direction in the MOF's favor, generally endorsing the ministry's imposition of taxes on interest income.

Nonetheless, *yūsei zoku* continued to resist and persuaded Secretary General Kanemaru Shin to modify the plan.[27] As a result, LDP leaders, including Kanemaru and PARC Chair Fujio Masayuki met in December 1984, and came up with a compromise. According to the compromise plan, the MOF and MPT would negotiate to establish a monitoring system where the MPT would have to withhold tax on interest income from illegal use of PSF. The plan indicated the possibility of the tax authorities' audit of PSF accounts, but postponed its implementation for the time being. With this compromise, the intra-party battle ended, leaving the MOF, MPT and banks to determine concrete measures for stricter enforcement of deposit limit at the PSF and that of *maruyū* rules at banks.[28]

Because of this agreement, as well as the Diet elections in 1986 in which LDP politicians refrained from discussing politically unpopular tax reforms,[29] the MOF had to halt its pursuit of tax reform. Since the LDP won the elections, the MOF later resumed the discussion of tax reform. This time the MOF included (wage) income tax cut as a major component of tax reform, and Prime Minister Nakasone regarded it as an important political agenda. In order to make up for the loss incurred by income tax cuts, MOF and LDP leaders looked to taxation on interest income as an alternative source of government revenue, and decided to introduce flat tax on interest income. Facing the development of a political trend for taxation on interest income, the MPT and LDP recognized the inevitability of taxation on PSF accounts and sought to explore ways to obtain concessions from the MOF in return for its acceptance of taxation on PSF accounts.

In the political domain, *yūsei zoku* members continued to fight against the taxation, passing resolutions against the taxation in various LDP meetings. Meanwhile, Vice Prime Minister Kanemaru sought to cut a deal that would provide quid pro quo for the MPT.[30] Kanemaru met Chief Cabinet Secretary Gotoda Masaharu on November 5. Kanemaru accepted Gotoda's request for the support of taxation on the PSF in return for quid pro quo, which would benefit MPT and *tokutei* postmasters.[31] Following this agreement, the MPT's Administrative Vice Minister, Sawada Shigeki, met the MOF's counterpart, Yoshino Yoshihiko, on November 13. Sawada proposed to negotiate between its Postal Savings Bureau and MOF's General Affairs Bureau to iron out differences. As a result of interministerial negotiations between the MPT and MOF, these ministries reached an accord on December 4.[32] This MPT–MOF accord was later finalized by LDP leaders, ending the MPT's and *yūsei zoku*'s opposition movement against taxation on PSF accounts.

In this accord, the MPT agreed with the MOF on taxation on the PSF, but the former obtained major concessions from the latter including the MPT's independent investment of a portion of the PSF, increasing the maximum limit of the PSF deposits from ¥3 million to ¥5 million per depositor, and the MPT's sales of ¥1 trillion of government bonds at post offices. In particular, the independent investment of a portion of the PSF had been the MPT's earnest desire since the late 1970s, because it was frustrated at its lack of authority to invest funds from postal savings. Also, the independent investment was crucial for the MPT to cope with ongoing financial liberalization, the topic discussed in the following section, as it made it possible for the MPT to increase its profit unlike in the preceding arrangement where it had to lend all funds of postal savings to the MOF at a predetermined interest rate. Through its opposition to the taxation, the MPT strengthened its operation.

Rōjin Maruryū Controversy

After political turmoil, the new system of interest income taxation began in April 1988.[33] Generally tax exemptions for interest income from PSF and bank deposits were abolished, but, from the standpoint of social welfare, the new arrangement included tax exemptions for the elderly (65 or above), single mothers, and handicapped people, collectively termed as *rōjin maruyū* (preferential tax treatment for the elderly). *Rōjin maruyū* exempted each qualified person from tax on interest income from PSF deposits, bank deposits, and government bonds, up to ¥3 million each.[34] Toward the scheduled minor revision of the new tax system five years after its enactment to evaluate its effectiveness, the MPT began to demand the increase of the limit on *rōjin maruyū* in August 1992.[35]

As discussed later in this chapter, a result of negotiations with the MOF on the liberalization of deposit interest was that the PSF deposit limit per person was increased to ¥5 million in April 1988, to ¥7 million in February 1990, and to ¥10 million in November 1991. In contrast, the *rōjin maruyū* limit for the PSF, ¥3 million, was the same as the old PSF limit, which had been effective from 1973 through 1988.[36] Although the MOF's financial deliberation council deemed the increase unnecessary,[37] LDP leaders became sympathetic to the MPT, and it seemed that the LDP would allow the MPT to increase the limit by ¥1 million to ¥2 million. However, the tide turned for the MPT when Koizumi Junichiro, the MPT's nemesis, was appointed as MPT minister in December 1992. At the press conference immediately held after the (unofficial) decision of his appointment, Koizumi clearly stated that the increase was unnecessary, to the dismay of MPT bureaucrats.[38] This prompted LDP leaders to change its position. Citing that the head of the MPT was not supporting the increase, the leaders became reluctant to approve the MPT's request.[39]

In response to MPT Minister Koizumi's opposition, LDP *yūsei zoku* politicians fought back. Political MPT Vice Minister Sasagawa Akira resigned in protest, and the politicians pressed major LDP leaders to support the MPT's request; some of them openly criticized PARC Chair Mitsuzuka's lack of control over Koizumi. The intra-LDP conflict was settled by the LTSRC decision on December 16, 1992. LTSRC chair and vice chairs decided to allow MPT to increase by ¥500,000 the limit of *rōjin maruyū* tax exemption for the PSF and others. MOF officials were not completely satisfied with the decisions, but these decisions compelled minimum concessions from the MOF while it offered token compromise to the MPT and *yūsei zoku* politicians.[40] This *rōjin maruyū* controversy suggests the limit of MPT's political power in PSF policymaking. The MPT–*yūsei zoku* political bloc was influential in LDP politics but it was far from dominant. Although it wielded strong influence in resisting changes in the existing arrangement, it was not strong enough to achieve drastic changes to strengthen the MPT's PSF operation.

The PSF and Financial Liberalization

Since the MPT's PSF operation is an integral part of Japanese personal finance, most major changes in the MOF's personal financial regulation require the MPT to adjust the operation. As the MOF's financial regulation changed in accordance with the global trend for liberalization in the 1980s and 1990s, it needed to make the PSF consistent with regulatory changes. Until the mid-1980s, MOF had tightly regulated Japanese finance, and the format of its regulation was characterized as "the convoy system," where the MOF emphasized the welfare of the financial industry on the whole and set specifics of its operation. This convoy system developed stability in Japanese finance and provided a positive financial environment for Japanese business during the post–World War II rapid economic development period. However, as shown in the chapter on the administrative reform involving the privatization of NTT, since the early 1980s, government involvement in economic activities began to be called into question. Along with this general trend for liberalization, the direct impact came from the U.S. government. MOF and U.S. Treasury reached an accord to liberalize the Japanese financial market in 1984. This accord stipulated that the MOF begin to allow banks, instead of the MOF, to set interest rates for bank deposits.[41] The MOF started the liberalization of bank deposit interest rates from large-scale bank deposits. Banks began to sell large-scale money market certificates (MMCs) in which the minimum was ¥50 million and with an interest rate that changed with the market trend in March 1985. Also, they started large-scale fixed deposits where the minimum was ¥1 billion with a maturation period that varied from three months to two years, with each bank setting their own interest rates.[42] As shown in table 4.1, the MOF gradually reduced the minimum amount for these financial commodities and expanded the area of financial liberalization.

From the late 1980s, the MOF began to liberalize interest rate of small-scale deposits and finished the liberalization in 1995. In this period, the MOF gradually liberalized financial activities to help small and medium-sized banks to cope with changes. Three major steps taken by the MOF were the introduction of small-scale Money Market, the liberalization of fixed deposits, and that of liquid deposits. In each step, the MPT and MOF engaged in extensive negotiations, where the former sought to gain concession to strengthen the PSF from the latter who tried to make the PSF consistent with the liberalization and the condition of competition comparable between the PSF and commercial banks to maintain equal footing.

Table 4.1 Progress of the liberalization of large-scale deposit interest rates

	Minimum deposit amount of a large-scale MMC (in ¥ million)	Minimum amount of a fixed deposit excluded from interest rate regulation (in ¥)
March 1985	50	
October 1985		1 billion
April 1986		500 million
September 1986	30	300 million
April 1987	20	100 million
October 1987	10	
April 1988		50 million
November 1988		30 million
April 1989		20 million
October 1989	Large-scale MMC abolished	10 million

Source: Zenkoku Ginkō Kyōkai (1997), *Ginkō Kyōkai 50 Nenshi*, 440.

The Introduction of Small-Scale MMCs

With gradual progress in the liberalization of large-scale deposit interest rate, the liberalization of small-scale deposit interest rates became
inevitable and the treatment of PSF needed to be examined. Since
total PSF deposits amounted to about half of the total bank deposits,
the MOF needed to make the government-operated PSF consistent
with the liberalized financial market. In particular, the MOF considered the PSF's *teigaku* deposit very problematic, which was a ten-year
fixed rate account with flexibility of withdrawal without penalty from
six months after the deposit. The MOF, as well as commercial banks,
argued that only PSF, as a government operation free of urgent concern for profitability, was capable of maintaining *teigaku*, and that it
was virtually impossible for banks to provide comparable financial
services particularly in the competitive market after liberalization.
Therefore, the MOF thought it was essential to revise the advantages
of the *teigaku* deposit for financial liberalization.[43] The MOF and
banks sought to impose restrictions on PSF to prevent it from taking
advantage of its privileged position of government operation in the
liberalized market.

The MPT had an opposite view about the relationship between
PSF and financial liberalization. It maintained that the revision of the
teigaku deposit was not only unnecessary but also contradictory to
liberalization. Rather, since liberalization would enable banks to

operate flexibly, the MPT argued that PSF as a government operation was so restricted that liberalization would put it in a disadvantaged position. Therefore, the MPT sought to add flexibility to PSF operation. In 1985, as a part of the fiscal year 1986 budget request, the MPT demanded that the MOF set aside a portion of PSF—what the MPT called *Kinyū Jiyūka Taisaku Shikin* (the fund for coping with financial liberalization)—to be used for the MPT's independent investment.[44] The MOF initially turned down the MPT's request, but, as shown earlier in this chapter, the MPT got approval from the MOF in December 1986 in return for taxation on PSF (and bank) deposits. Along with flexibility in investment, the MPT sought to gain flexibility in marketing PSF by introducing a new type of deposit whose interest rate would change in accordance with the market trend, and began to negotiate with the MOF in September 1985.[45] Yet, because of the opposite views held by each of the two ministries on PSF and financial liberalization, negotiations did not proceed quickly.

The first item that the two ministries dealt with was small-scale MMCs, which was introduced as a transition measure for liberalization of small-scale deposits in December 1985.[46] The MPT sought to start a similar commodity for the PSF to keep apace with the progress of liberalization. However, the MOF was unwilling to allow PSF to start small-scale MMCs.[47] The MOF demanded that, as a condition for the approval of the MPT's request, the latter should revise the format of the *teigaku* deposit.[48] However, the MPT argued that the revision of the *teigaku* deposit was irrelevant to the liberalization of small-scale deposit interest rate.[49] In addition to the difference of positions, MPT–MOF negotiations were also delayed by an external factor. Since, as discussed earlier in this part of this chapter, changes in taxation on interest income from bank and PSF deposits took longer than expected, the format of taxation on small-scale MMCs was uncertain, preventing the MPT and MOF from engaging in substantive negotiations for the introduction of small-scale MMCs. After September 1987 when the bills for the changes were passed by the Diet, the MPT and MOF began to negotiate for the introduction of small-scale MMCs.[50]

Still the two sides' positions remained in conflict. The MPT sought to establish a very long-term ten-year MMC, independently from bank MMCs, and refused to accommodate the MOF and banks' demand for revising the *teigaku* deposit's high interest rate and very long maturation period.[51] Yet, with the enactment of the abolition of tax exemption of interest income from PSF and banks' *maruyū* deposits in April 1988, each side began to soften its position. The abolition of *maruyū* led depositors to transfer funds from bank accounts to other high-yielding financial commodities, such as investment trusts. Banks wanted to stop further transfers and regain funds through small-scale MMCs. The abolition of the tax exemption status of PSF deposits wielded similar effects on the PSF. Moreover, the MPT had a special reason to expedite the introduction of small-scale MMCs. A vast number of high-interest *teigaku* deposits were made during the Green Card controversy in the fiscal year 1980, and they were going to mature in the fiscal year 1990. Since the total amount deposited in these accounts corresponded to about one-third of the total PSF, the MPT needed MMCs to prevent the funds from being transferred to other financial institutions. As a result, the MPT softened its stance on *teigaku* revision and began to include it as an item in its negotiations with the MOF.[52]

However, the MPT did not concede quickly, but patiently negotiated with the MOF to maximize its gains. Finally in December 1988, the MPT and MOF reached an agreement on the introduction of small-scale MMCs. In this agreement, the MPT and banks would establish five common types of small-scale MMCs in accordance with the maturation period, that is, three-month, six-month, one-year, two-year, and three-year MMCs. The minimum deposit for all of these would be ¥3 million. The interest rates of the first four types of MMCs would be linked to CD interest rates.[53] Also, this agreement stated that the interest rate of two-year MMCs would not surpass that of three-year MMCs. Regarding the *teigaku* deposit, the MPT agreed to set the upper limit on *teigaku* interest rates, which would, as a rule, be 80 percent of the three-year MMC interest rate.[54] Since the MPT agreed to set some limit on the *teigaku* deposit, this was epoch-making, but the MPT fended off the MOF and banks' demand to shorten the maturation period and abolish the calculation of yield at compound interest. Moreover, the MPT obtained a significant concession from the MOF, which was the increase of PSF deposit limit per person to ¥7 million from ¥5 million. A maximum deposit of ¥3 million made at a *teigaku* deposit in the fiscal year 1980 was to grow larger than the current deposit limit, ¥5 million, at the end of its maturation period in the fiscal year 1990, and the PSF was not going to be able to reabsorb it entirely. But the increase of the maximum amount would enable the MPT to lead *teigaku* deposit holders to deposit all of their money into a new *teigaku* deposit or other PSF accounts.[55] Thus, the MPT did not get all their demands met but secured the most essential.

The Liberalization of Interest Rates for Small-Scale Fixed Deposits

Following the MPT–MOF agreement in December 1988, the MPT and banks began to sell two types (six-month and one-year maturation) of small-scale MMCs in June 1989. They added three types: three-month, two-year, and three-year maturation MMCs in 1990, and reduced the minimum deposit to ¥1 million.[56] Although the expansion of small-scale MMCs was consistent with the liberalization of interest rate determination for small-scale bank deposits, individual banks and the MPT did not have the freedom to determine interest rates for small-scale MMCs; the introduction of small-scale MMCs were a transition measure before complete liberalization. The MOF tried to expedite the liberalization process, but faced resistance from small and medium-size banks, which were not capable of coping with quick liberalization.[57] Yet, the U.S. government pressed the MOF to quickly complete the liberalization within a year when the two governments held talks on finance in May 1990. Also, Kinyū Mondai Kenkyūkai (the Financial Issue Research Group, FIRG), an advisory group for the MOF Banking Bureau chief consisting of economists that set general guidelines of financial liberalization, issued a report in the same month that called for the completion of the liberalization of deposit interest rate. Following these requests, the MOF decided to complete the liberalization of interest rate for fixed deposits in about three years, and due to U.S. pressure, small and medium-sized banks came to accept the MOF's proposed schedule of liberalization.[58]

In pursuing liberalization, as was the case with the introduction of small-scale MMCs, the treatment of the PSF became a contentious issue, particularly the determination of interest rates for PSF's fixed accounts. Banks insisted on establishing rules that would follow changes in interest rate at bank deposits to prevent the PSF from holding unfair advantage by setting its interest rates higher than those at banks. Emphasizing the autonomy to determine interest rates as paramount to its PSF management, the MPT opposed the establishment of the rules.[59] Nonetheless, in December 1990, the MPT and MOF reached an agreement that included the synchronization of PSF interest rates with bank interest rates. According to this agreement, the MPT would introduce a new type of PSF fixed account, whose minimum would be ¥3 million, in conjunction with the liberalization of interest rate for fixed deposits of ¥3 million or above in banks in fall 1991. The MPT would set the interest rate for the new PSF fixed account based on the average interest rate of bank accounts released by the Bank of Japan. In return for its concession of interest rate synchronization, the MPT was allowed to increase the maximum of total PSF deposits per person to ¥10 million, as well as engagement in foreign exchange and travelers check sales at post offices.[60] Following the agreement, the interest rate of fixed deposits of ¥3 million or above was liberalized in November 1991.[61]

For further progress in the liberalization of fixed deposit interest rate, the MOF needed to make the *teigaku* deposit concurrent with liberalization. Although, as mentioned earlier, the MPT agreed to set the upper limit—about 80 percent of three-year MMCs—on the *teigaku* interest rate in December 1988, the MPT never kept this agreement. From February 1991, the *teigaku* interest rate had been higher than those of MMCs, and vast funds were transferred from banks to the PSF,[62] leading banks to demand a fundamental revision of the *teigaku* deposit in October.[63] With the beginning of this partial liberalization of fixed deposits in November 1991, the MOF began to negotiate with the MPT to determine the treatment of the *teigaku* deposit problem. Siding with the banks, the MOF sought to fundamentally change major advantages of the *teigaku* deposit, particularly the following three points. First, the *teigaku* deposit had longevity in that its maturation period was ten years without change of the initial interest rate. Second, the *teigaku* deposit had flexibility in that depositors were able to withdraw cash without penalty after six months, and transfer money to new higher interest *teigaku* accounts. Third and finally, the *teigaku* deposit had a high interest rate, set by the MPT in accordance with the official bank rate but not necessarily with the market rate. Although the MPT showed its willingness to link the *teigaku* interest rate to the market rate, it refused to change the longevity and flexibility of the *teigaku* deposit.[64] Again, MPT–MOF negotiations were stalled.

This time the MPT had no incentives to comply with the MOF's demand. In addition to the *teigaku* deposit, the MPT already had small-scale MMCs and the new fixed deposit that kept up with the market trend. Even if the *teigaku* interest rate happened to become much lower than that of banks' fixed deposits, the MPT was capable of keeping funds within the PSF by leading depositors to transfer funds to small-scale MMCs and the new fixed deposit. In contrast, the MOF had a time constraint—they had planned to finish by spring 1993. However, just after assuming the position in December 1992, Minister of Posts and Telecommunications Koizumi Junichiro took up the banks' demand for the fundamental revision of the *teigaku* deposit. The MPT was able to limit the reform of the *teigaku* deposit

Table 4.2   Computation of the *teigaku* deposit interest rate

		Market interest rate	
		When long-term interest rate is higher than short term	When long-term interest rate is equal to or lower than short term
Interest rate level of the *teigaku* deposit	Ordinary (lower than 6%)	3-year CD market interest rate multiplied by about 0.95	Government bond coupon interest rate subtracted by 0.5
	High (6% or higher)	3-year CD market interest rate multiplied by between 0.90 and 0.95	Government bond coupon interest rate subtracted by between 0.5 and 1.0

Note: All the figures are computed in annual percentage rate. The MPT and MOF agreed to allow small deviations from the exact computation.

Source: *Kinyū Zaisei Jijyō*, January 18, 1991, 30–31.

to interest rate synchronization and the MPT and MOF reached an agreement on December 25, 1992. This agreement specified the method to determine the *teigaku* interest rate, shown in table 4.2. To the disappointment of banks, the agreement did not include any modification on the *teigaku* deposit's longevity and flexibility, but it finalized the schedule for the liberalization of interest rates for fixed deposits.[65]

The Liberalization of Interest Rate for Small-Scale Liquid Deposits

In June 1993, the minimum requirement for the fixed deposit was abolished, and small-scale MMCs were terminated; the MPT did the same for the PSF. As for the *teigaku* deposit, the MPT began to change its interest rate twice a month in accordance with the market trend, based on the scheme shown in table 4.2.[66] With this change, the MOF finished the liberalization of fixed deposit interest rates, and the focus of financial liberalization shifted to liquid deposits (*ryūdōsei yokin*). By this time, discussion on the liberalization of interest rates for liquid deposits had already been in progress since July 1990, when the MOF's FIRG first raised the issue. In discussing the liberalization of interest rate for liquid deposits, whose major components were traditional savings and checking accounts and whose major functions were saving and settlement, the FIRG was concerned with a smooth transition. They were unsure of whether small and medium-sized banks would be able to handle competitive pressure that would be generated by the liberalization. When the FIRG released a report in May 1991 after hearings with the banks and MPT, it called for the introduction of a new type of savings deposit as a transition measure, similar to small-scale MMCs as a transitional measure for the liberalization of fixed deposit interest rates. The new savings deposit would emphasize the saving function of liquid deposits, restricting the automatic transfer of funds and setting a limit on the number of withdrawals per month.[67] This deposit would prevent banks from paying high interest rates to those customers who impose a high cost on bank operation by frequently transferring funds. Yet, the MPT had first opposed the introduction of the new savings deposit and demanded quick liberalization of liquid deposit interest rate. The MPT finally conceded to MOF and allowed the introduction of the new savings deposit when the ministries reached an agreement in July 1991, and the new savings deposit began to operate both at post offices and banks in June 1992.[68] However, at the same time, the MOF agreed to allow national government officials' payroll to be transferred to ordinary PSF saving accounts.[69]

The remaining task that the MOF had to undertake was to complete the liberalization of interest rates by allowing market competition to determine the interest rate of ordinary savings deposits at banks. Again, the central issue was the treatment of the interest rate of the PSF's ordinary saving deposit. The MOF sought to establish a mechanism that would lead the interest rate of the PSF's ordinary savings deposit to follow interest rates of banks' counterparts, preventing the PSF from pushing up the general interest rate level. The MPT resisted MOF's plan, citing the difference between the PSF's and banks' savings. Whereas corporations constituted a large portion of banks' savings deposit use, most depositors of PSF ordinary savings were noncorporate. Since noncorporate depositors did not engage in transactions as much as corporate depositors, the cost of the operation of PSF savings deposits was lower, and the MPT tried to justify the PSF's offering of a higher interest rate.[70] The MOF's introduction of the new savings deposit emphasizing the saving function was intended to undermine the MPT's claim in this aspect. The MOF tried to define the primary function of the ordinary savings deposit as account settlement, the same for the PSF and banks. Yet, the MPT did not back down.

In addition, the MPT questioned whether market mechanism would operate in the determination of interest rate among banks.[71] The MPT's concern was not groundless given that market competition did not seem to have operated in the determination of interest rate after the liberalization of fixed deposit interest rates. When the liberalization began in June 1993, interest rates for banks' fixed deposits were virtually the same, and continued to be devoid of variance despite differing financial conditions among banks. Since an economist suspected collusion among banks and submitted a request of investigation with the Fair Trade Commission, eventually banks became the subject of the commission's investigation.[72] Since it was uncertain if ordinary savings interest rate would be determined by market competition, the MPT opposed the synchronization of PSF ordinary savings deposit interest rate with banks' ordinary savings interest rate, and instead insisted on linking the PSF rate to other short-term financial products, such as three-month CDs.[73]

Neither the MPT nor MOF conceded on the treatment of ordinary savings deposit, and did not reach an agreement for a long time. The MOF planned to liberalize liquid deposit interest rates, except for checking, in June 1994.[74] For this, the MOF needed to finish negotiations with the MPT in December 1993 so that the former would be able to send bills for this change to the Diet in the following month.[75] However, the MPT did not change its position by the end of 1993, and negotiations continued in early 1994. At one point, MPT–MOF relations were severed. In March, the MOF presented a plan that would leave out the PSF regarding the liberalization of commercial banks. In return, the MPT threatened to formulate Diet bills to revise PSF-related laws and enable the MPT to freely determine PSF ordinary savings interest rates. Obviously, the bills would not gain approval from the MOF, preventing them from being sent to the Diet; however, by doing so, the MPT contemplated generating an image that the MOF was responsible for the delay in the liberalization.[76]

Since the Japanese government promised the liberalization of bank deposits to the U.S. government, both ministries could not prolong negotiations much longer and reached an agreement in April 1994. In general, the MPT agreed to link ordinary PSF savings deposit to banks' counterparts, but the MOF allowed the MPT to set the PSF rate approximately one percent higher than the average interest rate of banks' ordinary savings. Also, the agreement included two major exceptions to this rule. One was to separate PSF and bank ordinary savings interest rate and link PSF rate with three-month CDs when banks' ordinary savings interest rate was too low. The other was the assurance that the PSF rate would never fall below 1.32 percent, that is, current rate as of April 1994.[77] The agreement stipulated that PSF ordinary savings rate be linked to ordinary savings rate at banks and set similar rules on the relationship between the PSF's and banks' special savings deposit with limited settlement functions.[78] Yet it virtually guaranteed that the former would always be higher than the latter, again to the frustration of banks.

According to the agreement, the MPT and MOF would reexamine the agreement in December 1994 after its implementation in October. The National Banking Association and other peak associations of financial institutions submitted petitions with MOF's Banking Bureau chief just after the release of the agreement and demanded the modification of the rules to allow the PSF to maintain a higher interest rate. Even though the MOF, taking the agreement to be more a temporary arrangement than a definite resolution, tried to persuade the MPT to reduce the difference in the interest rates, the MPT did not allow a fundamental revision of the agreement when they finished negotiations in December 1994.[79] Nonetheless, the interest rate difference between the PSF and banks was ceasing to be a major controversy, because the MPT flexibly set PSF ordinary savings interest rates so as not to deviate from banks' savings rates.[80]

The MOF agreed with the U.S. Treasury to liberalize bank deposit interest rates in 1985, and completed liberalization of liquid deposits in October 1994. Despite repeated demand from the U.S. government for expedited implementation of the liberalization agreement, it ended up being a very long and complicated process, as summarized in table 4.3. This complication and delay derived in part from the MOF's concern about the stability of the banking industry. To help

Table 4.3 Chronology of small-scale deposits (over ¥10 million per account)

Interest rate liberalization	
May 1984	US–Japan agreement on the liberalization of bank deposit interest rates
June 1989	Small-scale MMCs introduced (¥3 million minimum with 6-month and 1-year maturation periods
November 1991	Liberalization of fixed deposits (¥3 million minimum with various maturation periods between 3 months and 3 years)
June 1992	Special savings deposit with limited settlement functions introduced at the PSF and banks
June 1993	The minimum-amount requirement for liberalized fixed deposits abolished and small-scale MMCs terminated
October 1994	Liberalization of liquid deposits (except for checking)
October 1995	Restrictions on the maturation period of liberalized fixed deposits

Source: Zenkoku Ginkō Kyōkai, *Ginkō Kyōkai 50 Nenshi*, 441.

small and medium-sized banks to cope with change, the MOF phased in liberalization measures gradually from fixed deposits to liquid deposits and provided transitional measures within the liberalization process of each type of deposit. However, the necessity to make the PSF concurrent with the liberalization made its process even more complex and time-consuming, due to opposing views on the relationship between the PSF and financial liberalization.

The MPT sought to receive the benefit of liberalization by freer PSF activities. In contrast, the MOF and banks regarded the PSF,

Table 4.4 Major MPT–MOF agreements on tax reform and financial liberalization and major concessions

Agreement	MPT's major concessions	MOF's major concessions
Reform of tax on interest income (December 1986)	Taxation on PSF deposits	Independent investment of the PSF Increase of maximum deposit limit per citizen from ¥3 million to ¥5 million Sales of government bonds at post offices Increase of limit of *Yū Yū* Loan from ¥1 million to ¥2 million
Small-scale Money Market Certificates (December 1988)	Setting upper limit on *teigaku* interest rate (never implemented)	Increase of maximum deposit limit to ¥7 million
Liberalization of interest rate of fixed deposits over ¥3 million (December 1990)	Linking the newly created fixed deposits to banks' rates	Increase of maximum deposit limit to ¥10 million Foreign exchange operation at post offices
Introduction of new savings deposit with limited settlement functions (July 1991)	Introduction of the new savings deposit	National government officials' payroll transfer to ordinary PSF savings accounts
Liberalization of interest rates for fixed deposits (December 1992)	Linking *teigaku* interest rate to CD interest rate	Interest rate setting advantageous for *teigaku* deposits
Liberalization of liquid deposits (April 1994)	Linking *teigaku* interest rate with market rate	Setting PSF ordinary savings interest rate higher than market rate

Source: Compiled by the author.

government operation, as fundamentally inconsistent with liberalization. The MOF and banks tried to make the liberalization an opportunity to correct the PSF's advantages, typified in *Teigaku*'s high interest rate, longevity, and flexibility, that were made possible because of its status as government business with few constraints regarding profitability. In the sense that the MOF persuaded the MPT to link PSF interest rates to that of banks, the MOF and banks were successful, but the MPT gained valuable concessions from the MOF that helped the PSF keep its competitiveness, as summarized in table 4.4. In the following part, this aspect will be further discussed in conjunction with the expansion of the PSF.

The Expansion of the PSF

In the process of the MOF's interest income tax reform and liberalization of bank deposit interest rates, the MPT strengthened the basis of PSF operation by obtaining concessions from the MOF. The most valuable concession for the MPT was the increase in the maximum amount of PSF deposit per person. The maximum amount was increased from ¥3 million to ¥5 million in 1988, to ¥7 million in 1990, and to ¥10 million in 1991. This rapid increase enabled the MPT to prevent many *teigaku* depositors from transferring their funds after maturation. The 1990 increase was particularly important because the fate of about ¥30 trillion was at stake. Between April and November 1980, massive amounts of money were deposited to *teigaku* as a result of the planned introduction of the Green Card system. Since these *teigaku* deposits had the annual compound interest rate of 8.0 percent, the maximum deposit of ¥3 million would be worth ¥6.4 trillion when it was to mature in 1990.[81] The 1990 increase helped MPT minimize the transfer of matured *teigaku* funds to other high-yield financial commodities, such as coupon bank debenture.[82] Thus, as shown in figure 4.2, the PSF deposit total steadily increased despite tax reform and financial liberalization.[83]

Another crucial concession that the MPT obtained from the MOF in this period was the former's independent investment of the PSF. In return for agreeing to taxation on PSF deposits in 1986, the MOF allowed the MPT to set aside a portion of the PSF for independent investment. The agreement allowed the MPT to gradually transfer a total of ¥15 million from the PSF to the independent investment account by the end of the fiscal year 1991. In its request for the fiscal year 1992 budget, the MPT tried to make the size of the independent investment fund significantly larger by establishing a rule that would

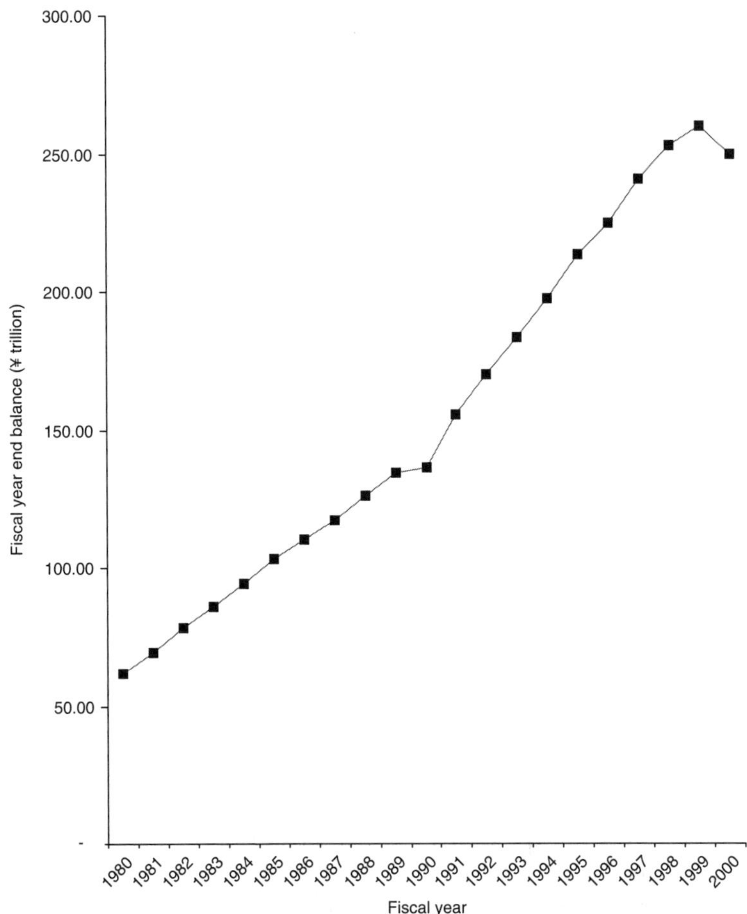

Figure 4.2   PSF account balance, fiscal year 1980–2000.

Source: Ministry of Public Management, Home Affairs, Posts and Telecommunications home page, http://www.zaimu.yusei.go.jp/tokei/2000/excel/chokin/caxx0017.xls (April 3, 2002).

allow the MPT to transfer half of the annual increase of the total of the PSF to the account. The MOF rejected this idea, but agreed to allow the MPT to continue to transfer funds—¥4.75 trillion annually in the fiscal years 1992 and 1993, and ¥5 trillion annually in the fiscal years 1994, 1995, and 1996.[84] As shown in table 4.5, the size of the independent investment account grew larger and the account occupied about one-fifth of the total at the end of the fiscal year 1996.

Table 4.5   MPT's independent investment

Fiscal year	Amount transferred from PSF (¥100 million)	Total of independent investment (¥100 million)	Total PSF (¥100 million)	Ratio of independent investment (%)
1988	45,000	45,000	1,258,691	4
1989	30,000	75,124	1,345,723	6
1990	35,000	110,203	1,362,803	8
1991	40,000	150,349	1,556,007	10
1992	47,500	204,398	1,700,906	12
1993	47,500	251,974	1,835,348	14
1994	50,000	302,057	1,975,902	15
1995	50,000	352,132	2,134,375	16
1996	50,000	402,145	2,248,872	18

Source: Ministry of Posts and Telecommunications Annual Whitepaper (Various Years).

In this period, the MPT improved the convenience of PSF services by adding new features as well as reinforcing new ones. Through the liberalization process, the MPT added new types of financial commodities, including government bonds, and gave customers more selections to choose from. In return for its concession to its agreement of taxation on PSF deposits, the MPT increased the limit of *Yū Yū* loans from ¥1 million to ¥2 million.[85] Through budget negotiations with the MOF in late 1991, the MPT obtained agreement from the MOF to further increase the limit to ¥3 million in 1992.[86] These improvements, which derived from its interactions with the MOT in financial reforms, were combined with improvement measures that the MPT had been implementing by utilizing on-line networks.

The MPT began to connect post offices via on-line networks in 1978, and all the nationwide post offices were connected by March 1984, laying the basis for the provision of various personal financial services comparable to those at commercial banks. The first 20 automated teller machines (ATMs)[87] were put into operation at post offices in Tokyo in 1981, and the MPT continued to set up ATMs at public places, such as department stores, train stations, and college campuses, as well as at post offices. To bring the PSF's service on par with that of commercial banks, the MPT started in many prefectures an automatic transfer system of funds from the ordinary PSF savings account toward the payment of utility bills in 1982, followed by the beginning of automatic transfer of pension and other benefits to the account in 1983. Commercial banks vehemently opposed the MPT's institution of these services, but the MPT continued and expanded nationwide the area of coverage.[88]

Furthermore, in July 1984, in cooperation with domestic credit card companies, the MPT introduced *Yūbin Chokin Kyōyō* Card (PSF Dual-Use Card) that worked not only as a cash card at the PSF's ATMs but also as a credit card to make purchases at member stores, which was in turn charged to ordinary PSF savings accounts.[89] Initially, the dual-use card was limited to use only in Japan, but the MPT made it international by partnering up with major international credit companies. In June 1986, the MPT along with a Japanese credit card company reached an agreement with Master Card to create a PSF dual-use Master Card,[90] and a similar deal was made with Visa Card and another Japanese credit card company the following September.[91] Despite opposition from commercial banks, the MPT implemented the agreement in the same year and created dual-use cards that could be utilized for purchases and cash advances internationally.[92]

In the 1990s, the MPT continued to add to the usefulness of the PSF by connecting its on-line networks with other financial institutions so that PSF depositors would be able to engage in ATM transactions at those institutions. The MPT began to submit budget requests to the MOF for this purpose in 1993 and approached the National Banking Association to gain cooperation. Yet, there were more than 100,000 ATMs in bank networks, and the banking industry as a whole, particularly major banks, had no strong incentive to connect bank networks with PSF networks, which only had about 20,000 ATMs. Therefore, MOF's Banking Bureau opposed the connection, and the MOF kept rejecting the MPT's budget request to allocate funds for it until 1996.[93]

Facing opposition from Japanese commercial banks, the MPT began to work with other financial institutions. The MPT proposed on-line network connections to security companies in September 1996; security firms also in negotiation with commercial banks for network connection deferred its decision.[94] But, the MPT reached an agreement for on-line network connection with Citibank and other credit card companies by the end of 1996, and it gained budget allocation from the MOF for the preparation of on-line network connections.[95] Many more financial institutions, including city banks, local banks, and trust banks, moved to establish on-line network connections with the PSF. As a result, in January 1999, PSF depositors were able to use ATMs at financial institutions whose networks were connected to the PSF's.[96] The MPT's effort to extend PSF on-line networks that began in the early 1990s bore fruit in the late 1990s.

The MPT was forced to accept major changes due to tax and financial market reforms from the mid-1980s. The MPT coped with these reforms quite adeptly and strengthened the PSF based on concessions from the MOF. As a result, the PSF expanded its size, increased its autonomy of management, and added a great deal of convenience in this period. An often-cited metaphor aptly describes the relationship between the PSF and the consumer financial market: a whale in a small pond, where the whale is bigger, more self-sufficient, and more attractive. Fishes—commercial banks—in the pond are threatened, crying for help from someone outside. The growth of the PSF ignited forces against the PSF in government reforms in the late 1990s and the early 2000s, discussed earlier in Chapter 3 on government reform.

Postal Life Insurance and Postal Service in the 1990s

Among the three postal businesses in Japan, the PSF is the most controversial, but each of the other two postal businesses—postal life insurance (PLI) and postal service—have had problematic relationships with private sector competitors. PLI, established in 1916, is designed to provide inexpensive life insurance to the public at the nationwide post offices. As its Japanese name, *Kan-i Hoken* (simple insurance), connotes, the procedure to purchase PLI is simpler than life insurance provided by private sector insurers in that PLI does not require applicants to submit a medical certificate and has no occupation-based restrictions. But the highest amount of insurance is ¥13 million (raised from ¥8 million in 1977), a modest amount for life insurance. Due to its affordability and convenience, PLI has continuously expanded. Its share has been at least 25 percent in the Japanese life insurance market measured by total asset, and has been increasing from the 1990s.[97]

Although this is not widely known, just like the PSF, the PLI is the world's largest insurance corporation. The ascent of PLI—¥117 trillion at the end of the fiscal year 1999—was about a half of the PSF and roughly three times as big as the asset (¥43 trillion) of the largest Japanese life insurer: Nippon Life Insurance Corporation (see figure 4.3). Unlike the PSF, the MPT transferred only one-tenth of funds from PLI to the MOF, but, based on the agreement with the MOF reached in the early 1980s, about two-third of the funds were used to purchase bonds issued by central and local governments or government-related corporations. The rest was invested in financial markets, toward purchasing stocks and bonds.[98] Although investment in financial markets amounted to only one-third of funds from PLI, it

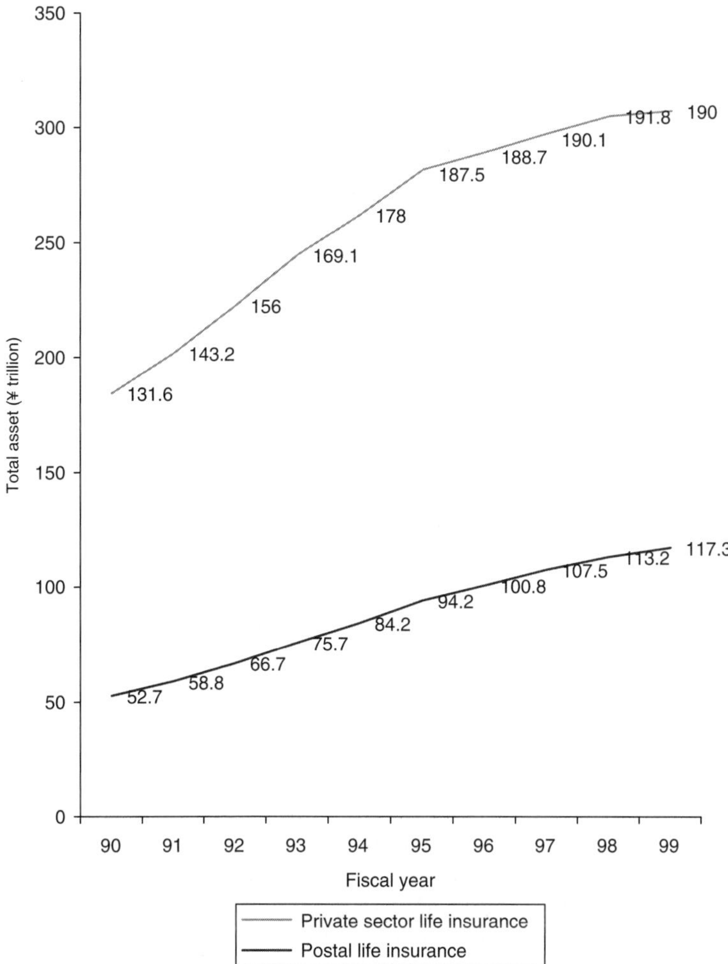

Figure 4.3 Total assets (PLI and private sector life insurance) in the 1990s.

Source: Ministry of Public Management, Home Affairs, Posts and Telecommunications.

was still a large amount of money to influence the markets. In fact, when the Japanese government tried to stimulate the Japanese stock market through so-called price keeping operation, funds from PLI along with government pension funds were invested in the stock market.[99]

Because of its large market share in the life insurance market, private sector life insurance companies have been critical of the operation of PLI. The existence of PLI has been particularly threatening to private sector insurers since the early 1990s when Japan's economic recession began with the burst of the bubble economy. Due to the stock market slump, private sector insurers had difficulty in making profits from investment, and were in financial trouble. In November 1996, the Life Insurance Association of Japan, the trade association of private sector life insurers, issued a report criticizing PLI. In this report, the Association called for the discussion for drastic reform measures such as the abolition of PLI and its privatization after breaking up.[100] Allied with commercial banks, private sector life insurers came to strongly advocate reforms in postal businesses.

Although the MPT was primarily known for its operation of postal services, the scale of business was much smaller and the postal service had its own controversy with private sector carriers, particularly Yamato Transport. In 1976, Yamato introduced home delivery service of packages, called *Takkyūbin* (express home delivery packages) and expanded its coverage nationwide, overcoming opposition from the Ministry of Transportation.[101] Since Yamato carried packages door to door quickly and reliably, it expanded its share at the expense of the MPT's parcel post system. Since 1986, the number of packages handled by Yamato has been larger than that by MPT.[102] Since other carriers followed suit and entered into the package delivery service market, the share of parcel post declined and constrained the business base of the postal service.

As long as Yamato and other carriers were carrying packages containing food, books, and cloth they had no trouble with the MPT. However, once Yamato began to target the delivery of things deemed to be letters or correspondence, the MPT intervened. The law governing postal service stipulated that *shinsho* (correspondence) should not be handled by any carrier other than the MPT. Although the law did not strictly define *shinsho*, the MPT specified it as a thing where the sender conveyed fact to and/or communicated with the addressee. The MPT objected to Yamato's expansion of package delivery business because of its monopoly on the delivery of *shinsho*. When Yamato's local subsidiary began to deliver credit cards at a price lower than certified mail in 1993, the following year the MPT demanded that the subsidiary should stop based on its position that credit cards were *shinsho* and the subsidiary violated the postal law. Yamato did not back down, and decided to begin credit card delivery service nationwide. Although the MPT threatened to take legal action against Yamato, the latter showed its willingness to fight in court and leaders of major business organizations, including Keidanren, supported Yamato.[103]

In reaction, the MPT set special certified mail for credit cards whose price was cheaper than Yamato's and credit card companies soon had no incentive to use Yamato, preventing this controversy from developing further. Yet, conflict between the MPT and Yamato was revived when local governments were planning to distribute Regional Promotion Tickets that were to be given to citizens as a measure to stimulate the economy in 1999. Yamato received orders to deliver the tickets from many local governments. Maintaining that the tickets were *shinsho*, the MPT requested the local governments not to use Yamato and the government complied. The MPT's action led Yamato to file allegation to the Fair Trade Commission. Yamato argued that the MPT's action to prevent Yamato from delivering the tickets violated the antitrust law and requested that the MPT be restrained.[104] The Commission denied Yamato's allegation on the ground that this issue was not an antitrust issue although it pointed out the MPT's action problematic in the context of fair competition and called for further discussion on the treatment of *shinsho*.[105] Thus, controversy developed not only regarding the PSF, but also with the MPT's other two postal businesses in the 1990s.

Among the three postal businesses, the PSF has been the most controversial. The PSF has been the largest and arguably the strongest player in Japan's personal banking. The MPT and MOF/commercial banks fought each other for a long time. In contrast, the MPT's conflict with private sector competitions in the other postal businesses, PLI and postal service, has been less intensive. However, these two businesses are recently becoming controversial. Since the late 1990s, reformers, such as Koizumi, have been targeting not only the PSF but also the entire postal business as the object of reform privatization.

Conclusion

Old guard politics in the postal business is multidimensional. Similar to showdown politics that develop during each of the three government reforms, described in Chapter 3, both reformist and old guard politicians got deeply involved in issues that changed taxation on PSF accounts. Although the strength of old guard *yūsei zoku* politicians prevented reformers from enacting measures that would have significantly weakened the MPT's operational autonomy and advantages given to the PSF, LDP leaders' determination to pursue tax reform forced the MPT to modify PSF operations. One major example is the MPT's acceptance of taxation on PSF accounts. Against the backdrop of political interactions, details were ironed out between the bureaucracies, the MPT and MOF. The interaction between the bureaucracies was central to the liberalization of the financial market, whose impact on electoral politics was much less direct than tax reform. In its negotiations with the MOF, the the MPT adeptly gained valuable concessions, albeit through long negotiations. Therefore, reform liberalization measures were enacted but the enactment was accompanied by measures that strengthened MPT's PSF operation. In addition to these political and interministerial interactions, the MPT enhanced its PSF operation by negotiating with private sector firms, as shown in its introduction of the PSF credit/debit card and the connection of the PSF on-line networks with other financial institutions. The MPT's pursuit of operational strength was also evident in its operation of the PLI and postal service, although the threat of the two postal businesses, particularly the postal service, to private sector rivals was much smaller than the PSF. The continued expansion of the MPT's postal business operation through the 1990s along with its connection to the FILP led Koizumi and other reformers—who believe that government operation should be secondary to private sector business—to pursue the privatization of postal business in the 2000s.

Chapter 5

Reforms in Transportation: Trains, Planes, and Automobiles

Transportation, the infrastructure that promotes the flow of goods and people, is an integral part of economic activities. Because of its importance, like other governments, the Japanese government has been deeply involved in the development of transportation systems, particularly road networks, railways, and airways. It has been using a significant amount of government funds, including those from the FILP, a major investment outlet for funds from the PSF. Since government spending on the construction of transportation networks brings in money and jobs, transportation involves a variety of influential LDP *zoku* (policy tribe) politicians and has developed distributive networks. Just like *yūsei zoku* in postal service, these *zokus* worked hard as old guard politicians to protect and develop the mechanism while trying to stall reforms. Yet, in the last two decades, reformers became increasingly concerned with the accumulating financial burden that the construction of transportation networks imposed on society. To make the operation and construction of transportation networks less costly, reformers promoted reform measures, including privatization, deregulation, and liberalization. In this chapter, I examine the progress of reform in each of the three transportation areas, which are highway construction and operation; national railway construction and operation; and airline service and airport construction. Through these analyses, I demonstrate that, similar to reforms in postal business, reformers, including the LDP leadership, and old guard politicians engage in long-term interactions in various dimensions.

Politics of Road Construction

Post–World War II Road Construction

Japan has a long history of developing nationwide road networks, which connected Edo—renamed Tokyo in 1868—with major cities in Japan. These networks were developed in feudal times, when people traveled on foot or horseback, so roads were narrow and unsuitable for auto transportation. Unlike its German counterpart, which developed the *autohbahn* for high-speed driving in the prewar period, the prewar Japanese government regarded the construction of road networks as secondary to the construction of national railway networks. Roads, except for those important for military use, were severely underdeveloped before the end of World War II, and most roads, including Route One—the first national road—were unpaved and suitable solely for horse buggy traffic. When the World Bank mission visited Japan to evaluate the government request for a World Bank loan for the construction of an expressway, its members were struck by the bad road conditions in Japan. In the early post–World War II period, there was an urgent need to upgrade and develop nationwide road networks in Japan.

The Ministry of Construction (MOC) established in 1948 was in charge of construction. Since the number of automobiles operating in Japan increased exponentially from about 140,000 in 1945 to more than a million in 1956, the MOC deemed it urgent to develop nationwide road networks. Yet, since most of government spending for public works was used for the development of infrastructure for agricultural production, securing funds for road construction was a crucial issue and its initial road construction plan was aborted due to the lack of funding. The MOC's pursuit of road construction was supported by LDP politicians, particularly Tanaka Kakuei, who later became prime minister and (even after his resignation due to his involvement in the Lockheed scandal) continued to influence Japanese politics as the leader of the LDP's largest faction. Tanaka played a leading role in enacting two important laws that made the MOC's road construction policy feasible. One was a law that designated revenue from tax on gasoline as the funds for road construction. The other was the law to establish the Japan Highway Public Corporation (JH), which was authorized to act as a government agency but was relatively free from Diet scrutiny. These laws set up the basic scheme for road construction in the 1950s.

The gasoline tax revenue, later combined with a part of revenue from automobile tax that owners paid at the time of purchase and periodical inspections, came to be called *dōro tokutei zaigen*; the revenue was to be used exclusively for road-related expense, and the MOF had no control over its use. Therefore, the MOC was entitled to the stable inflow of funds for the development of ordinary government roads, *kokudō*, which usually did not charge tolls. In building a new route, the central government paid two-third of its cost and the local government paid the rest. Once built, local governments were in charge of maintenance. JH, in contrast, was in charge of developing national expressway (toll way) systems. Its major funding sources were FILP and other loans as well as its revenue from tolls. In the construction of new routes as well as the operation of existing routes, JH used (central) government funds as well as revenue from expressway toll, freeing local governments from sharing construction costs. Since LDP politicians supported the use of FILP funds for expressway construction, JH aggressively pursued the expansion of expressway networks.

The first toll road built by JH was the Meishin Expressway that connected Nagoya and Kobe in 1965. The cost of construction was ¥116.4 trillion, of which ¥28.8 trillion was a loan from the World Bank. JH spent ¥342,5 trillion, including ¥108 trillion of another World Bank loan, to build Tomei Expressway between Tokyo and Nagoya, which came into service in 1969. These two expressways connected the three major urban areas, and significantly contributed to the improvement of auto transportation. Since these expressways attracted traffic, JH generated a great deal of profit from the operation of these expressways, especially Tomei, which became a major source of funding for the construction of new expressways.[1] For the construction of metropolitan expressway systems, the Metropolitan Expressway Public Corporation, established in 1959, was in charge of expressways in Tokyo and Hanshin Expressway Public Corporation began to build expressways in Osaka and Kobe in 1962. These expressways accommodated rapidly expanding automobile transportation in Japan's two metropolitan areas.

In the early period, the construction of expressways was very rational in that the construction was absolutely necessary for the smooth development of automobile transportation, a vital part of rapid economic development. Yet, toward the end of rapid economic development, the construction of expressway networks accelerated due to political reasons. Since the early 1970s, the LDP began to emphasize the development of social overhead capital, including the expressway networks. Also, the rapid economic development resulted in the concentration of industries and population in urban areas, especially Tokyo and Osaka, leaving rural areas relatively underdeveloped. To promote a balanced development by stimulating economic development in rural areas, LDP politicians, particularly Tanaka Kakuei and his followers, deemed it essential to connect rural areas and urban centers by expressway networks.

Along with the long-term goal of regional economic development, the construction of expressway networks generated valuable employment opportunities to residents in rural areas where job opportunities were decreasing with the decline of agriculture.[2] Creating jobs appealed to rural residents as a whole, and bringing construction projects to their districts benefited the LDP's core supporters in rural areas, namely construction companies. To cater to construction companies, which provided not only financial assistance but also electoral campaign support, LDP politicians wielded extensive influence over expressway construction projects. The selection of construction routes was determined in the Diet, and LDP politicians were the ultimate decision makers regarding expressway construction whereas the MOC bureaucrats determined specifics. Developing close connections with the MOC bureaucrats, LDP politicians were in a position to influence the selection of contractors.[3] As indicated earlier, financial constraints were few; funds were not from the general tax revenue over which the MOF had strict control but the FILP, and local governments had to pay nothing. LDP politicians rushed to expand expressway networks and resisted any attempt to delay the construction of expressways in their district.[4]

Honshu–Shikoku Bridges

The big expressway project in the early 1970s was to construct bridges between Japan's main island and Shikoku, a big island with four prefectures in the southwest of Osaka. There was no bridge between the two islands, and the major transportation that carried people and goods was ferry services. The lack of bridges was thought to be a bottleneck for the development of the Shikoku economy, and building bridges over Setonaikai, an inland sea famous for its beautiful scenery and abundant and high-quality fish catches, was thought to vitalize the Shikoku economy. In 1969, the Japanese government decided to build bridges to connect the main island and Shikoku and the construction of three routes was planned to begin in 1973. However, in the early 1970s, Japan went through economic hardships deriving from the rise in oil price, thus the plan to build the bridge was on hold until one route was started in 1978. The construction of this route was completed in 1988. The construction of the other two routes was resumed in the mid-1980s in response to pressure from the United States and other advanced industrial countries; the Japanese government agreed to stimulate domestic demand through public spending, which would presumably increase the import of foreign products and ease Japan's ever-accumulating trade surplus. These two other routes were completed in the late 1990s, and Shikoku and the main island were conveniently connected.[5]

Connecting the main island and Shikoku was a politically popular idea, particularly among LDP politicians and their constituents in Shikoku. As in JH's construction of expressway networks, the Honshu–Shikoku Bridge Authority had access to FILP funds and expected to pay back debt from tolls after the completion of bridges; hence there were few budget constraints. As a result, the commercial viability of toll bridges was not seriously examined in the process of construction, and JH presented such optimistic projections of expected traffic for each route that no one doubted each route's financial viability. Also, simultaneously constructing three routes prevented LDP politicians from fighting each other over the selection of routes, but it ballooned construction and operation costs while diffusing users among the three routes. As of the end of the fiscal year 2002, the Authority had nearly ¥3.83 trillion debt. Since its income was ¥95.6 billion in contrast to ¥142.2 billion expenditure, the debt was growing with no prospect of business recovery.[6] In the discussion of privatization of public highway corporations, in chapter 3 of this book, the treatment of the financially defunct Bridge Authority was one of the biggest issues, and the construction of the three routes was regarded as a symbol of the irrationality of expressway construction.

Continued Expansion and Adjustment

Similarly, in its construction of nationwide expressway networks, JH did not consider the economic viability of each route. Although major expressways, such as Chuo, Kanetsu, and Tohoku, directly connecting Tokyo and medium-size cities, significantly improved freight transportation, many other routes that were built recently in rural areas did not have any realistic prospect of generating profit due to the lack of sufficient traffic. Reformist LDP politician, Ishihara Nobuteru, who was the minister in charge of government reform and later became minister of Land, Infrastructure, and Transport (MLIT),[7] both in the Koizumi cabinet, once joked about an expressway in the rural area of Hokkaido, an island north of the mainland, saying that there were more bears walking than cars driving on the expressway. Nonetheless, both the LDP and JH had no sign of slowing down the construction of expressways. The fourth national comprehensive development plan approved by the Cabinet in 1987 stated that Japan should have 11,520 kilometers of expressways in the early twenty-first century. When Prime Minister Koizumi began to discuss the privatization of the public highway construction corporations in 2002, 6,976 kilometers were in operation and 2,366 kilometers had basic route plans (the total of 9,342 kilometers was the amount of expressway networks that old guard politicians wanted to construct).[8]

While pursuing the privatization of JH and other public highway corporations, discussed in Chapter 3, Prime Minister Koizumi explored ways to change the system such that a vast amount of funds could be channeled to expressway and other road constructions. Koizumi, an ardent critic of government waste, promised to contain the total amount of the issuance of government bond to ¥30 trillion for the fiscal year 2002, and looked to *dōro tokutei zaigen*, which was revenue from taxes on gas and automobiles designated to be used solely for road-related expenses. Koizumi sought to use this revenue for other non–road-related expenses. Also, Koizumi proposed to abolish the ¥300 billion budget allotment to JH, which supported its operation of unprofitable routes. Since LDP politicians and MLIT bureaucrats thought that the realization of either proposal would jeopardize the construction of the 9,342 kilometers expressway networks, they came up with creative solutions. In the fiscal year 2002 budget, the MLIT cut down spending on road projects by ten percent, as required by the government mandate for cuts on uniform spending; it saved ¥224.7 billion and transferred this fund to the general revenue as a temporary measure for the fiscal year 2002.[9] As for the termination of the budget allotment to JH, *dōro zoku* politicians manipulated the length of the redemption period. As a quid pro quo for the acceptance of the termination of the budget allotment, *dōro zoku* politicians persuaded Koizumi to change the current redemption period of 30 years to 50 years. The longer redemption period meant more funds available for expressway construction, and this extension, the *zoku* politicians thought, would generate enough funds (about ¥1 trillion per year) for most of the construction of planned expressways. While Koizumi claimed his feat of (apparently) containing the cost of expressway construction, the *zoku* politicians protected the plan for building expressways.[10]

LDP *dōro zoku* and the MLIT continued to handle flexibly the rise of Koizumi's reform movement. Since Koizumi focused on the privatization of JH and other public highway corporations, *zoku* politicians and MLIT bureaucrats explored ways to build expressways by not using JH so that they would minimize the impact on the construction of expressways caused by fundamental changes in JH operation. For this purpose, to make up for the expected reduction that would derive from the privatization of JH, the MLIT came up with a way to build expressways directly through the government. Before the discussion of JH privatization heated up, the Ministry of Construction, the MLIT's predecessor, once contemplated its direct involvement in expressway construction. However, due to resistance from JH president and a former administrative vice minister of construction, Fujii Haruho, the Ministry had to abandon the idea. When the MLIT rehashed this idea to protect the expressway construction, it gained approval from *zoku* politicians. In 2002, the LDP and the MLIT agreed to allocate a portion of *dōro tokutei zaigen*—a total of ¥3 trillion to be spent in 15 years—to the MLIT's construction of expressways. This led the MLIT to decide to build the expressway routes that were expected to be so unprofitable that the reformatted JH would never agree to construct them. Although the MLIT had to reduce the cost of construction by downgrading the facility of each route, including the number of lanes, the MLIT and *zoku* politicians secured means to build the entire 9,342-kilometer expressway networks despite the controversy over JH privatization.[11] Thus, the old guard bloc outmaneuvered Koizumi's reform attempt and conserved the basis of the distributive networks.

Tokyo Bay Aqua Line: The Future of Privatized Highway Corporations?

The construction of an unprofitable expressway route was not limited to rural areas. Thanks to lobbying from *zoku* members from Chiba, Tokyo's neighboring prefecture that included a great deal of rural areas, the Tokyo area has had a gigantic road project on Tokyo Bay, building an expressway commonly called the Tokyo Bay Aqua Line. The Aqua Line is a 15.1-kilometer long (a little less than 10 miles) expressway across Tokyo Bay, connecting Kanagawa and Chiba prefectures. Two-third of the route is an undersea tunnel and the rest is a bridge on the sea. The route was designed to ease the traffic congestion on major routes to Tokyo by letting those cars, buses, and trucks from Kanagawa to Chiba, and vice versa, bypass Tokyo. The original idea was slowly developed in the 1960s, but with the oil shock in the early 1970s, planning came to a standstill. Yet, in 1986, to stimulate domestic demand, as requested by the United States and other governments, the Japanese government decided to construct the Aqua Line, and in the following year, the Trans Tokyo Bay Road Authority was established. The Authority was a joint venture of government organizations and private sector firms. One-third of the fund or ¥20 billion was from JH, one-third from local governments—the area's prefectural and city governments—and the other one-third from private sector firms including major steel, auto, and electric power companies. In December 1997, the Aqua Line was opened for traffic.[12]

In the construction of the Aqua Line, Japan's state-of-art underground tunnel drilling technology was used and the leading artist of Japanese-style painting designed the entrance buildings. The expressway was of high technological and artistic quality but the construction cost was enormous, a whopping ¥1.438 trillion or ¥100 billion per kilometer. Just like JH, the Aqua Line Authority had access to vast amounts of funds; most construction funds came from government-guaranteed bonds or loans from the government. Although the inclusion of private sector investors was expected to make the Authority cost conscious, in reality there was no sign of cost-cutting efforts. The Authority closely communicated with prospective contractors in the selection process, and each of six major tunnel building blocs was awarded to different bidders at 99.7 percent of the highest price that the Authority set beforehand as acceptable, suggesting collusion among the Authority and construction companies. Because of high costs and the resulting debt payment, the Aqua Line continues to have a very low profitability.[13]

With a very optimistic and unrealistic estimate of traffic, the Authority had expected to pay back the debt in 30 years. Yet, when the Aqua Line began to operate, the actual amount of traffic was far below what the Authority had estimated. In a year after opening, about 3,840,000 autos used the line, less than half of the Authority's estimate. Due to this, the Authority changed its debt redemption period to 40 years. However, this is still a very optimistic estimate, and critics doubt the Authority will ever pay back the debt without rescue from the government.

The Aqua Line episode has a very important implication regarding the privatized JH. In the Aqua Line construction, the Authority was in charge of construction, but after the opening, the ownership of the Aqua Line along with its debt was transferred to JH. As discussed in Chapter 3, in the format that Koizumi and old guard forces agreed about public highway corporation reform, privatized expressway operation companies would be in charge of construction, but, on construction completion, ownership and debt would be moved to the government-owned expressway system organization. Just like the Aqua Line Authority, each of the expressway operation companies would not have to consider the repayment of debt accruing from expressway construction, allowing them not to be cost conscious. Critics claim that the reformed format of expressway construction would continue to be inefficient and costly, as shown by the experience of the Tokyo Bay Aqua Line.[14]

The politics of road construction that came to the fore of reform politics in the 2000s has a trajectory that starts from the early post–World War II days. As a result of prewar Japan's emphasis on the strengthening of economic and military power, Japan's road transportation system was severely underdeveloped. For economic recovery and development, the government needed to develop road transportation networks as a crucial segment of economic infrastructure, and came up with a mechanism that enabled the government to construct expressways without being limited by short-term budget constraints. Although this mechanism contributed to the rapid expansion of expressways, due to the availability of funds, the construction of expressways itself became the goal to benefit rural areas, not addressing the necessity and economic feasibility of each route.

Politics of National Railways

Labor Politics

The building of Japan's national railway networks began in 1872 when the government opened a railway between Tokyo and Yokohama. In the late nineteenth century, both the government and private sector firms built regional railway networks in many places throughout Japan. Yet, in the early twentieth century, the government bought up most railway operations and exclusively engaged in the construction of the national railway networks, which were completed in 1940. Before the end of World War II, the railway network was operated directly by the Ministry of Railways, but Japan National Railways (JNR), a government corporation established by the U.S. occupation forces in 1948, came to be in charge of the operation—passenger and freight—of the networks after the war. Just like NTT before privatization, JNR lacked operational autonomy. Crucial decisions, such as the revision of railway fares and the determination of the wage of railroad workers, required Diet approval and support from LDP politicians in the legislative process. Therefore, JNR management was susceptible to political influence, particularly from the LDP.

Being susceptible to LDP influence took away JNR management's business capability.[15] To make matters worse, JNR unions were closely connected with left-wing politics in a very complicated manner. JNR had numerous unions, and three unions, in particular, were very strong. Its largest union (for most of the period before JNR privatization) Kokurō was one of the most important unions in Japan and wielded significant influence over the Socialist Party. Dōrō, whose members consisted mainly of motormen and other personnel in charge of train operation, was under the influence of the Communist Party and other far Left organizations. Tetsurō supported the Democratic Socialist Party, and rejected adversarial labor relations, unlike the other two unions. Thus, JNR management faced two extremely uncooperative unions: Kokurō and Dōrō, each of which posited the ultimate goal of its movement as the achievement of a Socialist revolution and pursued an extremely confrontational approach. They constantly intimidated lower-level managers and defied their orders. In addition to management–labor confrontation, unions fought each other, even the left-wing unions, especially over the acquisition of new members. Within a union, except the moderate Tetsurō, different political groups, such as mainstream moderate Socialists, far Left Socialists, Communists, and radical left-wingers, competed to take the initiative. JNR managers at all levels had to deal with highly complicated and volatile labor relations.

Most Japanese unions in the private sector were known for their commitment to improve company business, because they recognized that they would benefit from the improvement and that decline in business performance would negatively affect their pay and labor conditions. In contrast, since JNR was a government corporation, business performance was of secondary concern for left-wing union workers (as well as for managers until the mounting deficit became a major problem). Regardless of JNR's business performance, the basic pay raise was determined by the general pay scale for government employees along with negotiations that involved LDP and JSP politicians and MOT senior bureaucrats in addition to JNR union leaders and executives. Union leaders paid little attention to company performance, concentrating on political activities.

In the early 1970s, faced with deteriorating company finance, the JNR management tried to improve company management by instilling awareness of productivity and efficiency among JNR workers through educational meetings—a movement commonly called *Marusei*. The introduction of the concept of productivity in the workplace itself was apolitical, but in reality, this resulted in the shift of members from left-wing unions to pro-management Tetsurō, and left-wing unions such as Kokurō and Dōrō fiercely opposed JNR management's attempts. Since a government board on labor relations determined that the JNR committed unfair labor practice in the process of *Marusei,* its president was forced to publicly apologize in 1971. With this victory, the JNR union movement gained momentum and became ever more aggressive, demanding the right to strike.

JNR workers, as government employees, were not allowed to go on strike. When unions illegally went on strike, the JNR management punished them by dismissing their leaders and through other punitive measures. The left-wing JNR unions set gaining the right to go on strike as their primary goal during this period. JNR's left-wing unions became offensive in the first half of the 1970s. Dōrō engaged in *junpō tōsō* (law-abiding struggle). Instead of going on strike and being absent from the workplace, Dōrō engineers significantly slowed down train operation by "strictly" following safety procedures. Dōrō used this tactic several times until the spring of 1973 when frustrated passengers rioted. In March, about 10,000 JNR commuters at Ageo Station in the outskirts of Tokyo became so frustrated with train delays that they stormed and destroyed station facilities. In the following month, similar incidents occurred in busy stations in Tokyo. Facing opposition from the public, Dōrō had to change its strategy. Dōrō and Kokurō went on strike in November 1975 and stopped the entire system for eight days. Although JNR managers were willing to concede to union demands, LDP leaders harshly criticized the unions for greatly inconveniencing the public through their illegal strike and refused to compromise, preventing the unions from achieving its goal.

After the strike, labor relations deteriorated further and business operations lacked discipline, exemplified by prevalent absenteeism and clandestine pay. This worsened the public image of JNR that had already been tarnished by the struggles and strikes in the first half of the 1970s. LDP leaders found an excellent opportunity to crash the left-wing unions, particularly Kokurō—one of the biggest unions that supported the biggest opposition party, the JSP. The leaders sought to weaken it through the privatization of JNR discussed in Chapter 3. During this process, Dōrō initially opposed privatization, but, sensing its inevitability, changed its position and supported the privatization, forming cooperative relations with JNR managers. In contrast, since Kokurō was a much bigger union with more internal factions, it could not be flexible and ended up maintaining its stance on opposing privatization. Due to lack of cooperation regarding privatization, many Kokurō members were not hired by privatized companies (JRs), and its moderate wing split. Through the privatization of JNR, left-wing unions were either dismantled or made to become pro-management. Privatization freed JRs from political disturbance from the Left and made it possible for them to engage in profit-oriented management. Thus, reformers succeeded in infusing efficient management into national railway operations.

Constructing New Railway Lines in Rural Areas: Old-Style Distributive Politics

When the privatization of JNR was discussed, the two major concerns were the accumulating deficit and conflict-laden labor relations that harmed JNR's business operation. It was widely believed among the public that JNR's labor relations were the cause for the accumulating deficit. Also, due to its status as a government corporation that required Diet approval for major business decisions, JNR lacked managerial autonomy essential for flexible business operation, and some pointed out that this prevented JNR from generating profit and developing stable labor relations.[16] JRs, into which JNR was divided, were given managerial autonomy as private sector companies, and JRs cut operation costs by selectively not hiring many former JNR employees who were the members of Kokurō. Since privatization, JRs in general have had stable management, and they have been enjoying a good reputation. However, the transformation of the railways into profitable private sector companies owes greatly to the fact that JRs were given a clean slate. JNR's huge deficit was transferred to a government organization. JRs are detached from the mechanism that trapped JNR into a deficit spiral: the construction of railway lines for political purposes. In actuality, the construction of railways without considering profitability was the real reason why JNR got into financial trouble in the first place.

The construction and improvement of railway lines were not without merit. Roads were severely underdeveloped in the early post–World War II period in Japan, and the railroad was the most widely used means of transportation. However, railways were damaged by the war, and the existing system was incapable of handling the high volume of passengers. Trains were so crowded that most passengers had to get in and out through the windows instead of the train deck and service was slow and infrequent, making train rides extremely unpleasant and cargo transportation very slow. Therefore, early in the post–World War II period, JNR invested greatly in the improvement of existing lines—such as changing single tracks to double tracks—to increase the capacity to carry passengers and cargo. Also, JNR extended networks to the (rural) areas that it had not served previously.

This strategy would have been reasonable if no other transportation had developed to take customers away from JNR. However, in reality, the use of cars and trucks increased exponentially, supported by the government's construction of expressways and other road networks. Also, the use of airlines slowly developed, becoming another threat to JNR's business. JNR's expansion of national networks did not pay off, resulting in ever accumulating deficit. Nonetheless, JNR continued to invest in expanding its railway networks until the early 1980s when discussions on the reform of JNR developed. This miscalculation was partially due to JNR management's optimistic prospect of its business accompanied by the lack of urgency to generate profit, deriving from its status as a government corporation that was designed to serve the interest of citizens.

Yet, the crucial reason behind the expansion was that LDP politicians strongly promoted the construction of new lines without considering their commercial viability. Likened to a common saying in Japanese *Gaden Insui* [selfishly drawing water to one's farm], LDP politicians' passionate lobbying for the construction of new railway lines in their district is called *Gaden Intetsu* [selfishly drawing railway lines to one's farm]. The political logic is similar to the one behind the construction of nationwide expressways. Constructing a new railway line benefits local communities by increasing convenience and stimulates their economy through the construction project's employment of residents, particularly in rural areas from which most LDP Diet members are elected. Since the immediate beneficiaries of railway construction projects are construction companies, LDP politicians expect to receive kickbacks from the contractors in the form of political donations, which is not illegal as long as it is properly reported to the authorities. Moreover, those politicians who have access to undisclosed route information at the very early stages profit by purchasing the land whose price is likely to go up after the disclosure of route information.[17]

Similar to expressway construction, Tanaka Kakuei played an important role in the expansion of national railway networks. In 1964, Tanaka established the Japan Railway Construction Public Corporation (JRCPC), detaching most of the railway construction function from JNR. Following the order from the minister of transport, the JRCPC pursued the construction of nationwide railways, using FILP funds. After the completion of construction, JNR came to be in charge of the operation of new railway lines. The JRCPC built some new lines in urban areas to ease congestions, but most of the new lines were in rural areas and JNR had to bear the financial burden of operating newly built unprofitable lines. When Tanaka became prime minister in 1972, he emphasized the importance of constructing new railway lines to stimulate economic development in less developed areas and had JNR expand its operation until 1974 despite the fact that it had already accumulated a huge deficit.[18]

Constructing Bullet Train Networks:
Persisting Distributive Politics

In the late 1970s, since the fact that JNR's deficit was out of control was widely recognized, it became increasingly difficult for LDP politicians to prey on the construction of new lines in rural areas. They shifted their focus to the construction of the bullet train (Shinkansen) networks. Bullet trains run faster than 150 miles an hour and compete for the fastest with French TGV. The bullet train system is one of the symbols of Japan's post–World War II technological success, of which many Japanese are proud. Unlike the conventional JNR (and private sector railway) trains that run on narrow gauge, bullet trains use broad gauge. Although they are not totally inconvertible, for maximum performance bullet trains require new railway networks, separate from conventional JNR networks.

Using loans from the World Bank for the reconstruction of the Japanese economy, JNR first built the bullet line between Tokyo and Osaka, which began to operate in 1964 when the Olympics were held in Tokyo. Bullet trains carried passengers between Japan's two urban centers in about three hours, significantly improving convenience, particularly for business travelers. JNR extended the Tokyo–Osaka line westward in 1972 to Okayama, and, in 1975, to Hakata, a major city in Kyushu, making it possible for passengers to travel from Tokyo to Hakata in about six hours. In 1982, two new bullet train lines began to operate. Unlike the Tokyo–Osaka line and its extension that connected a handful of major cities, each line connected Omiya at the outskirt of Tokyo and sparsely populated northeast Japan. One of them, the Joetsu line, reached Niigata prefecture, Tanaka Kakuei's political base, by placing a station in the middle of nowhere but near Tanaka's hometown. The other went mostly to the rural Tohoku area, which is where many LDP Diet members were from.[19]

Among these bullet train lines, the Tokyo–Osaka line conveniently connecting the city center of Tokyo to Shin-Osaka, a ten-minute train ride from downtown Osaka, was profitable in spite of the rapid development of airline services.[20] However, the other lines, including

Sanyo, the westward extension of the Tokyo–Osaka line, did not generate profit due to not having enough number of passengers. Despite the low expectation of profitability, the law enacted in 1970 for the extension of bullet train networks stipulated that five new bullet train lines (*Seibi Shinkansen*) be constructed or extended. Citing this law, LDP Diet members and local politicians promoted the construction of new bullet train lines nationwide. As JNR's mounting deficit became an important government agenda and the discussion on the JNR privatization developed, the construction of the new bullet train lines attracted the attention of finance-conscious reformers. Therefore, the LDP and the government decided to freeze the construction in 1982, but the issue was set outside of discussion on JNR privatization.

Though LDP transport *zoku* (policy tribe) politicians who would benefit from the construction of the new bullet train lines did not oppose the privatization of JNR, they continued to demand the construction, promising their constituents to bring the line to their districts in election campaigns. Construction companies were also actively lobbying with the government, the LDP, and JRs.[21] However, the construction of the new bullet train lines required more extensive negotiations than that of nationwide expressway networks by JH. Whereas, as shown earlier, JH and the Ministry of Construction had the special funding source for road construction that derived from gasoline taxes, funding for new bullet train line construction came from the general government budget. Concerned with the increase in the budget deficit, the MOF was adamant about increases in new spending, and objected to the resumption of the new bullet line construction, citing the lack of firm prospects for profitability. Also, JRs were not happy to have new bullet train lines, because their operation would imply further financial burdens. JRs objected to making financial contributions to the construction.

While discussion on JNR reform was proceeding, LDP transport *zoku* politicians refrained from having overt public campaigns for the resumption of the construction of the new bullet lines, but actively engaged in backstage lobbying. The JNR Reconstruction Administrative Committee—that eventually formulated a radical plan to privatize and break up JNR—initially supported the idea of freezing construction. However, conceding to pressure from the LPD, in its final report presented to Prime Minister Nakasone in July 1985, the Committee avoided including this issue in its JNR reform plan, merely stating it as an issue to be discussed further. As the format of the privatized national railways became clearer, transport *zoku* members began to be active in demanding the resumption of construction. When the government and the LDP agreed to continue to postpone the construction in August 1985, LDP politicians from Aomori prefecture, to which the Tohoku bullet line was planned to be extended, vehemently protested and LDP prefectural assembly members declared they would leave the party. To calm down the opposition, the government set up a budget arrangement to begin to build a new bullet train station in Aomori city. The *de facto* construction of the new bullet lines thus resumed in 1985, though officially the construction was still postponed because the funding of the construction in Aomori did not come from the bullet train construction plan.[22]

In the late 1980s, the movement for the construction slowly gained momentum. In December 1988, the government and the LDP reached an agreement to resume discussion on the construction order among the five planned bullet train lines as well as the share of construction cost to be charged to JRs, the national government, and prefectural governments.[23] Determining the construction order was a tricky issue. Because of budget constraints, it was clear that it was not feasible to construct all lines simultaneously. However, each LDP politician demanded speedy construction of the line that would benefit his or her district and prefecture. Therefore, the determination required extensive negotiations. In August 1988, an LDP–government agreement was reached on the construction of the Takasaki–Karuizawa zone of the Hokuriku line. In January 1989, the LDP and the government agreed on a basic scheme to allocate construction cost among JRs, the national government, and the prefectural governments. As a result, starting from three major planned routes, the construction of the new bullet train lines resumed.[24]

The 1989 agreement had restrained construction, but now construction progressed in those zones with high priority. In particular, the construction of the so-called Nagano bullet train was expedited after the 1998 Winter Olympics were determined to be held in Nagano. Using loans from the FILP for its construction, the Nagano line began to operate in 1997, connecting Tokyo and Nagano in a little less than two hours.[25] Although the MOT and LDP transport *zoku* politicians sought to expedite the expansion of construction to other areas, due to the difficulty in securing funding, they did not succeed in setting up a concrete plan. In 1993, the MOT tried to extend the use of FILP funding for other routes. However, reflecting on the JNR experience of operating nonprofitable lines that the government constructed using FILP funding, JRs opposed its extensive use.[26] After the LDP was thrown out of power in 1993, the non-LDP coalition government postponed the construction discussion for three years in February 1994.[27]

Once the LDP came back to power as a coalition partner in the summer of 1994, LDP transport *zoku* politicians resumed active lobbying in order to recover from the setback. In December 1994, nullifying the previous agreement, the coalition partners—the LDP, the Social Democratic Party, and the Sakigake Party—reached an agreement whereby they would formulate a concrete comprehensive plan for new bullet train lines construction by 1996 so that the construction of all the planned new bullet lines would be finished by the early twenty-first century. To formulate a plan, particularly the scheme for financing the construction, the LDP, MOF, MOT, and the Ministry of Home Affairs—the ministry that represented prefectural governments—negotiated extensively. Consequently, in December 1996, these political actors came to an agreement and set up a scheme to allocate construction cost among JRs, the government, and the prefectural governments.[28] When Hashimoto became prime minister and worked on administrative reform in 1997, the construction was disrupted again. Yet, in 1998, after the resignation of Hashimoto, the government allocated the budget for the continuation of new bullet train construction.[29]

Later, Koizumi's cabinet cut the budget allocation, but it did not terminate the plan itself. Thus, construction of the new bullet train has been progressing slowly, due to LDP transport *zoku* politicians' lobbying to benefit their rural constituents, especially construction companies, despite the fact that there is no firm prospect of JRs generating profit from operating these lines. The fundamental dynamics of the construction of the new bullet train lines as well as the construction of unprofitable rural railway lines during JNR days is similar to that of the construction of national expressways. Old guard politicians worked to distribute wealth to rural areas. Thus, although JNR privatization succeeded in rationalizing management by weakening labor unions, it did not fundamentally change the distributive mechanism that JNR was forced to perform.

Airline Deregulation and Airport Construction

Similar to road and railroad systems, air transport developed slowly with the end of World War II. Since air transport was closely connected to military operation, the Japanese were not allowed to operate aircraft until the conclusion of the peace treaty between the United States and

Japan. When Nihon Kōkū Kabushiki Kaisha (the predecessor to Japan Airlines) was established in 1951, the airline company consigned all air transport services, including flights between Tokyo and Osaka, to a U.S. carrier, Northwest Airlines. In the following year, the airline company began to operate air transport services with its personnel. In 1953, taking over the airline company, Japan Airlines (JAL) was established as a semigovernment corporation. The government invested ¥1 billion in JAL when it was established, and continued to provide subsidies and loan guarantees in order to help the airlines successfully operate both international and domestic services. JAL's domestic service was limited to major routes, and two other airlines extensively operated domestic routes. The MOT guided these two airlines, which merged into the All Nippon Airways (ANA) in 1958.[30]

ANA became a dominant carrier in the domestic airline market, but two smaller competitors eventually emerged as Japan's airline market rapidly expanded. In 1971, the smaller competitors merged and established Toa Domestic Airlines (TDA). Faced with the regrouping of the domestic airline service market, the MOT established an arrangement to manage the airline service market in the early 1970s, assigning each of the three airlines a segment(s) of the air transport market. JAL was assigned to operate international routes and major domestic routes that connected five major cities. ANA was in charge of major and nonmajor domestic routes as well as short-distance charter flights. The MOT designated TDA to operate mainly nonmajor domestic routes.[31] Although this arrangement was designed to help develop Japan's airline industry, it benefited JAL most because it only operated lucrative routes, helping it become one of the largest carriers in the world for a very short time.

However, the other two carriers, especially ANA, became increasingly dissatisfied with the arrangement as a large number of Japanese tourists went overseas. In the early 1980s, ANA actively lobbied for its entrance into international service while demanding JAL's exit from domestic service and opposed JAL's attempt to expand its domestic service. In addition to the carriers' demand for changing the arrangement, the MOT was facing new developments in the mid-1980s. One was the expansion of trans-Pacific flights between Japan and the United States. As a result of negotiations between the United States and Japan, the MOT secured the allocation of trans-Pacific flights for another Japanese carrier in exchange for its concession to allow more U.S. carriers to operate on trans-Pacific routes. The other was the development of a trend for deregulation and privatization, as shown in the NTT and JNR reforms.[32] The MOT thought it necessary to revise the arrangement to manage Japan's air transport industry and began to discuss this at its policy deliberation council on transportation in September 1985.[33]

The council recommended the reformatting of the arrangement. Major recommendations were: allowing ANA and TDA to enter into the international service market, the privatization of JAL, and the introduction of competition in the domestic service. Consequently, the MOT allowed ANA to begin operating flights between Japan and the United States in 1987. In the same year, JAL became a private sector company after the government completely sold its share. Also, the MOT relaxed limitations on domestic services by allowing more carriers to operate on the same route. Despite these changes, Japan's airline industry continued to be under the MOT's heavy regulation, exemplified by its exercise of strong control over airfare and its prevention of price competition.[34] Although the carriers wanted to have more managerial freedom, they did not like to have cutthroat competition and sought to keep the MOT's protective policy. During this time, deregulation and liberalization progressed very slowly in the airline industry. In the early 1990s, facing the carriers' financial problems after the burst of the bubble economy, the MOT relaxed its regulations, such as the limit on the number of carriers allowed to operate on the same route and restrictions on the use of foreign maintenance companies. These deregulatory measures were intended to help the carriers improve their businesses.[35]

In the mid-1990s, the MOT embarked on the deregulation of airfare. As of December 1994, airline carriers were no longer required to get approval for reduced fares from the MOT as long as the discount rate was 50 percent, or less, of the ordinary fare. The Japanese carriers introduced domestic discount airfare for pre-purchased tickets, already a very common practice for U.S. carriers, in March 1995.[36] In 1996, the MOT relaxed ordinary domestic airfare regulation, allowing each carrier to determine its airfare for each route within the range set by the MOT. The MOT set the upper limit computed from each carrier's average operation cost plus "appropriate" level profit and the lower limit was set to be 25 percent lower than the upper limit. When the carriers changed airfare based on this airfare determination system in March 1996, they generally set airfare to near the upper limit, resulting in price increases for many routes. Although the new system allowed carriers flexibility to set airfare, price competition did not develop and the change disappointed consumers who had expected it to reduce airfare.[37]

Nonetheless, the movement for airline deregulation continued to develop, and Prime Minister Hashimoto singled out the airline service market as one of the major target areas for regulatory reform. In response, during the fall of 1996, the MOT hammered out a comprehensive deregulatory plan for the airline service market, which included the eventual abolition of supply–demand control where the MOT determined the number of flights for each route based on expected air passenger traffic and allocated them among airliners. This prevented new carriers from entering into the airline service market. When a new runway was added to the Haneda airport—a large and convenient airport in Tokyo that handled mainly domestic air traffic—in 1998, the MOT allocated new flight slots to two new entrants. Since these new entrants introduced discounted airfares and existing carriers and the incumbent carriers matched their airfare, domestic airfare was significantly reduced.[38] In February 2000, the MOT abolished the supply–demand control as well as restrictions on airfare, allowing carriers to freely determine airfare. Thus, in the last 20 years, airline deregulation progressed significantly, albeit slowly, in Japan.

In contrast, airport construction, closely related to the development of the airline service market, did not proceed as quickly as expressway construction did in the post–World War II period. Air construction entailed large-scale construction projects and its potential benefit was immense particularly for rural areas. Nonetheless, LDP politicians concerned with the distributive networks have been much less active in promoting airport construction than they have been in promoting expressway construction. This seems to derive from the following three reasons. First, airports impose enormous social costs on surrounding areas. Airport construction requires large-scale appropriation of land, easily arousing opposition, as found in the construction of the Tokyo (Narita) International Airport, which had been delayed for a long time by fierce opposition from farmers who refused to give up their land. Second, merely constructing new local airports is not commercially viable. Most flights from local airports go to the airport in Tokyo or Osaka, which do not have additional slots to accommodate flights from new local airports. Therefore, major airport constructions have not been in rural areas but in Tokyo and Osaka—the construction and expansion of Narita and Haneda airports in Tokyo and the construction of Kansai airport in Osaka. Third and perhaps most importantly, funding is limited for airport construction. Similar to how the gasoline tax is designated to be used for road construction, airport-use fees and jet fuel taxes are used for airport construction. Yet, they are not high enough to cover the cost of the construction of local airports. With the development of competition in the airline service market, cost-conscious airliners have been pressing the MOT to reduce airport-use fees, making it even more difficult to construct new airports.

Conclusion

Reforms in transportation did not progress fast, but it is an exaggeration to say that nothing has changed. Indeed, responding to the growing demand for deregulation, deregulation/liberalization measures were implemented in the transportation industry during the last three decades. In the railway industry, JNR was privatized into JRs in 1987 and JRs significantly improved in terms of operational efficiency by weakening or subjugating left-wing unions. In the airline service market, JAL was privatized in 1987. Restrictions on airfare were gradually relaxed until they were abolished in 2000, and the MOT allowed new carriers to enter the market. In expressway operation, as a result of Koizumi's reform efforts, JH is scheduled to become a private sector company in 2005. As symbolized by the drastic reduction of airfare, these reform measures have generated benefits to consumers.

However, regarding the features essential to the development and maintenance of the distributive networks, reform did not progress as intended. As shown in airport construction, due to budget constraints, newly planned construction projects were becoming increasingly difficult to be implemented. However, reformers did not succeed in stopping those projects that had long been planned. Despite Koizumi and his supporting staff's efforts to fundamentally change the mechanism of national expressway construction through JH privatization, the basic feature of the mechanism was intact, making it possible for the government to continue to construct expressways. Due to budget constraints, the construction of new bullet train lines did not proceed as quickly as LDP politicians wanted. Yet, despite reluctance expressed by JRs, new bullet train lines have been built without the prospect of commercial viability. Thus, the existence of the distributive networks was the determinant of progress in government reform.

In this and previous chapters, I have looked at two major issue areas each of which is crucial to the maintenance of the distributive networks. The fundamental nature of interaction between reformers and old guard is the same as what was found in showdown politics during the three (Nakasone, Hashimoto, and Koizumi) reform periods. Reformers sought to enact measures that reduce government intervention or involvement with market activities but, when the issue was crucial to the distributive networks, old guard politicians and bureaucrats became active and forced reformers to compromise, which significantly watered down the effectiveness of proposed reform measures. At the same time, the detailed analysis of these two issue areas shows diversity and the complexity of reform politics. Although reform in general meant reduction in government activities, the nature of reform varied across issues in the two areas. In the tax reform and financial liberalization involving postal savings, the reform point in dispute was how to establish parity between the PSF and commercial banks in the application of rules on interest income tax and liberalization measures; reformers sought to undermine the advantages that the PSF held. In the postal service market reform, reformers demanded the extension of market competition to mail service. In transportation, reformers pursued the reduction of government spending on road and railway construction, whereas deregulation progressed in the airline market.

The interaction between reformers and antireform old guard was equally diverse and complex. Some issues, such as the introduction of interest income on PSF accounts and planning the construction of nationwide highways, were accompanied by full politicization whereby reformers and the old guard collided with each other. In contrast, the MPT and MOF extensively negotiated the treatment of the PSF in the liberalization of the personal financial market, which was devoid of overt political intervention. Also, the outcome varied across issues. In general, as shown in the MPT's success in strengthening the PSF through its interaction with the MOF as well as the MLIT's defense of its highway construction plan, the old guard minimized the progress of reform when reformers sought to change the existing system. On the contrary, when the old guard sought to add new policy measures, it faced uphill battles, exemplified by Koizumi's intervention in the issue of tax exemption for the elderly and the delay in the construction of the bullet train networks. Thus, the interaction by the dual state is complex and dynamic. The distributive networks have been under constant pressure from reformers and their political actors have had to resist them, adjust their system, or accept changes, resulting in the evolution of the networks.

Chapter 6

Telecommunications Regulatory Reform: Bureaucracy-Led Liberalization?

As shown in Chapters 3–5, reformers pursued diverse government reform in and around the Nakasone, Hashimoto, and Koizumi reforms. They reduced the government's physical size, as shown by NTT and JNR privatizations, and sought to improve operational efficiency through government reorganization implemented in 2001. They also tried to scale down the government's financial involvement in the reform of the PSF and the privatization of the Japan Highway Corporation while modifying regulatory intrusion into market activities, exemplified by the liberalization of telecommunications and airline deregulation. The immediate rationale behind these reforms was the ever-accumulating budget deficit and these reforms were thought to directly or indirectly ease the financial burden on the government. Yet, at the same time, these reforms were driven by neoconservative economic ideology that emphasized the superiority of market competition over government control for economic development. This aspect was particularly important for telecommunications and information technology when NTT privatization during the Nakasone reform introduced market competition. In this sector, government actors were more concerned with competition than protection and major business actors were much less dependent on government than those in the distributive sector, making it unnecessary for old guard politicians to intervene. Yet, political involvement occurred when government and business actors collided. Therefore, I examine the politics of the developmental networks in this chapter, focusing on regulatory aspects.

As shown in Chapter 3, through Nakasone's administrative reform, NTT was privatized and the telecommunications market began to be liberalized. Even though NTT privatization was crucial, market reform was much more of a long-term process where introduction of market competition progressed slowly accompanied by interactions and conflicts. In these interactions, the MPT, which was reorganized into the MPHPT, NTT, and new common carriers who entered into the telecommunications market after NTT privatization, were particularly important. Also, although telecommunications has been important throughout the last three decades, the proliferation of Internet use in the late 1990s made telecommunications even more important while political dynamics changed around that time. In the first section, I analyze interactions between these actors before the Internet age. In the second, I turn to interactions during the Internet age. Then, in the conclusion, I briefly summarize politics of deregulation in telecommunications.

The Politics of Telecommunications after NTT Privatization: NTT, MPT, and NCCs

As discussed in chapter 3 in the section on the background of telecommunications reform politics, prior to privatization NTT had been the sole operator and regulator of telecommunications. Through privatization, NTT lost its *de jure* monopoly status, but NTT continued to be the *de facto* dominant actor in Japanese telecommunications. Unlike JNR, which was broken up into regional companies and a freight carrier, NTT avoided its break-up. As discussed here, pressed by the MPT, NTT had to change its organizational format, but it has essentially preserved the unity as a telecommunications carrier and later as a group of carriers. Therefore, NTT has been the only carrier that operates all aspects of telecommunications, such as local, long-distance, and mobile telecommunications. In particular, since NTT monopolized local networks, so-called new common carriers (NCCs) were dependent on NTT to reach customers. Similarly, most Internet providers, such as DSL operators, needed to use NTT local networks, due to the underdevelopment of alternative networks, such as cable television. In addition to the operation of local networks, NTT boasts long-accumulated operational and technological knowledge of telecommunications, contributing to its market dominance.

However, NTT fully recognized that being an incumbent carrier with nationwide networks did not necessarily mean that it would never be challenged by new entrants. Telecommunications-related technology had been rapidly developing and newer equipments were far faster and far less costly than old ones. Although NTT kept upgrading its network technologies, it could not afford to use the most advanced technologies for the entire network. In contrast, NTT expected new entrants to fully utilize the new equipment and to provide high-quality service at a competitive price. Moreover, unlike NTT, which was required to provide nationwide services rather evenly regardless of profitability, NCCs were in a position to choose its operation areas based on profitability and to concentrate on high-profit operation, commonly known as "cream-skimming." NTT thought it was highly vulnerable to competition from NCCs.

NTT, therefore, sought to maintain its business advantage primarily in three ways. First, NTT sought to preserve its unity as a carrier, resisting the MPT's pressure to break it up. Second, NTT tried to utilize its position as the local network operator to eliminate as many of NCCs' advantages as possible. NTT required them to submit detailed information of their new service when they applied for the use of its local networks. NCCs charged that NTT often deliberately delayed processing new service requests so that NTT would have a headstart over NCCs. Third and finally, NTT used the logic of liberalization to demand freer and flexible operation. NTT argued that the fundamental purpose of NTT privatization was to let private sector carriers compete freely. Although a significant portion of NTT's share continued to be held by the government, NTT was supposed to work as a private sector carrier and NTT claimed that it needed to have operational and managerial flexibility, trying to fend off MPT's intervention with excessive government involvement in private sector business.

Due to its background as a government corporation whose management had been under Diet scrutiny, NTT has maintained close relations with LDP politicians. Since NTT, as a government corporation, was not allowed to give financial contributions to political parties, including the LDP, NTT channeled money to the LDP via so-called NTT family companies, from which NTT exclusively procured high-priced telecommunications equipment. NTT topped up money for LDP donation to the equipment price, which NTT family companies in turn donated to the LDP. After privatization, NTT set up a slash fund based on managers' "voluntary" contributions and channeled money to LDP politicians.[1] Also, NTT family firms were influential members of *Keidanren* (the Federation of Economic Organizations), a peak business organization consisting of big business, and it was able to develop some support from the business community.

NTT was a very strong political actor, but it was not strong enough to dominate telecommunications policymaking. NTT had strong connections with LDP leadership, but, unlike construction companies in the distributive networks, it did not have strong district-specific influence. NTT had about 300,000 employees and its electoral impact was substantial, but most of the employees were the members of Zendentsu, which consistently supported opposition parties. Unlike JNR, the union and the management took cooperative relations. LDP members were often unhappy about NTT management's conciliatory stance toward the union, exemplified by its reluctance to drastically and rapidly cut down its labor force. Therefore, NTT and the LDP formed stable but complex relations. NTT could not count on the LDP as a cheerleader for them to protect its interest though NTT could influence LDP leaders at crucial junctures.

Facing the dominant incumbent NTT was the MPT, which had been downplayed as a third-class ministry due to subordination to NTT in telecommunications regulation. The MPT initially opposed the privatization, but recognizing the prospect of becoming a policy-making ministry in charge of a rapidly developing industry, it changed its position and actively supported NTT privatization. Since the MITI, known as the architect of Japan's industrial strength, also tried to take over a government agency overseeing telecommunications, the MPT fought hard with the MITI for the status of a primary government agency in telecommunications. Although the MPT was given the status in the NTT privatization process, the MITI continued to work to seize jurisdiction over telecommunications.[2] Therefore, the MPT sought to demonstrate its effectiveness in telecommunications policymaking and strength over telecommunications carriers, particularly NTT.

MPT used the logic of liberalization to strengthen its position and emphasized the promotion of market competition as a primary object of telecommunications reform. This logic was convenient for the MPT, which was trying to contain NTT. Portraying NTT's dominance as the biggest obstacle to the development of market competition in Japanese telecommunications, the MPT legitimated its strong actions to weaken NTT's dominance for market reform and thereby increased its influence over telecommunications. Also, this logic of reform for market competition worked well in dealing with many new entrants, particularly NCCs directly competing with NTT. The MPT closely scrutinized their applications and monitored their business to nurture the competitiveness of new entrants helping them effectively compete against the gigantic incumbent NTT. With the development of competition in telecommunications, the MPT's relative role decreased but it strengthened its position as the government ministry in charge of telecommunications, forming "reciprocal consent" between the government and business actors.[3]

For the pursuit of its "reformist" policy, which NTT criticized as continued government intervention in market activities, the MPT's close connection with the LDP generated a favorable policy environment. As shown in Chapters 3 and 4, because of its operation of postal business, the MPT maintained cozy relationships with LDP's *yūsei zoku* (postal tribe), and the same *yūsei zoku* members also dealt with telecommunications policy; the MPT counted on *yūsei zoku* in passing Diet bills related to telecommunications. Since, unlike postal business, telecommunications policy rarely had district-specific impact, *yūsei zoku* did not support the MPT in telecommunications policy-making as strongly as they did for the postal business. While its connection to *yūsei zoku* helped the MPT to counterbalance NTT's political power, the more direct and effective policy tool that the MPT had was specific legislative mandate that it had gained through the NTT privatization, including a specific agreement to allow the MPT to discuss the break-up of NTT. Citing specific provisions in telecommunications-related laws, MPT confronted NTT and controlled NCCs.

Observing the interaction between NTT and the MPT, NCCs and other business organizations took a rather passive stance. NCCs and business organizations were not happy about the MPT's intrusive regulations toward them and often criticized the excessive regulations. However, NCCs were dependent on the MPT's support of NCC in competing with NTT. For example, NCCs looked to the MPT for their smooth and expedited connections of their networks with NTT's local networks. In fact, to enhance its connections with the MPT, most NCCs hired ex-MPT senior bureaucrats as executives, the practice known as *amakudari* (decent from heaven).[4] In addition, since many NCCs were somehow related to Japanese big business, a major source of LDP finance, NCCs had indirect connections with the LDP, but their political strength was no match for NTT and the MPT, leading them to play a passive role.

Each of the major actors in telecommunications: NTT, MPT, and NCCs, interpreted liberalization and reform in telecommunications to its own benefit, and tried to maximize its interest, generating complex interactions among them. At critical junctures, their interactions involved the LDP's intervention. This was the basic format of interactions, but the general policy environment surrounding the interactions changed with the diffusion of Internet technologies in the late 1990s. I analyze interactions among major policy actors in the two separate phases, the early phase and the Internet phase.

The Early Phase of Telecommunications Liberalization

In the early phase of telecommunications liberalization, NTT was the sole, incumbent telecommunications carrier and boasted overwhelming strength. In contrast, due to the prospect of the expansion of the telecommunications market and high profit, many companies were interested in entering into telecommunications, but none of them had the potential to effectively compete with NTT immediately. For the development of market competition, it was necessary for the MPT to create a level field by both containing NTT and nurturing NCCs, which was the fundamental goal of telecommunications reform. For this purpose, the MPT used provisions in telecommunications laws legislated through the NTT privatization process to introduce competition into the telecommunications market, especially in its regulation of market competition and its pursuit of NTT reorganization, as shown in the following two sections.

MPT's Regulation of Market Competition

The MPT effectively used its legal authority to select new entrants to the market. Given that new entrants would have to compete against the highly experienced telecommunications giant, NTT, the MPT thought it necessary to scrutinize the feasibility of each prospective new entrant and to deny applications with low viability or force entrants to modify unsatisfactory business proposals. In particular, the MPT used the so-called *jyu-kyū chosei* (supply and demand adjustment) authority stipulated in the NTT laws as the basis of its sanction power in limiting the number of new entrants.[5] Using this authority, MPT was able to effectively restrict the number of new entrants by forcing the merger of prospective new entrants in the long-distance telephone service market, by delaying the entrance of new carriers into the local telephone service market, and by allowing only one cellular phone company to compete with NTT in each local area.[6]

Those new entrants into the long-distance telephone market that had cleared the MPT's scrutiny and obtained licenses to operate telecommunications business still faced the powerful, incumbent NTT, which had a monopoly over customers when these new entrants began offering their services. In order to nurture competition, the MPT assisted the new entrants by giving them preferential treatment and by preventing NTT from resorting to predatory business practices by taking advantage of its exclusive operation of local public telephone services. The MPT also used its authority to approve changes in telephone charges for the promotion of competition. Although the MPT pressed the new long-distance carriers to coordinate price levels, it did not allow NTT to reduce its long-distance telephone charges, allowing the new carriers to maintain price competitiveness.[7]

As mentioned earlier, NTT had a distinct advantage over the new long-distance carriers. NTT virtually monopolized the local telephone networks, which the new carriers also had to use. The MPT tried to prevent NTT from taking advantage of the new carriers' reliance on these local telephone networks; it did not allow NTT to impose high access charges on the new long-distance carriers for the use of local networks.[8] Furthermore, when it allowed NTT to introduce new services, the MPT ensured that the new carriers would also be able to offer comparable services. For example, in the late 1980s, both NTT and the new carriers planned to introduce the Virtual Private Network—called Software Defined Networks in the U.S.—a public telephone system that can be used as private extensions for lower connection fees. This service was based on the integration of long-distance and local networks. NTT needed little technical modification and began to offer the service in February 1994. In contrast, in order for the new carriers to offer the service, NTT had to modify its internal systems to accommodate the new carriers. NTT was reluctant to let the new carriers connect their Virtual Private Network facilities to NTT's without substantial interconnection charges, and intentionally delayed connection. The new carriers requested that the MPT order NTT to connect its telephone networks with the new carriers' Virtual Private Networks on November 8, 1994. In response to this, after holding a hearing based on the Telecommunications Business Law, the MPT issued an order that required NTT to establish connections with the new carriers. As a result, the new carriers began Virtual Private Network long-distance services in May 1995.[9] Thus, just as the MPT used its authority to reduce the number of competitors in the newly liberalized telecommunications markets, to approve changes in telephone service charges, it ordered NTT to connect its networks with the networks of the new carriers.

NTT Reorganization

In the original plan to privatize NTT, released in 1982, the advisory committee for administrative reform recommended that NTT be broken up into long-distance and regional local telephone companies. LDP leaders and the MPT tried to stipulate the breakup of NTT in one of the laws related to NTT privatization, but NTT management and labor prevented the MPT from mandating by law breakup as a requirement for NTT privatization. The law instead included a provision for reviewing NTT's organizational structure by March 1990. Following this provision, the MPT and its Telecommunications Council examined the format of NTT operations in the late 1980s. The Council released its interim report in March 1990, and recommended the break-up of NTT into a long-distance telephone company, a local telephone company, and a mobile phone service company, arguing that competition had not fully developed in the Japanese telecommunications market because of NTT's predominant strength and the NCCs dependence on NTT's local telephone networks.[10]

The MPT lobbied LDP politicians to implement the breakup of NTT, but faced opposition not only from private sector organizations but also from government organizations. NTT opposed the breakup, which, it argued, would jeopardize the quality of service it provided through its comprehensive service operations, delay the progress of digitalization of networks, reduce its R&D capabilities, and create losses for current stockholders because breakup would negatively affect stock prices.[11] Telecommunications equipment manufacturers supported NTT's position because breakup would make it more costly for them to engage in R&D activities with multiple NTT firms. Furthermore, *Keidanren* expressed reservations and argued that more time was needed to finalize the breakup. This position reflected the coexistence of support for and opposition to NTT breakup within the business community.[12]

Taking positions similar to that of *Keidanren*, government organizations, such as the MITI, the Fair Trade Commission, and the Economic Planning Agency, argued that it was too early to implement the breakup and called for more detailed discussions.[13] The most intensive opposition to the breakup came from the MOF, whose primary interest in this issue was to keep NTT's stock prices high in order to maximize government revenue. After the plan to breakup NTT was released, its stock price fell below the initial price at which the MOF had sold NTT stock. This significantly reduced the marketability of

NTT stocks, and led the MOF to postpone further sales of NTT stock. Emphasizing the interest of NTT shareholders, the MOF asked the MPT to revoke its pursuit of the NTT breakup in order to prevent further declines in NTT stock prices.[14]

The MOF, along with NTT, was successful in mobilizing opposition to the MPT's efforts, and LDP leaders, concerned with the impact of breakup on both the large number of NTT shareholders and government revenue, began to express their disapproval of the breakup. This growing opposition threatened the MPT to the degree that it almost had to totally abandon the breakup attempt. However, the MPT was able to respond by mobilizing pro-MPT LDP *zoku* Diet members. After a series of negotiations, the MPT agreed with the MOF and the LDP to postpone the discussion of NTT's breakup until the 1995 fiscal year, which would start on April 1, 1995, and end on March 31, 1996. In agreeing to this postponement, the MPT obtained a number of concessions on NTT policy measures as quid pro quo. These measures included the adoption of the division system (*jigyōbusei*) in which each division, for example, long-distance and local telephone divisions, would operate independently, disclosing unit-based financial statistics; the separation of NTT's cellular phone service by the end of 1991; and the disclosure of NTT's telephone network information.[15] Although the MPT had to delay its effort to break up NTT, these measures actually enhanced the MPT's position over NTT.

With the end of the cooling-off period in April 1995, the MPT renewed its attempt to break up NTT, asking its Telecommunications Council to discuss NTT breakup in April.[16] NTT countered the MPT's moves by making it easier for NCCs to establish connections to NTT's local telephone networks, by issuing a large-scale rationalization plan that would reduce its approximately 200,000-employee workforce by one-fifth, and by embarking on a nationwide multimedia service for which its integrated structure was essential.[17] In addition, just before the release of the Council's final report, to enhance its position, NTT disclosed its plan to begin an Internet service that would make access more convenient and less expensive.[18] Along with these defensive measures, NTT strongly criticized the MPT, pointing to MPT regulation as a major obstacle to the development of competition in Japanese telecommunications, and argued that deregulation was more important than NTT breakup.[19]

NTT's request for deregulation attracted support from not only the business community, which wanted freer entrance into telecommunications businesses, but also from government actors because the deregulation of economic activities had become a major policy issue. Facing growing demands for deregulation, the MPT began to couple NTT breakup with deregulation. In December 1995, the MPT made public its intention to deregulate telecommunications by allowing free entrance into various areas of telecommunications business. This lessened the business community's opposition to the NTT breakup. Although major Japanese electronics manufacturers that supplied telecommunications equipment to NTT continued to oppose the breakup, the business community did not take a clear unitary position against it.[20] As a result, the MPT Telecommunications Council's final report in February 1996 proposed to break up NTT into a long-distance company and two local companies to stimulate competition in the telecommunications market.[21]

The release of the report did not end the controversy. Neither the MPT nor NTT showed any sign of compromise. In opposing the breakup, NTT's union gained support from the SDP. As discussed earlier, even though the LDP and the SDP were rivals in the Diet in the 1980s, the union had been successful in influencing the privatization of NTT. In 1996, the union had even better access to the policy-making process, because the LDP and the SDP were partners in the coalition government. Given this delicate situation, the LDP did not aid MPT efforts to realize the Council's proposal, but rather tried to postpone the decision. In March 1996, the LDP and the coalition partners agreed to postpone the decision for a year, asking the MPT and NTT to settle the issue themselves.[22]

Even after the government's decision, the MPT and NTT did not interact to try to settle the dispute until September 1996 when they began preliminary discussions in response to Prime Minister Hashimoto Ryutaro's demand that the MPT vice minister explore NTT's entrance into the international telecommunications business. After the HR elections in October, Hashimoto formed a new government without the participation of the SDP, and the influence of the NTT union's rigid position toward NTT breakup significantly decreased, making compromise feasible. Through extensive negotiations, the MPT and NTT sought to reach a consensus on the establishment of a shareholding company that would oversee the operations of a long-distance carrier, two regional carriers, and other companies. In December 1996, NTT and the MPT reached a final agreement that the newly reorganized NTT would commence operation in July 1999.[23]

Based on the agreement, in July 1999, NTT was reorganized into a shareholding company called NTT; two regional carriers, NTT East and NTT West; and a long-distance and international carrier, NTT Communications. MPT made concessions to NTT by letting NTT maintain its unity in this format, by treating NTT Communications as an ordinary common carrier free from special regulations, and by allowing NTT Communications to enter into the international telecommunications business. However, the MPT kept each of the three other NTT companies under detailed supervision by screening the appointment of executives and monitoring major business planning and budgeting. The MPT maximized the degree of separation among these companies by restricting personnel exchanges among them and prohibiting preferential treatment of NTT group companies over other non-NTT companies.[24]

The interaction between the MPT and NTT also affected NCCs and potential entrants. In the period before the reorganization, the MPT eased regulations. First, it abolished the system under which each carrier had to obtain approval from the MPT for price changes, and set aside the rule that required carriers to submit reports regarding price modifications. The one exception concerned NTT's local telephone service, changes that still required the MPT's approval. Second, the MPT abandoned the segmentation of the telecommunications market and allowed new carriers in each segment.[25] These measures were consistent not only with the preferences of NTT but also with those of the business community.

In addition to promoting competition via deregulation, the interaction between the MPT and NTT (indirectly) impacted on the large-scale expansion of the mobile communications market and the proliferation of Internet use, two major events in the development of Japanese telecommunications. The 1990 agreement mandated the spinoff of the mobile phone division of NTT, resulting in the establishment of NTT DoCoMo in 1992.[26] NTT DoCoMo, freed from making its business strategy consistent with that of NTT as a whole, began to pursue flexible business strategies.[27] After the spinoff, NTT DoCoMo drastically reduced the initial payment that new customers paid for mobile phone service initiation, making mobile phone service much more accessible. NTT DoCoMo's adoption of flexible management was also a background factor in introducing the *i*-mode technology that made e-mail exchanges possible via mobile phones and greatly accelerated the expansion of mobile phone use. Further, to counter continued pressure to break up the company, NTT introduced a new Internet service that included the establishment of Internet networks separate from existing telephone networks. Since other factors, such as technology development, were also involved in the expansion of mobile communications and Internet use, the interaction between the MPT and NTT was not the only driving factor, but interaction between the two at the very least helped to make the business environment more consistent with the development of these two phenomenon.

The MPT, NTT, NCCs, and other business organizations interacted with each other throughout the early phase of telecommunications liberalization, showing the essence of complexity of reform politics. The MPT used the logic of reform to weaken NTT, and it sought to increase control over telecommunications, contrary to the logic. NTT wanted to keep the strength that it inherited from its government corporation days as much as possible, but it used the logic to counteract the MPT's pursuit of breakup. As for NCCs, they made use of the MPT's preferential treatment, but they still tried to free themselves from detailed regulation. Along with these major actors, other actors, such as the LDP, MOF, and *Keidanren*, participated on interactions on various occasions. Unlike reform politics in the distributive networks, reform politics in this phase involved complex interactions and resulted in complex outcomes, reflecting diverse interests.

MPT's Regulation in the Age of Global Info-Communications

The MPT's regulation changed since NTT was broken up into regional carriers, NTT East and West (NTTEW), a long-distance carrier, NTT Communications, and other communications companies in 1999. Even after the reorganization, these NTT companies, along with NTT DoCoMo, were under the control of a shareholding company, NTT. Since NTT tried to maintain the strength of the NTT group as a whole, NTT carriers were still dominant in the telecommunications market, and the MPT needed to continue to promote competition by containing NTT's activities. Although the MPT maintained its status as the primary regulator of telecommunications and did not face any strong rivals within the government, its pursuit of the regulatory policy goal was becoming increasingly difficult in this period because of changes in telecommunications that had been developing in the late 1990s. Therefore, this section shows that the MPT was faced with the growing need for conciliation to cope with changes in telecommunications. The following section specifies major changes in telecommunications, followed by the case studies sections that discusses the relationship between the changes and telecommunications regulation.

Changing Policy Environment in the Late 1990s

Three basic features of telecommunications in the period between the privatization and the reorganization of NTT were as follows. The first feature was segmented markets. The MPT's regulation segmented telecommunications into local, long-distance, mobile, and international services. The second feature was relative seclusion from international forces. Although occasional international pressure came from the U.S. government, foreign carriers made no attempt to enter into the telecommunications service market in Japan. The third and final feature was the importance of voice-based telephone as the core telecommunications service, although the importance of data communications was increasing rapidly. The new policy environment of telecommunications regulation was the complete opposite of each feature; telecommunications became integrated, internationalized, and Internet based, as discussed in the following three sections.

Integration

The interaction between the MPT and NTT over NTT breakup caused not only the reorganization of NTT but also significant changes in telecommunications regulation in general. When NTT breakup discussions were held about a decade after its privatization, NCCs had developed business strength and began to feel that the MPT's regulations were harmful to their business activities despite their original intention to protect NCCs. Taking advantage of this sentiment, NTT countered the MPT's pursuit of NTT breakup by demanding deregulation, and the MPT began to work on deregulation to gain support for its pursuit. Momentum for telecommunications deregulation was accelerated by the Japanese government's deployment of deregulation as its central agenda. As a result, the MPT took a series of deregulatory measures, including the following.

Regarding entrance restrictions, in January 1996, the MPT officially abandoned the principle of segment-based regulations for NCCs that separated telecommunication services, such as local, long distance, and international, preventing NCCs from pursuing integrated service provision. In June 1997, the MPT abolished a provision of the Telecommunications Business Law on supply–demand control that authorized MPT to limit the number NCCs. Along with these two drastic deregulatory measures in entrance restrictions, the MPT significantly reduced its control over telecommunications charges. Following the shift of mobile communication charges from a permission system to a report system in December 1996, the MPT liberalized common carriers' telecommunications charges by just requiring them to report charge changes in advance except for NTT's local services company.[28] Also, the MPT reduced control over Kokusai Denshin Denwr (KDD), a former government-related carrier specializing in international telecommunications. Since the agreement on NTT reorganization stipulated that NTT's long-distance division enter into the international telecommunications service market, the MPT modified the KDD Law in June 1997 and allowed KDD to operate domestic services to maintain parity between NTT and KDD.[29] In the following year, the MPT abolished the KDD Law that authorized the MPT to exercise detailed control over KDD's operations, and KDD began to be treated in the same way as other NCCs.[30]

Deregulation made it possible for each NCC to freely choose its areas of operation, and it was necessary to establish integrated services in order to effectively compete against the NTT group. Since each NCC still lacked the capacity to independently establish integrated services, rather than simply spreading its operation to another segment, it sought to expand its service through a merger. The anticipated entrance into the international telecommunications service market by NTT Communications, NTT's long-distance carrier, prompted international carriers to negotiate with long-distance carriers for a possible merger. As a result, ITJ merged into Nippon Telecom in October 1997 and Nihon Kosoku Tsushin (TWJ) merged with KDD in December 1998. Although IDC, the other international communications carrier, had held talks with NTT, it was acquired by Cable and Wireless, a major British telecommunications carrier, in September 1999, as discussed below in the section on the internationalization of Japanese telecommunications.[31]

Whereas vertical integration between international and long-distance NCCs progressed, mobile NCCs had to start from horizontal integration because of the fragmented structure of the mobile communications market. Since the MPT limited the number of carriers in each regional market and issued permits on region basis, no NCC had coherent nationwide networks. Disadvantaged against the mighty NTT DoCoMo group with coherent and high-quality networks, mobile NCCs felt it was necessary to integrate operations. Among the five major groups of mobile carriers, Daini Denden Incorporated (DDI), whose subsidiary Cellular operated mobile communications, and Nihon Ido Tsushin (IDO) decided to form an alliance in March 1997, and began to develop nationwide mobile telecommunications operations using a new digital technology format, called cdmaONE, in 1998.[32] The integration of mobile communications was further enhanced by the exit of the financially troubled Nissan from the mobile communications business. Nissan was one of the core investors in the Tuka group, consisting of nine regional companies. DDI was a major partner for three Tuka companies operating in Tokyo, Osaka, and Nagoya, and Nissan's partner was Nippon Telecom for the other six. In order to reduce its financial burden, Nissan decided to sell its shares of the companies. In October 1999, DDI took over the former three and Nippon Telecom, in cooperation with Vodafone-Airtouch who invested in Nippon Telecom's mobile communications operation, acquired the other six. The acquisition was particularly important for Nippon Telecom because it led Nippon Telecom to establish a coherent nationwide mobile service, named J-phone.[33] After this acquisition, the number of major mobile communications groups was reduced to three—NTT DoCoMo, the DDI–IDO alliance, and Nippon Telecom.

Through the consolidation of the mobile communications market, Nippon Telecom became a carrier with a wide variety of services covering long-distance, international, and mobile communications. In contrast, neither the DDI–IDO alliance nor KDD had such a high level of integration. But the merger of KDD and TWJ and the formation of the DDI–IDO alliance laid the foundation for a merger of the two groups, because Toyota was a core investor in each group. Also, there existed an urgent necessity for DDI and IDO to merge because of the beginning of the next generation mobile communications system—IMT-2000—capable of transferring video data and usable worldwide. In July 1998, the MPT made public its intention to limit the number of carriers to three due to the limited availability of radio waves.[34] Since NTT DoCoMo and Nippon Telecom each with consolidated nationwide networks were better positioned to gain slots, only one slot was left for DDI and IDO in 2000. Consequently, DDI and IDO began exploring the option to consolidate operations in order to pursue the development of the new mobile communication system.[35] However, each of these three had different backgrounds—a former government corporation (KDD), a maverick NCC (DDI), and a subsidiary of a major auto manufacturer Toyota (IDO), and negotiations did not proceed smoothly. However, the three carriers reached an agreement in December 1999,[36] and a new company, publicly known as KDDI, began to operate in October 2000, including its mobile communications division called *au*.[37] The KDDI merger reconfigured the telecommunications business, triggered by NTT reorganization and the MPT's deregulation, at least for the time being.

As summarized in figure 6.1, the reconfiguration process consolidated major telecommunications carriers into two groups, Nippon Telecom and KDDI, in addition to NTT. In a way, this simplified the MPT's policy environment by reducing the number of actors. Yet, the trend for integration made the MPT's policymaking more complex than before. In particular, NTT reorganization was designed to give its business segment operational independence, and this segmentation was against the consolidation trend, leading the MPT to face friction deriving from this contradiction. Also, as shown in movements toward mergers, reconfiguration made the policy environment fluid and uncertain. This fluidity was further enhanced by the internationalization of telecommunications.

Internationalization

Concurrent with the consolidation of carriers in the domestic domain of telecommunications, international influence on the MPT's regulation grew due to the WTO agreement on basic telecommunications in 1997. This agreement covered various aspects of telecommunications, including the treatment of foreign carriers, conditions of interconnections, and the independence of the national telecommunications regulatory agency, in order to foster the liberalization of telecommunications both in international and domestic arenas.[38] The most immediate impact of this agreement was on the foreign ownership of telecommunications carriers. With the agreement coming into effect in 1998, the restriction on foreign ownership eased significantly, and it became possible for Japanese telecommunications carriers to establish operations in other WTO member countries.

Taking advantage of this new international business environment, Japanese carriers began to expand their international services. In 1998, KDD and Nippon Telecom began to provide international telecommunications service in the United States, mainly for communications to Japan.[39] NTT began its international services through its subsidiary in 1998. Taking over the subsidiary's international business after NTT reorganization, NTT Communications expanded its international business, exemplified by its acquisition of Verio, a U.S. Internet service company, in 2000.[40] NTT DoCoMo sought to expand its presence in the international mobile communications service market through its investment in mobile carriers in Western Europe and East Asia.[41] Other carriers greatly expanded their presence in the international markets as well, and the MPT became aware of the dimension of international competitiveness in its pursuit of telecommunications policymaking.

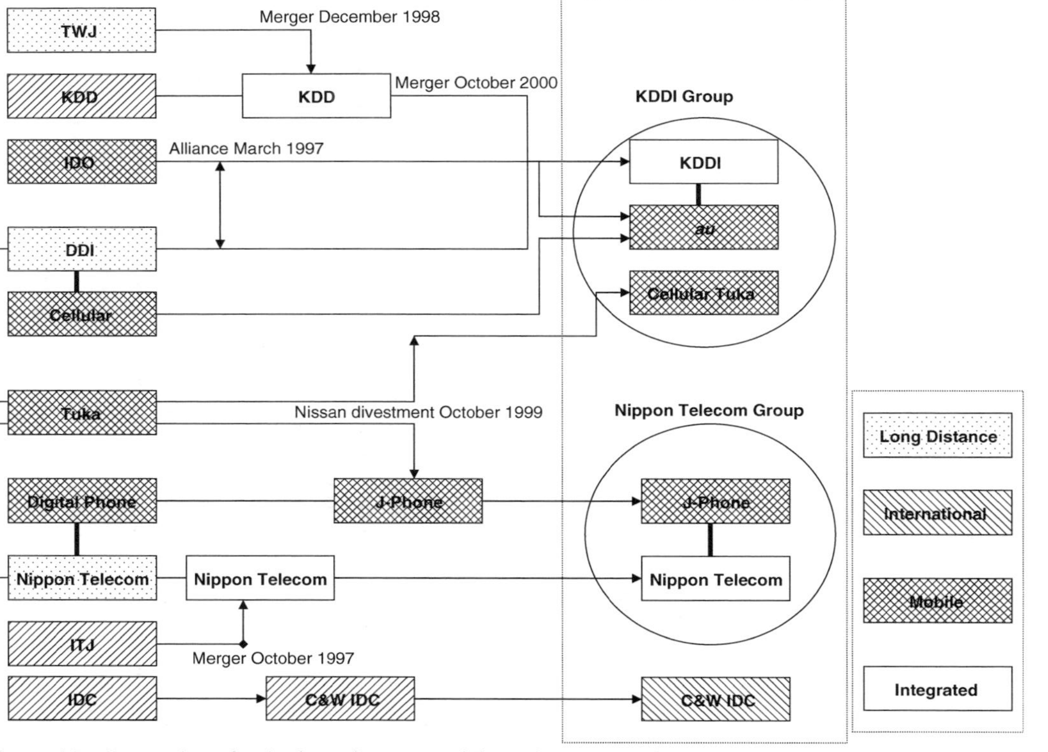

Figure 6.1   Integration of major long-distance, mobile, and international New Common Carriers.

The WTO agreement freed not only an outward stream of transactions but also an inward one. WorldCom, which had developed its telecommunications networks by targeting business customers in major cities around the world, was the first major carrier to set up business operations in Japan. Soon after the MPT liberalized the ownership and operation of foreign companies in Japan in February 1998, WorldCom began to operate in October 1998,[42] constructing fiber optic networks in central business districts in Tokyo and Osaka.[43] Cable and Wireless was already one of the leading investors of IDC, an international telecommunications NCC. Even though NTT had been negotiating with IDC to acquire the latter as a part of NTT Communications, Cable and Wireless sought to increase its share with the liberalization in early 1999. Despite opposition from IDC executives who preferred a merger with NTT Communications, Cable and Wireless overbid NTT and gained control over IDC in June.[44] British Telecom and AT&T also strengthened their business in Japan through investment in Nippon Telecom in 1999, but they took a less direct, less confrontational approach. Each of them agreed to invest in a 15 percent share so that Nippon Telecom would keep JR East with 15.1 percent share as its largest stockholder.[45] Their combined total share of 30 percent was less than the threshold of 33.4 percent necessary for a stockholder to exercise veto over a business plan at a shareholders' meeting.[46] Under this loose arrangement, Nippon Telecom marketed telecommunications services provided by Concert, an international communications company jointly established by AT&T and British Telecom in 2000.[47] Other major international carriers, such as Sprint, German Telecom, and French Telecom, followed suit and entered into the Japanese market.[48] Thus, the liberalization stimulated foreign carriers to expand business in various segments and in various ways in Japan.

The internationalization of telecommunications made the MPT deal with international demand particularly from the United States. The U.S. government had been applying pressure on the MPT, exemplified in its actions in international and mobile communications issues, and demanded specific market opening measures. With the internationalization, the U.S. government began to target regulatory issues. At the US–Japan Talks in 1995, the U.S. government insisted the Japanese government establish open interconnection between NTTs' and other carriers' networks.[49] At WTO negotiations in telecommunications, the U.S. government criticized Japan's restriction on the ownership and operation of major common carriers by foreign companies.[50] After the issuance of the WTO agreement on telecommunications, KDD and

Nippon Telecom applied for permission to operate an international communications business in the United States. As the condition for approval, the FCC required each of them to reduce its international interconnection charge for U.S. carriers in Japan.[51] In 1997, the U.S. and Japanese governments began talks over deregulation of telecommunications in Japan,[52] which developed into the interconnection dispute between the United States and Japan.[53]

Ironically, the internationalization of the telecommunications market increased the importance of telecommunications in national security. The development of global alliances, such as Global One and Concert, made it feasible for foreign carriers to acquire dominance in the Japanese telecommunications market and control basic telecommunications networks. This new prospect began to play an important role in the MPT's interaction with NTT. LDP politicians began to recognize NTT as the national flagship carrier and felt that the extreme fragmentation of NTT's operation would cause national insecurity.[54] It was becoming harder for MPT to promote competition simply through the weakening of NTT. Thus, the internationalization of telecommunications added another complexity in the MPT's regulatory policymaking.

Internet

In the late 1990s, telecommunications began to shift from voice to data-based communications due to the diffusion of Internet throughout the world. Especially in the United States, the expansion of the Internet stimulated the development of Information Technology (IT)-related industries, helping its economy recover from recession, and regain its prominence in the world market. Japan was late in adopting Internet use, and lagged behind the United States and other countries in 1998. As shown in table 6.1, Japan was the second in the number of users (16.9 million), but the number of users in Japan was about one-fourth of that in the United States (60.0 million). The degree of diffusion of Internet use was much lower than that of the United States and other countries, such as Sweden, Canada, and Australia.[55]

The MPT recognized this trend and explored the format of telecommunications policy in the age of the Internet and IT. In March 2000, the MPT's Telecommunications Council released a report that emphasized IT as the driving force behind industrial transformation that would make economic transactions quick and efficient. This comprehensive report dealt with various economic and social aspects related to the development of the Internet, including the

Table 6.1 Internet users in select countries in 1998

	Estimated Internet users (in thousands)
U.S.	60,000
Japan	16,940
Germany	8,100
U.K.	8,000
Canada	7,500
France	3,700
South Korea	3,103
Taiwan	3,011
Australia	3,000
Sweden	2,961
Italy	2,600
Brazil	2,500
China	2,100
Spain	1,733
Netherlands	1,600

Source: International Telecommunications Union.

following three aspects pertinent to telecommunications regulation. First, the report emphasized the importance of high-speed, uninterrupted, and low-cost Internet access available to the public. It suggested that the promotion of competition in local telecommunication markets would increase the number of carriers providing Internet access, force down Internet access charges, and stimulate the use of new technologies, such as fiber optic networks and digital subscriber lines (DSL). Second, the report recommended that the MPT change its regulations to make them consistent with the trend of fusion between telecommunications and broadcasting. Third and finally, the report pointed out the necessity for the MPT to take measures to cope with problems deriving from the development of IT, particularly the digital divide among geographical locations and social segments, and to guarantee universal service.[56] This report basically suggested that the MPT make an adjustment to its regulatory format.

At the same time, the promotion of the Internet in Japan was a big social issue, and business leaders demanded a more drastic reform of telecommunication regulations to stimulate the expansion of Internet use in Japan. *Keidanren* called for the establishment of a new regulation format that would emphasize the promotion of competition, limit the regulator's role, and integrate various communications services.[57] This sentiment for deregulation was also reflected in the political process. Responding to the business community's sense of urgency, Prime Minister Mori Yoshiro placed IT promotion as a central policy agenda and established a policy discussion forum, called IT Senryaku Kaigi (the Committee for IT Strategy) in July 2000, which, consisting of business leaders knowledgeable of IT industries, interacted with IT-related organizations including the MPT.[58] In November, the Committee issued a report that defined the promotion of Internet use and IT technology, termed "IT Revolution," as a national goal. In addition to recognizing the necessity for the reform of telecommunications regulation that *Keidanren* advocated, the report included the following as important measures to achieve the goal—the construction of high-speed communication networks; the arrangement of business environment for e-commerce; the development of e-government that, utilizing digital technology and the Internet, would simplify government operations and improve their efficiency; and the reinforcement of the system to increase IT literacy and develop talents to lead IT development.[59] Thus, the MPT's regulations began to involve a broad range of policy actors, due to the importance of IT in the economy.

Thus, integration, internationalization, and the Internet were the three new factors in the MPT's new policy environment, and each of them added complexity and fluidity to the environment. The complexity and fluidity were ever more enhanced by the MPT's enmeshment into the environment, exemplified by the merger among KDD, DDI, and IDO prompted by the MPT's policy on the next generation mobile communications. Also, integration, internationalization, and the Internet were intertwined. The Internet was the basis of seamless communications, promoting integration and internationalization. Internationalization and integration were closely linked because more and more foreign carriers began mergers and acquisitions, in addition to alliance formation. The MPT had to pursue its regulatory policymaking in this highly complex and fluid environment.

Changes and Conflicts in the MPT's Regulatory Policymaking

This section provides an analysis of the two major cases, each of which involved major development after NTT reorganization in 1999, highlighting the new complex and fluid policy environment. In the first case, the L-mode controversy, the MPT needed to face the essence of its policy contradiction—fragmented NTT in the age of integration and the Internet. In the second case, MPT sought a comprehensive reform that would make its regulation more consistent with the current trend, but LDP's opposition forced the MPT to make amendments.

From i-mode to L-mode

NTT DoCoMo introduced a new mobile communications service called *i*-mode in February 1999. The *i*-mode used HTML and transformed a handheld mobile phone into a tool to use the Internet anywhere in Japan. The *i*-mode system enabled its subscribers to send and receive e-mail messages, and access World Wide Web home-pages adjusted for *i*-mode use. The *i*-mode became extremely popular among the Japanese, and the number of its subscribers increased exponentially to 1 million in August 1999, and to more than 10 million in August 2000. NTT DoCoMo's competitors, DDI, IDO, and Nippon Telecom, followed suit and began to provide similar service, which, along with *i*-mode, greatly contributed to the proliferation of Internet use in Japan.[60]

Witnessing NTT DoCoMo's success of *i*-mode, NTT's regional carriers, NTTEW, in October 2000, made public its plan to introduce a similar service, called L-mode, for its subscribers. The basic content of service was the same as that of *i*-mode, including sending and receiving e-mail messages as well as access to information related to every day life, with the only difference being that L-mode subscribers would use fixed phones connected to NTT's local networks, instead of mobile phones.[61] Setting March 2001 as the beginning date, NTTEW quickly proceeded with preparations, including public meet-ings with communications equipment manufacturers and Internet service providers for the clarification of technical details.[62] The L-mode would be a very simple tool for those who were not familiar with computers to use the Internet and it would help the proliferation of Internet use in Japan—the most important government agenda, but its introduction was controversial.

The L-mode system was a network based on the integration of local, long-distance, and Internet services, and NCCs and other busi-ness organizations thought the L-mode was well beyond the service of the carriers whose business was restricted to local communications. Since NTTEW needed to use inter-prefecture networks to connect L-mode users and Internet gateway, NCCs pointed out that the serv-ice would violate the NTT Law that limited NTTEW's business to intra-prefecture local telecommunication services. Also, NCCs argued that the NTTEW's service expansion into Internet service would limit market competition because of NTTEW's dominance in the local telecommunications service market, causing them to request the MPT not to approve the L-mode.[63]

As a result of the development of the movement against the introduction of the L-mode by NTTEW, the MPT solicited opinions from the public after NTTEW submitted the first version of the L-mode business plan to the MPT in December 2000. Although a substantial number of potential L-mode users and business organizations submitted opinions supporting NTTEW, the MPT/MPHPT determined that the L-mode service specified in the first plan would violate the NTT Law because NTTEW set the overall charge including the portion for inter-prefecture communications. The MPHPT notified its intention of disapproval to NTTEW in February 2001.[64] In response to MPHPT's instruction, NTTEW submitted a revised request of service approval in the same month based on a second plan. According to the plan, NTTEW would set charges for local communications and let NTT Communications' two subsidiaries be in charge of the operation of inter-prefecture communication and Internet connection services including setting charges for these services. With this second plan, NTTEW claimed that the L-mode would not violate the NTT Law.[65]

After receiving the request from NTTEW, the MPHPT had the Telecommunications Council evaluate it. NCCs continued to oppose NTTEW's provision of the L-mode, claiming that it was still beyond the area of business service approved for NTTEW even in the second plan. Also, NTTEW's control of the gateway facility was called into question. Based on the operation of the gateway facility, NTT DoCoMo controlled Internet service providers' access to *i*-mode users by designating certain sites as official ones listed in the *i*-mode menu, making it easier for users to access. Since NTTEW held much stronger market dominance than NTT DoCoMo, Internet service providers were particularly concerned with NTTEW's potential predatory activities using the L-mode, and demanded safeguard measures. When the Telecommunications Council issued its decision, it showed general intention to approve the service, but, as a condition for approval, instructed NTTEW to make the part of its plan on the operation of gateway facilities consistent with the current regulatory format that limited NTTEW's operation to intra-prefecture telecommunications. Also, the Telecommunications Council requested NTTEW to take measures to open access to the L-mode networks by competitors and Internet service providers, although these measures were not specified as conditions for approval.[66]

In response, NTTEW resubmitted a third business plan for the L-mode in April. According to this plan, NTTEW would separate the part of the gateway facility related to inter-prefecture communications and consign its operation to other carriers, which would independently set service charges for that part.[67] The MPHPT gave its approval after a week,[68] and NTTEW began the L-mode service in June 2001. NCCs were still bitter about the approval,[69] but the service flourished immediately, acquiring 19,000 subscribers in a month.[70] The L-mode controversy involved the fundamental contradiction in the MPHPT's regulation, that is, the segment-based regulation of NTT in the age of integrated telecommunications based on the Internet.[71] Although the MPHPT managed to come up with a solution to approve the service in the existing regulatory format, the MPT recognized problems with the existing format and pursued a comprehensive reform as discussed in the following section.

Revision of Telecommunications-Related Laws

The broad macro trend to promote the diffusion of the Internet in Japan was the background force for the revision of telecommunications-related laws (TRLs), whose major parts were the Telecommunications Business Law and the NTT Law. But imminent momentum for change emerged in the process of the U.S.–Japan interconnection charge dispute. As a result of the U.S.–Japan interconnection charges dispute, NTT regional companies were forced to reduce interconnection charges.[72] Since this would constrain each regional company's finance, it would require the expansion of its business. However, as a result of NTT reorganization, its business was restricted to local telephone networks, and prohibited them from providing potentially lucrative integrated telecommunications services by utilizing the Internet. NTT argued that restrictions imposed on NTT derived from the logic of telephone-based communications, but not on that of the Internet, and that these restrictions were obsolete. For this reason, NTT wanted the MPT to loosen restrictions through the revision of TRLs, particularly the NTT Law in exchange for agreeing to reduce interconnection charges.[73]

Concurring with NTT, the MPT thought necessary the revision of telecommunications regulations, particularly the treatment of NTT regional companies. The MPT's reasoning for change was related to the Internet but it was different from NTT's. The MPT recognized that Japan lagged behind the United States in the diffusion of Internet, and attributed this delay to deficiency in Internet access— Internet connection in Japan was slow and expensive. According to the MPT, NTT regional companies were responsible for this deficiency. Since NTT regional companies virtually monopolized local telephone markets, they had no incentive to be engaged in innovation for high-speed Internet access and to rationalize their operation to reduce telephone charges (for dial-up Internet connection). MPT thought that by introducing competition into local telephone markets, it would be able to press NTT regional companies to take measures that would promote the diffusion of Internet use in Japan.[74]

Thus, the MPT and NTT had a common interest in revising TRLs, and the MPT began to discuss TRL revisions at the Telecommunications Council in July 2000. In order to deal with its urgent policy agenda for the promotion of IT, the Council established a special committee for IT (IT committee, hereafter)[75] to formulate a draft for TRL revisions. The IT committee set up three subcommittees—Competition Policy, Universal Service, and International Competitiveness, reflecting the focuses of discussion.[76] Focusing on revision of the format of telecommunications regulations, the Competition Policy Subcommittee's discussion agenda included the introduction of dominant carrier regulation, the reinforcement of dispute resolution mechanisms, the promotion of competition in local telecommunications markets, and the reorganization of NTT.[77] Addressing the fact that telecommunications was closely related to public welfare, the Universal Service Subcommittee discussed how the nationwide provision of basic telecommunications was to be secured and how the cost of the provision was to be shared.[78] The International Competitiveness Subcommittee discussed the promotion of research and development in telecommunications, and ensuring national security in telecommunications.[79] In general, through discussions at the IT committee, the MPT sought to formulate the basis of Diet bills for TRLs revision that would enhance competition in telecommunications, reformat NTT regulations, and set up a business environment that would improve the information infrastructure.

Since the revision would require extensive examinations of telecommunications policy and its impact on the market, the Telecommunications Council's long-term schedule was to come up with a final report in two years. Yet, because of the urgency to formulate policy for IT promotion, the Council decided to issue the first report in December 2000 to formulate probationary revision measures as a short-term action program. Based on the evaluation of the effectiveness of these measures, the final report would be released in two years.[80] The IT committee's deliberation on the measures proceeded quickly. It held its first meeting in September 2000, and provided an arena of discussion among the MPT, IT committee members, who were mainly college professors and business leaders, and major business organizations concerned with telecommunications, such as NTT, NCCs, and *Keidanren*. Based on this discussion, the IT committee released its first report, entitled *Programs for the Promotion of Competition in the Age of IT*, in December 2000, about three months after its first meeting.

Reiterating the MPT's position, the report pointed out that the high-level competition essential for Internet access did not exist in local telephone markets and argued that competition enhancing policy measures were necessary to stimulate price reduction and technological innovation in telecommunications. Based on this recognition, the report proposed a number of policy measures to be implemented or discussed in 2001, if necessary, through the revision of relevant TRLs. With regard to changes in competition rules, the following three proposed measures were particularly important and later became controversial. First, the report called for the introduction of a dominant carrier regulation system. This system would designate specific telecommunications carriers, such as NTTEW, with crucial control over access to telephone networks and overwhelming market share. Based on scrutiny of the major aspects of each dominant carrier's business, such as price setting, terms of contract, and interconnections with other nondominant carriers, the MPT would take measures to prevent the dominant carrier from engaging in anticompetitive practice, if necessary. Second, coupled with the introduction of the dominant carrier regulation system, the report suggested that the MPT relax regulations for nondominant telecommunications carriers in response to requests from these carriers. However, despite requests from business leaders to end the distinction between different types of telecommunications carriers, the report did not call for its end. Instead, it recommended the establishment of rule-based regulation without much room for arbitrary discretion. Third and finally, for the effective application of rule-based regulations, the report suggested the establishment of a commission to quickly settle disputes among telecommunications carriers.[81]

Also, the report specifically discussed the treatment of NTT as the central issue in the reform along with general competition policy. The report termed its measures for NTT regulation change as incentive-based competition enhancement measures. The essence of these measures was taken from the FCC's approach to ease restrictions on regional telephone carriers' business activities in the reform of telecommunications laws in 1996 in the United States. The FCC allowed regional telecommunications carriers, that is, so-called Baby Bells, to enter the long-distance market in return for their acceptance of new competition rules in local markets. Similarly, the report proposed to ease restrictions as quid pro quo for NTT's voluntary measures for competition enhancement in local telephone markets. The report suggested that NTT should open local telephone networks to NCCs, grant autonomy to NTT Communications and NTT DoCoMo (by reducing stocks held by the NTT shareholding company), and make NTTEW's operation efficient. According to the report, if these measures result in competition in local telephone markets in two years after their enactment, current restrictions imposed on NTT should be lifted; if not, a fundamental revision of NTT format should be explored.[82] Although these were termed incentive-based measures, the report pressed NTT to take drastic measures.

Nonetheless, the report contained policy proposals congruent with NTT's interest. Since restrictions on NTT stocks made it very difficult for NTT to pursue business development through joint venture as well as merger and acquisition in foreign markets, the report suggested relaxing these restrictions by allowing the NTT shareholding company to flexibly issue shares, increasing the limit of the shares of the NTT shareholding company held by foreigners from 20 percent to one-third, and making it unnecessary for the NTT shareholding company to obtain the MPT's authorization in selling its shares of NTT Communications. To financially support the provision of telecommunication services throughout the country, the report called for the establishment of the universal service fund. In this universal fund system, the MPT would impose surcharges on those telecommunications carriers concentrated on urban areas and would use funds to subsidize NTTEW's telecommunications operation in the unprofitable and sparsely populated rural areas.[83]

The report proposed other policy measures, and presented a comprehensive framework of short-term action programs. But, at the same time, it was complex and ambiguous, arousing various responses from major business actors concerned with telecommunications. *Keidanren*, which had been vocal about the revision of telecommunications policy because of its importance to the economy, expressed disagreement with the IT committee. Since *Keidanren*'s basic position was to transform telecommunications regulation from one that controlled business activities to one that would enhance competition, it endorsed the IT committee's undertaking of revision of TRLs in the direction to promote competition. Yet, *Keidanren* thought that drastic liberalization through the reduction of the MPT's involvement with telecommunication businesses was essential and that the IT committee's discussion did not go far enough. *Keidanren*'s specific demands to the IT committee included the following. First, *Keidanren* argued that the division of common and noncommon carriers in telecommunications businesses was groundless and imposed unnecessary restrictions to common carriers. *Keidanren* called for the abolition of this division. Second, *Keidanren* considered government ownership of NTT stocks unnecessary, and suggested its divesture by the government. Third and finally, in order to prevent arbitrary use of power deriving from the MPT's status both as regulator and promoter of telecommunications, *Keidanren* proposed to set up an independent regulatory committee detached from the MPT.[84] Thus, *Keidanren* demanded the liberalization of telecommunications much further than proposed in the report.

Similar to *Keidanren*, NCCs welcomed deregulation aspects including the relaxation of restrictions on NTT stocks, but had more specific responses to the measures that the report proposed. NCCs maintained that NTT's reorganization in 1999 had not brought about a competitive telecommunications market but instead enhanced NTT's dominance. Therefore, NCCs supported the IT committee's proposed measures to weaken NTT's market dominance, such as the introduction of dominant carrier regulation. But incentive-based measures to NTT were unacceptable to NCCs since they were to be introduced without fundamentally changing the current format of the NTT group. NCCs considered it essential to abolish the NTT shareholding company and to give each NTT company managerial autonomy so that NTT companies would compete with each other. NCCs also thought that, without the breakup of NTT and the development of genuine competition in the telecommunications market, proposed measures favorable to NTT[85] were unjustified.[86] Although the content of the report incorporated NCCs' interests, NCCs thought the proposed reform did not touch upon the core of the problem in Japanese telecommunications, that is, the dominance of NTT.

Whereas NCCs thought the proposed reform was too soft on NTT, the latter felt that the proposed reform was too harsh. NTT approved the measures, such as the relaxation of restrictions on NTT stock transactions, the establishment of the universal service fund, and the revision of the rule that NTT was required to disclose results of NTT's technical research.[87] However, NTT did not approve of other competition enhancement measures. Maintaining that the current format of the NTT groups functioned well to generate competition in telecommunications, it argued that no new regulations targeted at NTT companies were necessary. With regard to dominant carrier regulation, the report specified the following two factors as important criteria for designating a carrier as the dominant one—the carrier's market share size and its close connections with bottleneck carriers, such as NTT regional companies, which controlled access to telecommunications. Therefore, it was likely that the dominant carrier regulations would be applied to NTT Communications and NTT DoCoMo. But NTT argued that the designation of these two NTT carriers as the dominant carriers would neglect the fact that these two carriers were facing severe competition in each segment of the domestic market, and that the imposition of extra regulations on these carriers would impair their global business activities.[88]

Furthermore, NTT was against the central idea of the report, which is to promote competition among NTT companies by weakening financial and personal ties among them. In order to cope with the development of discussion for the fragmentation of the NTT group at the IT committee, NTT began to lobby LDP Diet members, particularly *yūsei zoku* (postal tribe) members, in September when the IT committee's deliberation began.[89] After the release of the Telecommunications Council's report, NTT's managers engaged in pre-election campaign for LDP candidates for the HC elections expected to be held in July 2001, laying the foundation for *yūsei zoku*'s support for the NTT counteroffensive against the MPT's attempt to weaken the unity of the NTT group.[90] When NTT executives contacted *yūsei zoku* members, they emphasized that the current format of the NTT group was necessary for the support of NTT regional companies in the domestic market and the promotion of the NTT group's competitiveness in the international market.[91]

NTT's lobbying paid off when it tried to prevent the MPHPT from pursuing the weakening of the NTT group by passing bills for the revision of TRLs at the Diet. After the release of the IT committee's first report, the MPHPT formulated bills to be submitted to the Diet in late March. The draft of bills included the reform measures discussed earlier and stated that further reform measures, including the complete breakup of NTT, would be discussed if high-level competition does not develop in two years. Also, the draft set the basic criteria for the designation of the dominant carrier as the market share of 50 percent or more, and, in effect, made NTT DoCoMo the dominant carrier in the mobile telephone market and a target for specific regulations, including the requirement of government approval for interconnection charges.

Unlike NTT, the MPHPT (or MPT) did not fully inform *yūsei zoku* members of the content of TRLs revision in a timely manner, concentrating on policy formulation based on the Telecommunications

Council. When the MPHPT presented the draft plan of TRL revision at the LDP's administrative affairs policy subcommittee (*Sōmu Bukai*), a party organization of *yūsei zoku*, in March 2001,[92] the MPT faced tough opposition to the plan from the subcommittee members. Congruent with NTT's position, LDP members at the committee emphasized NTT as Japan's national flagship telecommunications carrier. Maintaining that dominance in telecommunications operation by a Japanese carrier was crucial for national security, the members considered it problematic to significantly reduce the unity of the NTT group because doing so would cripple NTT's ability to compete against foreign mega carriers that were emerging as a result of mergers and acquisitions on the global scale. For the same reason, the Members opposed the imposition of extra regulatory measures on NTT DoCoMo, since they deemed it an internationally competitive carrier. In addition, they summoned NCC presidents at their session, and criticized them for being overly dependent upon regulatory measures to weaken NTT in pursuing to expand their businesses.[93]

The MPHPT initially planned to send the bills to the Diet by the end of March, but this had to be postponed because of the growing of opposition toward them among LDP Diet members. Since a long delay in passing the bills might arouse criticism that the LDP was obstructing major reform in telecommunications, LDP leaders mediated to generate a compromise.[94] In response to suggestions from LDP leaders, the MPHPT agreed on the following three points of modification. First, the MPHPT dropped the idea of evaluating the progress of competition in the telecommunications market in two years. The bills did not specify a timeframe for the evaluation, and the MPHPT agreed to consider both NTT's global competitiveness and national security aspects of telecommunications in assessing the effectiveness of reform measures. Second, the threshold for the designation of the dominant carrier was reduced from 50 percent market share to 25 percent so that major NCCs became candidates for the targets of dominant carrier regulations. Third and finally, NTT DoCoMo would not have to gain approval from the MPHPT on interconnection charge but, instead, it would just report it to the MPHPT.[95] Also, LDP leaders negotiated with NTT executives to obtain NTT's support for this compromise. LDP leaders assured NTT that should the MPHPT forcefully pursue NTT breakup, they would punish the MPHPT by detaching the telecommunications conflict resolution function from it and making it more like a Japanese version of the FCC, which the MPHPT vehemently opposed for fear of losing control over telecommunications.[96] As a result of LDP leaders' mediation, the bills for TRLs revision were sent to the Diet in April and passed in June 2001.[97]

As a result of the political counteroffensive by NTT, the MPHPT had to drop one of the major components of the reform that the MPHPT (or MPT) envisioned, that is, stimulating competition among NTT companies through the provision of incentives. The MPHPT had to give up strong leverage to enforce NTT to take pro-competition actions, that is, the clause indicating that the lack of progress in competition in local telecommunications markets might lead to the complete breakup of NTT. The MPHPT had to make it much easier for NTT regional companies to expand their business into Internet services. Nonetheless, policy outcomes did not point to the MPHPT's total defeat, because most of the reform measures proposed by the TC remained. Although LDP politicians opposed the breakup of NTT, they were generally supportive of the MPHPT's policy for the proliferation of Internet use in Japan.[98] Through the use of dominant carrier regulations, the MPHPT would be able to press NTT regional companies to open up their networks and, if requested, promptly establish connections with NCCs at a low price. Thus, despite the growth of opposition against the MPHPT, the latter kept the existing level of control over NTT through the revision of TRLs.

Conclusions and Implications

Since the introduction of competition into the telecommunications market meant the weakening of NTT's market dominance and the relative strengthening of the MPT/MPHPT's influence over the telecommunications market, the MPT/MPHPT pursued regulatory reform for competition while trying to maintain strong regulatory control over NCCs. This strategy worked very well during the period between NTT privatization and the Mid-1990s when the telecommunication market included interactions among a limited number of carriers and separated them from international competition. However, in the 1990s, the policy environment became much more complex due to a growth in the integration of telecommunications, the internationalization of the telecommunications business, and the use of the Internet. Although the MPT/MPHPT continued to be very important in telecommunications regulation, it needed to negotiate more extensively and provide more consensus in order to achieve consensus.

The MPT/MPHPT's interactions with various business and government actors concerned with telecommunications regulation slowed down the MPT/MPHPT's pursuit of deregulation and liberalization of the telecommunications market. Also, by slowly implementing changes, the MPT/MPHPT tried to maintain as much control over telecommunications as possible. In this sense, the MPT/MPHPT was not a radical reformer. Yet, the MPT/MPHPT was generally supportive of deregulation and liberalization. *Yūsei zoku* politicians who vehemently opposed reforms in postal business only sporadically intervened in the telecommunications reform process. Even when they got involved, they did not try to stifle reform. Rather, they were generally supportive of reform. Since telecommunications firms were not dependent on government support and protection, they did not use LDP politicians to resist reform. Consequently, reform progressed significantly in telecommunications, exemplifying reform politics in the developmental networks.

Conclusion

Results of Reforms

In Japanese politics since the early 1980s, one of the most important issues has been government reform. Similar to government reform movements in other advanced industrial countries, such as the United States, Britain, and France, the fundamental goal of government reforms was to correct problems in government operation that came to be recognized, consisting of the following three aspects. The first aspect is government's restriction on economic activities. Before the reform period, government regulation emphasized stability for the orderly development of Japanese firms while deemphasizing competition. When the Japanese economy was in the process of economic recovery and the major goal of economic activities was to catch up with the United States and other advanced industrial countries, this protective regulation helped firms accumulate wealth that was reinvested to enhance competitiveness. With the maturation of the Japanese economy, protective regulations became obsolete because Japanese (export-oriented) companies gained strong competitiveness and because knowledge-intensive industries, for which flexibility was more important than stability, became the center of the Japanese economy. The second aspect is related to the internal rigidity of government operation. Government operation was rule-bound and, in many cases, any substantive change in its operation required Diet approval. In addition, the Japanese bureaucracy was notorious for vertical administration whereby there was no effective communication among different ministries, often causing an interministerial turf battle for an issue spanning across ministries' jurisdictions. The third and final aspect is the cost of government operation. In general, unlike private sector companies, profit making is not important for government operation, and government agencies are not cost-conscious, tending to make government operation costly. Although the cost of government operation in this narrow sense was not negligible, more important was government spending. Since government spending was used to boost the economy after the end of rapid economic development in the early 1970s, spending itself tended to be the purpose and the size of spending increased significantly, resulting in ballooning budget deficits. Government's restrictions on economic activities, the rigidity of government operation, and rising cost of government are the three major aspects that government reform intended to rectify.

The progress of reform varied across the three aspects. Among the three aspects, reform advanced most in order to deal with government restrictions. In various policy areas, the government significantly (often reluctantly) eased restrictions on business activities through deregulation. Telecommunications was a prime example of deregulation. Before reform, telecommunications had been one of the most regulated industries and the operation of telecommunications business was monopolized by NTT. Yet, with NTT privatization, the telecommunications business began to be deregulated. Non-NTT telecommunications carriers began long-distance services (and local services, to a very limited degree). Fierce competition developed between NTT and non-NTT mobile communication carriers, fostering the diffusion of mobile communications in Japan as well as the advancement of mobile communication technologies. Although reform was stalled or slowed down, it promoted market competition in telecommunications.

Reform results in the second aspect is rather mixed. Through privatization, major government corporations, particularly NTT and JNR, improved its operation by ceasing to be government organizations. Since these corporations engaged in business essential for public interest, even after privatization, they continued to be subject to more stringent government regulations than other ordinary private sector firms to ensure their stable provision of service or, as in NTT's case, to prevent corporations from predatory practice based on their former monopoly status. Nonetheless, government control over their operation, typified by the Diet's scrutiny of budget and personnel matters, was significantly reduced. Privatized NTT flexibly expanded its business whereas JRs, successor to JNR, became highly customer oriented and emphasized competition with rival railways.[1] Also, after privatization, both NTT and JNR reduced the size of their labor force without lowering the quality of service. Similarly, Japan Post, separated from the MPHPT as a government corporation in April 2003, had its first president from the private sector, and extensively adopted private sector management methods.

However, in general, government agencies seem to have made progress in their internal management in a much less significant way. The government reorganization implemented in January 2001 was remarkable, considering the pervasiveness of vertical administration in the Japanese government. Yet, vertical administration continues to be a big problem. The promotion of IT industries was still divided between the MPHPT, in charge of regulation and promotion related to telecommunication networks and the Ministry of Economy, Trade, and Industry dealing with computer and high-tech manufacturing, which were the two ministries that fought each other to protect their turf when government reorganization was discussed in the late 1990s. When Prime Minister Koizumi reportedly ordered the discussion of the unification of IT promotion in January 2004, the two ministries secretly communicated with each other and aborted the development of discussion.[2] The separation between the agricultural ministry's regulation of the livestock industry and the welfare ministry's food safety regulation was thought to be one of the major reasons why the mad cow disease became a big problem in 2001.[3] Vertical administration hampers effective policymaking on important issues, such as job creation and official development assistance.

As for the third and final aspect, the costliness of government, reformers have been much less successful. The privatization of government corporations, such as NTT and JNR, generated a large amount of government revenue through the sales of government shares on the market. Also, the privatization of JNR prevented further accumulation of financial burden that would have been imposed by JNR's inefficient operation. In this sense, privatization contributed to the reduction of the cost of government operation. However, reforms did not reduce distribution of wealth to nonurban areas. JNR privatization that reformers boast as a prime example of their success story did not alter the structure that inflated government spending through the further extension of bullet train networks. Critics point out that the privatization and breakup of the JH would not stop the continued expansion of highway networks in rural areas. Although funds from the PSF and PLI were no longer directly channeled to the FILP—the source of wasteful government projects, including highway and bullet train line constructions, a significant portion of the funds still went to the FILP. Government reforms have not succeeded in changing the structure of transferring resources to rural areas.

The pattern that characterizes outcomes of reform is that the more closely the issue is related to the distribution mechanism of wealth to the rural and uncompetitive segment of the Japanese society, the less successful reform becomes in that the reform process takes longer and that reformers have to make more compromises. This reform outcome is due to the politicoeconomic mechanism of post–World War II that the LDP uses to maintain its power. The LDP developed its electoral base in rural areas, which had been overrepresented compared to urban areas, through the provision of regulatory and other protections and spending in the rural areas. Rural business organizations in return offered financial and/or electoral campaign support to local LDP politicians. Bureaucrats were actual field managers in charge of the smooth operation of this mechanism, helping both LDP politicians and rural business organizations. In the construction of national highway networks and the expansion of the bullet train networks, LDP *dōro* (road) *zoku*, construction companies, and the ministry in charge maintained a cozy triangle. The postal business has political structure that is a little different but the essential characteristics are similar. LDP *zoku* politicians, rural *tokutei* postmasters, and postal ministry senior bureaucrats formed a coalition and helped each other. Thus, distributive networks were formed around issue areas that benefit both rural areas and the LDP.

LDP *zoku* politicians in these distributive networks actively opposed reform attempts that threatened the mechanism of resource transfer to rural areas. Even though each reform was pursued by the LDP leadership, especially the LDP prime minister, LDP *zoku* politicians, both senior members and backbenchers, did not hesitate to express their disagreement with the leadership from the early stages, and continued to develop opposition movements by holding meetings and forming study groups among the *zoku* politicians. Backbenchers took an extremely antagonistic position toward the reform not only to intimidate reformers but also to appeal to their constituents. Against the backdrop of the development of opposition, senior *zoku* members (and senior bureaucrats from the ministry in charge) engaged in backdoor negotiations with reformers. As a result, old guard *zoku* politicians protected the essential features in exchange for some modifications that reformers later claimed as their feat. In the case of JNR privatization, LDP *zoku* politicians thought the expansion of the bullet train networks, which would bring construction projects to rural areas, was crucial and prevented the termination of the bullet train networks plans while allowing the JNR to be privatized. In JH privatization, LDP *zoku* politicians preserved the mechanism, which continued to build national highways although JH had broken up and privatized. Throughout a series of reform of postal business, LDP *zoku* politicians preserved features vital for the protection of rural *tokutei* postmasters although the format of postal business changed dramatically. Each set of these distributive networks was not strong enough to expand its strength during the recent period when the government was under heavy financial constraints, but it was successful in aborting or at least delaying the progress of reform in its area.

Reforms that targeted issues and areas that were less essential to the distributive mechanism were more successful, involving drastic changes in a relatively short period of time. A good example was the privatization of NTT. Unlike JNR, NTT had maintained stable financial condition, not dependent upon government subsidies for its operation. On the contrary, taking advantage of its monopoly status as well as its close connections with Japanese telecommunication manufacturers, NTT had acquired business strength. As the importance of telecommunications in the economy developed and more and more new business opportunities for NTT began to emerge in the early 1980s, it was not necessarily beneficial for NTT to remain a government corporation because it was subject to extensive restrictions. While NTT executives had little incentive to oppose privatization, LDP *zoku* politicians had much smaller stakes in NTT operation than they had in JNR and JH, leading them to generally support the privatization. Also, MPT bureaucrats saw NTT privatization as a chance to upgrade their ministry into a regulator of a leading industry. Though MPT and NTT continued to fight after privatization, privatization itself proceeded rather smoothly and the telecommunications market was being deregulated significantly. Similarly in other industries less essential to the distributive mechanism, such as airlines, electric power, and gas industries, deregulation proceeded without causing political turmoil, based on negotiations among government bureaucrats and business executives to create consensus.

Thus, the outcome of each major government reform since the early 1980s in Japan was determined by its closeness and embeddedness in distributive networks. In a reform that touched upon the distributive networks, reformers faced fierce opposition from old guard politicians from the distributive networks, took a long time to go through the process, and made a great deal of concessions. In a reform that was less essential to the distributive networks but closely related to the developmental networks, reformers were more successful in changing the format of government operation and regulation although they still had to engage in extensive negotiations.

Problems with Government Reform

Although critics emphasize the lack of progress in some crucial areas, it must be noted that the Japanese government system has changed significantly. In this sense, reformers have made significant contributions for the improvement of the Japanese government. Nonetheless, future reform movement needs to overcome three deficiencies in decision making that reformers have not handled effectively.

The first deficiency is LDP party fragmentation. Each of the three major government reforms was pursued by the prime minister. Each prime minister sensed the rise of frustration with the government among the business community and/or the public and showed his commitment to reform. Prime Minister Hashimoto reportedly said he would pursue reform even if covered with flames and Prime Minister Koizumi declared he would destroy the LDP if the party obstructed his reform. At the early stage of reform policy formulation, each reformist prime minister developed reform plans at the policy deliberation council or with other government organizations related to reform without much consultation with the LDP, except for those LDP members who had government positions, such as ministers and vice ministers. After formulating concrete plans, the prime minister and his reformist staff presented the plans to LDP organizations to obtain party authorization to send bills based on the plans to the Diet.

Although each prime minister was also the LDP president, he did not exercise strong control over the party, typically leaving party business to the LDP leadership consisting of the secretary general, the chair of the Policy Research Council, and the head of the Executive Council. Since each of these subleaders was more like a broker who mediated diverse interests of party members, individual LDP members were constrained minimally by the LDP leadership in expressing their dissent. Therefore, when reform bills were discussed in the LDP, reformers faced fierce opposition from LDP Diet members. Since reform bills could never pass the Diet without support from the LDP, reformers needed to offer concessions to satisfy opposing old guard LDP members. As a result of compromise, reform bills passed the Diet, and the prime minister and reformers claimed victory. However, many of these concessions were contradictory to the essence of reform, and the reform plan that came out of this process was its severely watered down version. The lack of party cohesion resulted in hypocrisy on reformers' side, exaggerating their feat.

The second deficiency is the fragmentation of the (reform) policy-making process. In Japanese policymaking known for its pervasiveness of vertical administration—where communications are limited across ministerial jurisdictions, government reforms have been rather exceptional in that policy was initiated not by bureaucrats but political leaders; that policy was developed in a centralized way by organizations close to the prime minister; and that their policy goal was not constrained by jurisdictional boundaries. Yet, in most cases, bureaucrats from government ministries influenced the development of reform policymaking. They tried to protect their ministries' interests. In the privatization of government corporations, particularly NTT and JH, the MPT and the MLIT strengthened their influence, taking over functions that each corporation had had as a government agency. These ministries blended their particularistic preferences to the reform programs. Also, the ministries were reluctant to cooperate with other ministries when their own ministry's interest was threatened, exemplified by fierce conflict between the MPT and MITI over the jurisdiction of telecommunications. Since bureaucrats held expertise in policymaking, their involvement was essential for the realization of reform. Given that Japan's administrative system was fragmented, reform measures became rather piecemeal.

Similarly reformers have their own fragmented decision making. Reformers tended to concentrate so much on a particular reform issue that discussions on related issues were not well integrated. In the Nakasone reform, the privatization of the PSF was discussed in one division of the administrative reform council but FILP, through which FILP money was channeled to costly and wasteful government programs, was discussed in another division. Since the latter decided not to recommend any fundamental changes in the Program, the reform of the Fund did not proceed even though reformers, including prominent advocates of postal businesses reform, strongly believed it was important to privatize the Fund along with NTT and JNR. In the other two reforms, the issues related to the Fund, such as postal savings and highway construction, were discussed separately, making the reform process complicated and therefore difficult for the public to understand the true intent of reform. Even though it was necessary to focus on certain reform issues in a period of time, this rather fragmented approach delayed the progress of reform and generated inconsistencies.

The third deficiency is reformers' simplistic adoption of the neoliberal economic ideology based on which Margaret Thatcher in Britain and Ronald Reagan in the United States pursued government reform emphasizing the negative side of the government. Therefore, the basic tenet of Japan government reform was the reduction of government activities. As the neoliberal economic ideology suggests, government organizations have inherent weaknesses, such as inflexibility deriving from their rule-based operation, and inefficiency due to their lack of urgency to generate profit. The reduction of government involvement in economic activities was necessary. The privatization of NTT and the deregulation of telecommunications contributed to the development of telecommunications and information businesses in Japan. The privatization of JNR significantly resulted in a remarkable improvement of customer service by JNR's successor companies. Deregulation of the airline industry reduced airfare. There were numerous benefits that the adoption of the neoliberal economic ideology brought about in Japan through government reform.

Nevertheless, reduction in the size of the government became the reform goal itself rather than cutting specific obsolete government functions. As a result, reform measures included some government programs that were more suitable to be operated by the government rather than by the private sector. In the reform of postal businesses, it was legitimate to argue for the privatization of the PSF and PLI, which threatened respective private sector competitors, but the privatization of the operation of postal (mail) service was questionable because its provision of universal service was very important, making it difficult for a private sector corporation to operate it. In the Hashimoto reform, these businesses were discussed separately and postal service was not to be privatized. However, in the Koizumi reform, because of reformers' (or Koizumi's) "obsession" with the neoliberal ideology, the privatization of postal service was included in the package of postal business privatization, leading LDP politicians (and the public) to raise legitimate concerns about the provision of universal service after privatization.

Since the reduction in government involvement in economic activities itself became the reform goal, reformers tended to be content with the appearance of the reduction. The privatization of JNR significantly resulted in the improvement in the efficiency of railway operation, but it did not touch upon the mechanism of cost accumulation through the construction of bullet train networks. Although Nakasone and his reformist staff may be praised for defeating JNR unions (particularly by conservatives), their contribution to government reform has been exaggerated. Similarly, it is highly probable that JH's privatized operation companies will achieve operational efficiency. However, JH privatization did not change the mechanism to continue to build highway networks. Yet, Koizumi claims it as a great victory for reform. This is ironic because Koizumi once rightly criticized Prime Minister Hashimoto who measured the success of his reform by the number of government ministries that he reduced without considering the real impact of his reform on society and economy. Reformist leaders tended to exaggerate the result of reform by emphasizing its apparent congruence with neoliberal ideology, concealing their unhealthy compromises that fundamentally contradicted their reform intent.

The simplistic adherence to the neoliberal ideology created some confusion in the implementation of reform measures, particularly in dealing with former government corporations. Although reformers wielded a great deal of influence on legislating reform measures in the reform period, actual long-term implementation was left to government bureaucrats. In some reforms, fundamental changes were made in the reform period, requiring no explicit involvement by the government in the management of privatized corporations. Yet, in others, reform measures required government's continued commitment, particularly when reformers made compromises in the reform period. The breakup of NTT is the case in point. Although reformers intended to break up NTT into several regional companies through privatization, they postponed the breakup due to pleas from NTT management (and the labor union), leaving the MPT to pursue it. The MPT vigorously pursued NTT breakup because it would strengthen its influence over the telecommunications market, but "privatized" NTT resisted vehemently. Though reformers consistently maintained that NTT should be broken up, they did not support the MPT's breakup attempt, concerned about the increase of the MPT's influence. MPT and NTT fought for more than ten years, delaying the progress of the telecommunications market. It is not likely that JH (and postal business corporations, when privatized) would fall into this kind of intensive conflict. Privatized (government) corporations would be likely to resist reform attempts by a government agency, citing their quasi private sector status. The simplistic adoption of the neoliberal ideology and the obsession with the reduction of government involvement in the economy prevents government agencies from implementing reform measures.

Contemporary Japanese Government Reform and Comparative Capitalism

The analysis of contemporary Japanese government reform provided in this book is highly relevant to discussions of comparative capitalism,[4] including the varieties of capitalism approach, which is one of the most important analytical issues in comparative political economy. Each of these discussions focuses on the institutional aspect of market activities. Rather than regarding the market as an arena for monolithic competition among economic actors, it emphasizes social aspects of economic activities that differ across national economies and highlights that advanced industrial countries react differently to similar recent economic circumstances including competition from newly developed countries, the progress of globalization, and low economic growth. These discussions examine neoliberal economists' convergence argument: advanced industrial economies converge on the market-dominant economy where economic actors seek short-term profit maximization without being impeded by extra-market factors because the enhancement of global-scale competition eliminates extra-profit to reallocated among citizens and the interpenetration of business across nations brings about the homogenization of economic activities. They argue that national economies still keep distinctive national characteristics in adapting to ever changing global economic environment.

In general, these discussions distinguish between two types of market economies, that is, coordinated market economies from liberal market economies. Whereas major economic activities such as resource allocation, technology innovation, and employment, rely more exclusively on the market mechanism, in the latter, they involve more extra-market social interactions, such as employer–labor negotiations, intermediation by (peak) business organizations, and interfirm arrangement, in the former. The United States and Britain have liberal market economies. Along with the economies of West European countries, such as France and Germany, the Japanese economy is a prime example of coordinated market economy. The discussions present a rather general view of Japan's coordinated market economy, and the analysis of contemporary government reform in Japan provides more specific information on the dynamics of politicoeconomic interactions.

In contrast to a liberal market economy where economic actors compete for short-term profit, economic actors form stable formal and informal long-term relationships in a coordinated market economy. Therefore, changing the existing format of economic interactions requires more negotiations in the latter; reform of a coordinated market economy involves incremental change. This is mostly true in Japan if "incremental" means slow. As in other coordinated market economies, reforms involving the developmental networks, such as deregulation in telecommunications, airline, and finance, proceeded slowly because changing the existing format of economic interactions required extensive negotiations among government and business actors. In some specific reform issues, such as the break up of NTT, interactions became very confrontational, stalling reform progress, but conflict was mostly contained among those who had direct stakes in each issue, preventing politicization. Also, the reforms that sought to alter the distributive networks were very slow to progress. But, unlike reforms with the developmental networks, delays and stalemates occurred mostly in the political process where old guard politicians confronted reformers, using their political might. The end result was small change, but in the reform process, reforms had sought radical change only to be content with small progress due to opposition from old guards. The analysis of the contemporary political reforms shows that gradual change may be brought forth through dynamic political process, not just gradualism shared among economic actors preferring long-term stability.

Also, this analysis directly tackles the quintessential analytical issue of comparative capitalism, that is, convergence (toward the liberal market economy). In the Japanese government reforms, reformers adopted the neoliberal ideology and pursued the reduction in the size and involvement of the government in the economy. Since the government has been an integral part of Japan's coordinated market economy, the government reforms are attempts to move the world's largest coordinated national economy toward a liberal market economy, and the slowness of reform in general as well as the lack of progress in certain issues shows the resilience of the coordinated market economy. In particular, the development of resistance against neoliberal reforms shows political implications of Japanese-style social protection and skill formation discussed by scholars of varieties of capitalism.[5] Compared to other arrangements, they point out that Japanese firms encourage workers to acquire firm-specific skills that have low transferability by providing employment protection—lifetime employment, but that, unlike West European systems, the Japanese system does not have a high level of unemployment protection that guarantees income for unemployed workers for a long time. In contrast, the U.S. and British systems compel workers to invest in developing transferable general skills because both employment and unemployment protections are low. The political significance of the difference is demonstrated by the pervasiveness of resistance against reforms involving the distributive networks.

The neoliberal reform ideology that has developed in the United States (and Britain) implicitly assumes that workers have transferable skills, and that workers find it relatively easy to change jobs. Since Japanese workers are more likely to have firm-specific skills, they change jobs much less frequently than Americans. The circumstances surrounding unemployed workers in Japan are harsher than those in the United States. Unemployment insurance offers income a very short period. Japanese companies' commitment to protect their current employees means their reluctance in hiring older workers particularly in times of economic downturn, such as the period since the 1990s. Therefore, deregulation (and government reorganization) that did not directly impact on employment progressed rather quickly. In adapting to their new regulatory environment, companies avoided abrupt reductions in labor force. On the other hand, reform measures—which were expected to somehow cause unemployment particularly among LDP supporters—caused the mobilization of old guard politicians to resist change. In the reform of JH, old guard politicians were concerned with the continued construction of national highway networks because its abridgment would be detrimental to construction companies and their employees. *Yūsei zoku* politicians vehemently opposed the privatization of Japan Post, because it would involve the downsizing of national postal networks, causing job loss among *tokutei* postmasters in rural areas—invaluable supporters of *yūsei zoku* politicians. In either case, employers and workers have company-specific skills and face a very rigid job market, prompting them to act against reforms. Political turmoil that developed during the reform period demonstrates the difficulty of the pursuit of neoliberal reform in a coordinated market economy.

Thus, the analysis of government reforms in Japan shows political interactions are still important for the evolution of capitalism, at least in Japan. The discussion of contemporary capitalism emphasizes the importance of societal-level interactions, such as corporate governance, inter-firm arrangement, and labor relations, while regarding the discussion of politics (or the government) and economy to be rather secondary in importance. This is rightly so because discussions preceding comparative capitalism exclusively dealt with the government and economy, and the discussion of societal interactions should be expanded further. However, at the same time, the examination of the political environment needs to be developed. This is particularly important for the analysis of Japanese capitalism. As shown throughout this book, various dimensions of political interactions influenced the evolution of contemporary Japanese capitalism not because the government bureaucracy played a dominant role but because the government and business maintained symbiotic relationships. My discussion shows that the government continues to be an integral part of the Japanese economy.

This book analyzed Japan's contemporary government reform, one of the key issues in contemporary Japanese politics that has greatly influenced the evolution of Japan's contemporary capitalism. In general, due to the fragmentation of the LDP leadership and the segmentation of the policymaking process, reform progressed very slowly. Nonetheless, in some areas, deregulation progressed significantly so that competition developed to stimulate economic activities although little fundamental change occurred in other areas, thus continuing inefficient resource allocation. This difference in the progress of reform derives from the dual structure of the Japanese economy that created developmental and distributive networks. The distributive networks that relied heavily on government protection and expenditure resisted reform whereas the developmental networks called for reform in order to gain more business freedom and less economic burden to help support the less developed segment of the Japanese economy. This pattern of resistance against reform persisted because reformers adhered to the neoliberal ideology that emphasized the market principle. Reformers lacked systematic consideration of the possible impact of reform measures on those who were expected to bear their consequence. Reformers optimistically thought that reduction in the size of the government would solve most economic and social problems. To overcome these deficiencies, future reforms must aim at not just the reduction of the government but the reformation of the government as well. The government has been and will be the important ingredient of the Japanese economy. Reformers should not be preoccupied with reduction, but they sometimes have to seek to expand government activities to stabilize and improve society.

Notes

Introduction

1. David Asher, "What Became of the Japanese 'Miracle,' " *Orbis* 40, no. 2 (1996): 215–234.
2. Statistical Bureau & Statistical Research and Training Institute, the Ministry of Internal Affairs and Communications, http://www.stat.go.jp/data/sekai/03.htm.
3. Aurelia George Mulgan, *Japan's Failed Revolution: Koizumi and the Politics of Economic Reform* (Canberra, Australia: Asia Pacific Press, 2002).
4. Edward Lincoln, *Arthritic Japan: The Slow Pace of Economic reform* (Washington, DC: Brookings Institution Press, 2001).
5. Andrew Dewit and Sven Steinmo show how redistribution is accomplished through government spending in Japan. See Andrew Dewit and Sven Steinmo, "The Political Economy of Taxes and Redistribution in Japan." *Social Science Japan Journal* 5, no. 2 (2002): 159–178.
6. Richard J. Samuels, *The Business of the Japanese State: Energy Markets in Comparative and Historical Perspective* (Ithaca: Cornell University Press, 1987), 8–9.
7. Gregory W. Noble, *Collective Action in East Asia: How Ruling Parties Shape Industrial Policy* (Ithaca, NY: Cornell University Press, 1998), 36–37.
8. Kazuhisa Maeno, *Nijyū Isseiki wa Yūseishō no jidai* [The Twenty-First Century Is the Age of the Ministry of Posts and Telecommunications] (Tokyo: Bizinesu-sha, 1993), 44–50.
9. Chalmers Johnson, *MITI and the Japanese Miracle: The Growth of Industrial Policy, 1925–1975* (Stanford: Stanford University Press, 1982).
10. Mark J. Ramseyer and Frances M. Rosenbluth, *Japan's Political Market Place* (Cambridge: Harvard University Press, 1993).

Chapter 1   A Comparative Perspective

1. Peter Gourevitch, *Politics in Hard Times: Comparative Responses to International Economic Crises* (Ithaca: Cornell University Press, 1986), 24–29.
2. For a detailed analysis of the trajectory of Keynesianism in post–World War II Britain, see Peter Hall, *Governing the Economy: The Politics of State Intervention in Britain and France* (Cambridge, UK: Polity Press, 1986), 69–99.
3. Paul Pierson, "The New Politics of the Welfare State," *World Politics* 48, no. 2 (1996): 161.
4. Steven K. Vogel, *Freer Markets, More Rules: Regulatory Reforms in Advanced Industrial Countries* (Ithaca: Cornell University Press, 1996), 43–50.
5. Gourevitch, *Politics in Hard Times*, 176–178.
6. Hall, *Governing the Economy*, 164–191.
7. Ibid., 244–245.
8. Douglas Ashford, *Policy and Politics in France: Living with Uncertainty* (Philadelphia: Temple University Press, 1982), 230.
9. Ibid., 193–194, 202–208.
10. Hall, *Governing the Economy*, 236–239.
11. Peter J. Katzenstein *Policy and Politics in West Germany: The Growth of a Semisovereign State* (Philadelphia: Temple University Press, 1987), 186–187.
12. Wolfgang Streek, "German Capitalism: Does It Exist? Can It Survive?" in *Political Economy of Modern Capitalism: Mapping Convergence and Diversity*, ed. Colin Crouch and Wolfgang Streek (London and Thousand Oaks, CA: SAGE Publications, 1997), 39.
13. Takaaki Suzuki, "Keynesianism, Monetarism, and the Contradiction of Japan's Modern Welfare State," *The Japanese Economy* 30, no. 2 (2002): 56–57.
14. The harbinger of civil service reform is New Zealand, where a sweeping government reform was initiated by the Labor Party, a Left-leaning party usually regarded as a bastion of anti-privatizing forces. In the early phase of the reform, recognizing the problems inherent in public sector management, Labor Party reformers infused private sector style management to public sector organization to not only cut costs but also improve operational performance. They privatized state-owned enterprises and forced them to adopt private sector management. At the same time, the reformers introduced elements of private sector management in government operation, giving civil service managers flexibility in hiring and spending while making them more responsible for policy performance by evaluating to check if they meet specific targets. Donald Kettle, *The Global Management Revolution: A Report on the Transformation of Governance* (Washington, DC: Brookings Institution Press, 2000), 10–12. For an extensive analysis of government

reform in New Zealand, see Bary Schick, *The Sprit of Reform: Managing the New Zealand State Sector in a Time of Change* (Wellington, New Zealand: State Service Commission, 1996).

15. Kettle, *Global Management Revolution*, 13; Rod Rohdes "Reinventing Whitehall 1979–1995," in *Public Management and Administrative Reform in Western Europe*, ed. Walter J.M. Kichert (Cheltenham, UK: Edward Elgar, 1997), 45–52. For an overview of the Next Steps initiative, see Patricia Greer, *Transforming Central Government: The Next Steps Initiative* (Philadelphia: Open University Press, 1994).

16. Kettle, *Global Management Revolution*, 15–29, Joel D. Aberbach and Bert A. Rockman, *In the Web of Politics: Three Decades of the U.S. Federal Executive* (Washington, DC: Brookings Institution Press, 2000), 134–160.

17. Ezra Suleiman, *Dismantling Democratic States* (Princeton: Princeton University Press, 2003), 168–187.

18. Werner Jann, "Public Management Reform in Germany: A Revolution without a Theory?" in Kichert, *Public Management and Administrative Reform*, 83–84.

19. Christoph Reichard, "*Neues Steuerungsmodell*: Local Reform in Germany," in Kichert, *Public Management and Administrative Reform*, 61–65.

20. Suleiman, *Dismantling Democratic States*, 148–151.

21. For the analysis of cross-national transfer of agencification from Britain to Japan, see Koichi Nakano, "Cross-National Transfer of Policy Ideas: Agencification in Britain and Japan," *Governance* 17, no. 2 (2004): 169–188.

22. Regulatory reform has begun to involve the reform of social regulation, such as education and health care; Gregory Noble, "Trends in Economic and Social Regulation and Implications for Japan," *Shakai Kagaku Kenkyū* [Social Science Research] 54, no. 2 (2003): 53–54. However, since the main focus of this book is economic reform, I primarily discuss the reform of economic regulation.

23. Vogel, *Freer Markets, More Rules*, 41.

24. Ibid., 26–42.

25. Martha Derthick and Paul Quirk explain political factors, such as consumerism and the necessity to fight inflation, which helped the trend for deregulation to develop in the United States. See Martha Derthick and Paul J. Quirk, *The Politics of Deregulation* (Washington, DC: Brookings Institution Press, 1985), 39–57.

26. Ibid., 1–13.

27. Joseph Stiglitz dsicusses the serious consequences that resulted from deregulation in the 1990s. See Joseph Stiglitz, *The Roaring Nineties: A New History of the World's Most Prosperous Period* (New York: W.W. Norton and Company, 2003), 87–114.

28. Vogel, *Freer Markets, More Rules*, 70–92.

29. Ibid., 123.

30. Ibid., 100–114.
31. Ibid., 125–127.
32. Vivien Schmidt, *From State to Market? The Transformation of French Business and Government* (Cambridge and New York: Cambridge University Press, 1996), 114–118.
33. Ibid., 147–157.
34. Martin Fransman, *Telecoms in the Internet Age: From Boom to Bust to . . . ?* (Oxford and New York: Oxford University Press, 2002), 161–162.
35. Vogel, *Freer Markets, More Rules*, 239–240.
36. Fransman, *Telecoms in the Internet Age*, 158.
37. Schmidt, *From State to Market*, 97–100.
38. Suleiman, *Dismantling Democratic States*, 96–97.
39. Vogel, *Freer Markets, More Rules*, 247–250; Fransman, *Telecoms in the Internet Age*, 127.
40. *Journal of Commerce*, October 15, 2003, 1.
41. Mitchell P. Smith, "Europe and the German Model: Growing Tension or Symbiosis," *German Politics* 10, no. 3 (2001): 126–130.
42. Vogel, *Freer Markets, More Rules*, 252.
43. Christophe Knill and Dirk Lehmkuhl, "How Europe Matters: Different Mechanisms of Europeanization," *European Integration Online Papers* 3, no. 7 (1999); <http://eiop.or.at/eiop/texte/ 1998-007a.htm>
44. Raniner Eising and Nicolas Jabko, "Moving Targets: Institutional Embeddedness and Domestic Politics in the Liberalization of EU Electricity Markets," *Comparative Political Studies* 34, no. 7 (2002): 742–767.
45. For example, Theodore Lowi argues that government agencies are dependent upon interest groups in implementing policy in the United States. See Theodore Lowi, *The End of Liberalism: The Second Republic of the United States* (New York: W.W. Norton & Company, 1979).
46. T.J. Pempel, *Regime Shift: Comparative Dynamics of the Japanese Political Economy* (Ithaca: Cornell University Press, 1998), 35–36.
47. Schmidt, *From State to Market*, 148–152.
48. Robert Gilpin, *Global Political Economy: Understanding the International Economic Order* (Princeton: Princeton University Press, 2001), 152–155.
49. Michael Loriaux, "The French Developmental State as Myth and Moral Ambition," in *The Developmental State*, ed. Meredith Woo-Cumings (Ithaca: Cornell University Press, 1999), 237–246.
50. Streek, "German Capitalism," 38–39; Richard Deeg, *Finance Capitalism Unveiled: Banks and the German Political Economy* (Ann Arbor: University of Michigan Press, 1999), 10–11, 22–23; Katzenstein, *Policy and Politics in West Germany*, 22–23.

Chapter 2   The Politics of the Dual State

1. Hall, *Governing the Economy*, 139–163.
2. Ashford, *Policy and Politics in France*, 228–235.

3. Gerald E. Curtis, *The Japanese Way of Politics* (New York: Columbia University Press, 1988), 13.
4. Ibid., 4–14.
5. Ibid., 16–18; Pempel, *Regime Shift*, 104–106.
6. T.J. Pempel, *Policy and Politics in Japan: Creative Conservatism* (Philadelphia: Temple University Press, 1982), 71–78.
7. Pempel, *Regime Shift*, 42–58.
8. Ibid., 60–63.
9. Ichiro Miyake et al., *Nihon Seiji no Zahyō: Sengo 40-nen no Ayumi* [The Locus of Japanese Politics: Progress in the 40 Years after the War] (Tokyo: Ōkura Zaimu Kyōkai Zeino Shirube Sōkyoku, 1985), 135–136.
10. Masaru Mabuchi, *Ōkurasho Tōsei no Seijikeizai-Gaku* [Political Economy of the Ministry of Finance's Control] (Tokyo: Chūō Kōron Sha, 1994), 214–215.
11. Michio Muramatsu and Ellis S. Krauss, "The Conservative Policy Line and the Development of Patterned Pluralism," in *The Political Economy of Japan: Volume 1—The Domestic Transformation*, ed. Kozo Yamamura and Yasukichi Yasuba (Stanford: Stanford University Press, 1987), 528–530.
12. Samuels, *Business of the Japanese State*, 8–9.
13. Pempel, *Regime Shift*, 53–58.
14. The Ministry of International Trade and Industry, renamed the Ministry of Economy, Trade, and Industry in 2001, has been active in promoting deregulation, especially in industries that come under the jurisdiction of other ministries.
15. Dewit and Steinmo show how redistribution is accomplished through government spending in Japan. See Dewit and Steinmo, "The Political Economy of Taxes and Redistribution in Japan," 159–178.
16. In the single nontransferable voting system for HR elections that had been used until the mid-1990s, since each district has two or more seats, two or more candidates were from the LDP and they competed against each other.
17. Government operation of telecommunications service was justified mainly for the following three reasons. First, since telecommunications service was essential to social and economic activities, the government needed to stabilize its operation. Second, since the telecommunications industry had the feature of natural monopoly where launching cost was high and the economy of scale played an important part, it was difficult for private sector companies to develop telecommunications business. Third and finally, the government's monopolized operation was suitable for the maintenance of a unified standard, crucial for the nationwide development of telecommunication networks. See Nippon Denshin Denwa Kabushikigaisha, *Nippon Denshin Denwa Kōsha Shashi* [The History of NTT Public Corporation] (Tokyo: Nippon Denshin Denwa Kabushikigaisha, 1986), 34–35.

18. Ibid., 1–9.
19. *Nihon Keizai Shimbun*, June 17, 1981, 1.
20. Since NTT was a government corporation, it was prohibited from making monetary contributions to political parties. NTT family firms provided funding to the LDP on NTT's behalf. A portion of the payment for telecommunications equipment was arranged to be transferred to the LDP.
21. As discussed in Chapter 5 on transportation reforms, the assessment of the outcome of the highway system reform was divided among reformers.

Chapter 3   The Dual State and Government Reforms

1. Richard J. Samuels, "Leadership and Political Change in Japan: The Case of the Second Rincho," *Journal of Japanese Studies* 29, no. 1 (2002): 3.
2. The first Commission was established in 1962 to discuss ways to improve government operation. It issued reform recommendations, including the strengthening of the prime minister's leadership, in 1964. But, this was not implemented due to resistance from the bureaucracy. See Yasuo Maruyama, *Shōgen: Daini Rinchō* [Eyewitness Report on the Second Provisional Administrative Reform Commission] (Tokyo: Shinchi Shobō, 1984), 2–3, 18–20.
3. The leaders of five major business organizations formed *Gyōkaku Suishin 5-nin Iinkai* [Five-Man Committee for the Promotion of Administrative Reform], which pressed the government to work on reductions in government spending. See Hiroshi Kato and Yoichi Sando, *Dokō-san to tomoni 730nichi* [730 Days with Mr. Doko] (Tokyo: Keizai Ōrai-sha, 1983), 20–22; Masaru Kanbara, *Tenkanki no Seijikatei: Rinchō no Kiseki to sono Kinō* [The Political Process at a Turning Point: The Trajectory and Functions of the Administrative Reform Council] (Tokyo: Sōgō Rōdō Kenkyū-sho, 1986), 19.
4. Taro Maki, *Nakasone Seiken 1806 Nichi Jō* [Nakasone Administration's 1806 Days, Volume 1] (Tokyo: Gyoken, 1988), 37.
5. Masao Komori, *Den Den mineika no butaiura* [Behind the Scenes of NTT's Privatization] (Tokyo: Gōdō Tsūshinsha, 1988), 80–81.
6. Yomiuri Shimbun Seijibu, *Dokyumento Gyōsei Kaikaku* [Documentary Administrative Reform] (Tokyo: Yomiuri Shimbunsha, 1983), 74–77.
7. Kato and Sando, *Dokō-san to tomoni*, 41–43.
8. In the fiscal year 1981, the Railroad's cumulated deficits amounted to ¥16.42 trillion and about 30% of the general account government budget was used for financing the deficits. See Atushi Kusano, *Kokutetsu Kaikaku* [JNR Reform] (Tokyo: Chūō Kōronsha, 1989), 18–19.

9. Kato and Sando, *Dokō-san to tomoni*, 104–106.

10. Jun Iio, *Min'eika no seijikatei: Rinchō-gata kaikaku no seika to genkai* [The Political Process of Privatization: The Accomplishment and Limit of Rinchō-style Reform] (Tokyo: Tokyo Daigaku Shuppankai, 1993), 62–63.

11. Since NTT privatization was one of the major political events in the 1990s, it has been extensively analyzed by scholars of Japanese political economy. See Chalmers Johnson, "MITI, MPT, and the Telecom Wars: How Japan Makes Policy for High Technology," in *Politics and Productivity: How Japan's Development Strategy Works*, ed. Chalmers Johnson, Laura D'Andrea Tyson, and John Zysman (New York: Harper Business, 1989), 177–240; Steven Vogel, *Freer Markets, More Rules*; Iio, *Min'eika no seijikatei*.

12. Akira Yamagishi, *NTT ni ashita wa aruka.* [Is There a Tomorrow for NTT?] (Tokyo: Nihon Hyōronsha, 1989), 104–105.

13. Iio, *Min'eika no seijikatei*, 141–172.

14. Along with JNR and NTT, based on *Rinchō* recommendation, the government company that sold tobacco and salt exclusively was privatized.

15. *Asahi Shimbun*, October 7, 1993, 2.

16. The Japan Socialist Party changed its name to the Social Democratic Party in 1996.

17. *Nihon Keizai Shimbun*, January 11, 1997, 1.

18. The most symbolic was government regulation that prevented Swiss body-searching dogs from participating in rescue efforts after the Hanshin earthquake. See Pempel, *Regime Shift*, 141.

19. Interministerial coordination was difficult since communications were held mainly within the boundary.

20. Pempel, *Regime Shift*, 142–143.

21. *Asahi Shimbun*, October 10, 1996, 1.

22. Masahiro Horie, "Shōchō Saihen Tō no Igi to Kadai" [The Significance and Subject of Government Reorganization, etc.], paper presented at the Japan Public Policy Association, 2000, 3–4.

23. *Asahi Shimbun*, Evening Edition, November 29, 1997, 1.

24. Gyōsei Kaikaku Kaigi Jimukyoku Ob-Kai, *21 Seiki no Nippon no gyō sei* [Japan's Public Administration in the Twenty-First Century] (Tokyo: Gyōsei Kanri Kenkyū Sentā, 1998), 552–557.

25. *Asahi Shimbun*, August 21, 1997, 2.

26. *Asahi Shimbun*, November 10, 1997, 2.

27. The ARC recommended that the Ministry of Construction be divided into two and incorporated into the Ministries of Land Development and Land Maintenance. *Asahi Shimbun*, August 22, 1997, 2.

28. *Asahi Shimbun*, September 10, 1997, 7.

29. A senior official at the Management and Coordination Agency recalled that the Sato–Muto switch was a turning point. Interview, June 2000.

30. *Asahi Shimbun*, September 23, 1997, 2.
31. *Asahi Shimbun*, November 11, 1997, 2.
32. *AERA*, September 29, 1997, 19.
33. *Asahi Shimbun*, November 16. 1997, 2. MPT and *yūsei zoku* LDP politicians had no objection to the abolition of this fund transfer because the MPT wanted to be engaged in the independent investment of the PSF.
34. Gyōsei Kaikaku Kaigi, *Saishū Hōkoku* [Final Report] (1997), http://www.gyoukaku.go.jp/siryou/souron/report–final/index.html.
35. As for the MPT's telecommunications policymaking, the final plan withdrew the idea of separating regulatory and promotional functions of telecommunications policymaking, and instead transferred the MPT's telecommunications policymaking functions to *Sōmushō*, tentatively called the Ministry of General Affairs and later officially named the Ministry of Public Management, Home Affairs, Posts and Telecommunications (MPHPT). Although the ARC report required the MPT to reorganize the three (tele-) communications-related bureaus into two in this transition, the MPT avoided its absorption into its archrival, the MITI. Moreover, the Postal Agency that oversees the proposed postal business government corporation was going to be a part of the MPHPT. The MPT as whole was going to be incorporated into *Sōmushō*. The MPT not only avoided its breakup but also became an essential part of a big powerful ministry.
36. It is important to note that the law specifically stated that the privatization of postal businesses would not be discussed in the future. As shown below, Koizumi completely ignored this provision in his pursuit of postal privatization.
37. Even after the MPT's incorporation into the MPHPT, I continue to use the term *yūsei zoku* politicians (postal tribe) because they continued to fight for the protection of the postal businesses.
38. According to a senior LDP Diet member, it was fortunate that the arrangement to establish the postal service corporation had already been made because Koizumi might have implemented a more drastic reform more quickly, utilizing public support. Interview, June 2001.
39. *Asahi Shimbun*, April 25, 2001, 1.
40. *Asahi Shimbun*, April 6, 2002, 3.
41. The report presented the following three formats as alternatives: a special government-owned company engaged in the three postal businesses; a private sector company operating the three businesses; and a private sector only in charge of postal service with the abolition of postal savings and postal life insurance.
42. There were issues involving postal savings and postal life insurance, e.g., the contribution to general government revenue and the acceptance of inspection by financial authorities. Since the MPHPT conceded these issues albeit reluctantly, no major controversy developed.

43. According to the MPHPT, only express delivery is liberalized in the United States; a letter beyond a certain price or a certain weight can be handled by nonpostal service carriers in France and Germany. *Asahi Shimbun*, December 13, 2001, 9.

44. *Asahi Shimbun* Evening Edition, December 13, 2001, 1.

45. The MPHPT relaxed regulations on large-size mail and express mail. *Asahi Shimbun*, April 4, 2002, 13.

46. *Asahi Shimbun*, March 27, 2002, 13.

47. *Asahi Shimbun*, April 28, 2002, 3.

48. *Asahi Shimbun*, April 6, 2002, 3.

49. *Asahi Shimbun*, April 26, 2002, 1; April 27, 2002, 2.

50. *Asahi Shimbun*, May 22, 2002, 3; *Yomiuri Shimbun*, May 24, 2002, 4.

51. *Asahi Shimbun*, May 28, 2002, 9.

52. *Asahi Shimbun*, July 3, 2002, 3.

53. *Nihon Keizai Shimbun*, July 2, 2002, 1.

54. *Asahi Shimbun*, July 2, 2002, 2.

55. *Nihon Keizai Shimbun* homepage, http://www.nikkei.co.jp/sp2/nt47/index.html.

56. *Nihon Keizai Shimbun*, October 4, 2003, 1.

57. To soften opposition from the old guard, the manifesto included a sentence indicating that the LDP would hold a nationwide discussion on Japan Post privatization and it specified April 2007 as the time set for completion of privatization. The old guard thought that it would be possible to postpone privatization in the discussion. *Nihon Keizai Shimbun*, October 28, 2003, 33.

58. *Nihon Keizai Shimbun*, Evening Edition, August 11, 2004, 3.

59. *Nihon Keizai Shimbun*, September 11, 2004, 2.

60. Takenaka was a professor of economics, and he was not an elected official when he was appointed to be a government minister. Yet, he became a member of the HC after winning the elections in July 2004 with the largest vote that an LDP candidate had in the nationwide district.

61. *Nihon Keizai Shimbun*, April 5, 2005, 1.

62. *Nihon Keizai Shimbun*, June 29, 2005, 1.

63. *Yomiuri Shimbun*, July 6, 2005, 4.

64. One of the LDP members who changed his position due to persuasion from the LDP leadership was Nagaoka Yoji. Nagaoka later commited suicide apparently because he felt bad about his change of position.

65. Unlike the HR, the HC has a fixed term. Many LDP members were perplexed about Koizumi's intention to dissolve the HR even though bills were passed through the HR.

66. *Nihon Keizai Shimbun*, November 19, 2001, 1.

67. One of the LDP *dōro zoku* politicians likened the writer to a Taliban member, for his radical criticism of the government.

68. *Nihon Keizai Shimbun*, December 7, 2002, 4.

69. In the discussion on PHC privatization, JH's financial condition was a big issue, and JH president Fujii was asked to present the JH financial statement that used the accounting method for a private sector company and showed its sizable deficit. Fujii denied the existence of the financial statement in many occasions, including his response to a question from an opposition party politician at a Diet committee meeting. Yet, one reformist JH employee, who had been demoted due to his support of reform, disclosed that JH did formulate the financial statement; pressure against Fujii grew among the public. Soon after reformist LDP politician Ishihara Nobuaki became MLIT minister with a cabinet shuffle in September 2003, Ishihara demanded Fujii's resignation, resulting in his dismissal.
70. *Nihon Keizai Shimbun*, Evening Edition, December 22, 2003, 1.

Chapter 4   Postal Business

1. Its yield is computed on the compound interest rate every six months, making *teigaku* even more attractive vis-à-vis commercial banks' long-term accounts.
2. See Zenkoku Ginkō Kyōkai, *Ginkō Kyōkai 50 Nenshi* [The 50-Year History of the Banking Association] (Tokyo: Zenkoku Ginkō Kyōkai, 1997), 446; and Kent Calder "Linking Welfare and the Developmental State: Postal Savings in Japan," *Journal of Japanese Studies* 16 (1990): 39–45.
3. Ministry of Posts and Telecommunications, *Yūsei Hyakunen Shi* [The One-Hundred Years History of Posts and Telecommunications] (Tokyo: Teishin Kyōkai, 1971), 752–753.
4. Kazuhisa Maeno, *Yūseishōtoiu Yakusho* [A Government Agency Called the Ministry of Posts and Telecommunications] (Tokyo: Suna Shobo, 1993), 44–50.
5. Calder, "Linking Welfare," 46–47.
6. From 1983 through 1998, the HC elections, a proportional representation system, was used for the nationwide district, and the LDP determined the rank of each candidate. The MPT's candidates were generally placed high on the list, reflecting the LDP's respect for *Tokutei* postmasters' electoral strength.
7. *Yomiuri Shimbun*, August 26, 2001, 1.
8. A rapid expansion of the PSF in 1954 led the peak association of financial organizations (Kinyū Dantai Kyōgi Kai) to submit a petition to Prime Minister Yoshida Shigeru and called for restraint on the expansion of the PSF. Zenkoku Ginkō Kyōkai, *Ginkō Kyōkai 50 Nenshi*, 446–447.
9. Koizumi Junichiro is regarded as one of the few *ginkō zoku* members.
10. Zenkoku Ginkō Kyōkai, *Ginkō Kyōkai 50 Nenshi*, 378.
11. Masaru Mizuno, *Zeisei to tomoni Ayunda 30 Nen: Kishikata Yukusue* [30 Years with Taxation: Past and Future] (Tokyo: Gyōsei, 1993), 271–272.

12. Also, at the time of bill passage, *yūsei zoku* politicians were not capable of wielding influence because of the KDD scandal, made public in 1979, involving illegal payments to many *yūsei zoku* politicians. See Frances M. Rosenbluth, *Financial Politics in Contemporary Japan* (Ithaca: Cornell University Press, 1989), 183.

13. The *teigaku* account is a long-term savings account with high interest rates, and is most popular among the PSF accounts.

14. *Kinyū Zaisei Jijyō*, October 6, 1980, 24.

15. *Kinyū Zaisei Jijyō*, April 13, 1981, 8.

16. *Kinyū Zaisei Jijyō*, May 17, 1982, 14.

17. Junko Kato, *The Problem of Bureaucratic Rationality: Tax Politics in Japan* (Princeton: Princeton University Press, 1994), 231.

18. The LDP TSRC operates within the LDP PARC and discusses tax policy. See Kato, *Problem of Bureaucratic Rationality*, 95–97.

19. Mizuno, *Zeisei to tomoni Ayunda 30 Nen*, 272–274.

20. Mizuno, *Zeisei to tomoni Ayunda 30 Nen*, 274–276.

21. *Nihon Keizai Shimbun*, May 19, 1984, 1.

22. *Nihon Keizai Shimbun*, February 10, 1983, 3.

23. The seven plans were as follows: strict enforcement of the current regulation on tax exemption for savings, the introduction of the *maruyū* Card used only for PSF and bank accounts, the application of tax exemption for interest income to low income earners, withholding tax on interest income, tax exemption computed per household, low interest across the board taxation, and the abolition of all the tax exemptions. See *Nihon Keizai Shimbun*, September 12, 1984, 1.

24. *Nihon Keizai Shimbun*, May 17, 1984, 3.

25. PARC Chair Fujio Masayuki stated in public that fiscal austerity without tax increase, the slogan for government reform in the early 1980s, was impossible, and intended to make interest income taxation a steppingstone for more extensive tax increase. Also, recognizing tight government finance, Secretary General Kanemaru Shin, the boss of *yūsei zoku*, also supported the imposition of more tax on interest income as a temporary measure effective for three to five years. *Nihon Keizai Shimbun*, November 19, 1984, 2.

26. LDP *yūsei zoku* and the MPT's *tokutei* postmasters held a rally against the reform, attended by some 300 LDP Diet members, and passed a resolution calling for the maintenance of the tax exemptions status of PSF accounts, which was handed in to LDP leaders and the chief cabinet secretary. *Nihon Keizai Shimbun*, December 8, 1984, 3.

27. *Nihon Keizai Shimbun*, July 15, 1985, 1.

28. Zenkoku Ginkō Kyōkai, *Ginkō Kyōkai 50 Nenshi*, 392; *Nihon Keizai Shimbun*, December 18, 1984, 1; Rosenbluth, *Financial Politics in Contemporary Japan*, 198–199.

29. During the Diet elections in July 1986, LDP leaders became quiet about tax reform because the reform plan included the introduction of the value added tax, unpopular among one of the LDP's core

constituents, small and medium-sized merchandise company owners, as well as taxation on interest income. Rosenbluth, *Financial Politics in Contemporary Japan*, 200–201.

30. Vice Prime Minister Kanemaru, who was the leader of old guard LDP politicians, ordered a *yūsei zoku* leader Ozawa Ichiro to mediate interests among *yūsei zoku* members to promote the tax reform. Yet, at the same time, Kanemaru directed another *yūsei zoku* leader, Obuchi Keizō, to fight against it to the end in order to satisfy backbenchers who were eager to act against taxation on the PSF. *Kinyū Zaisei Jijyō*, December 15, 1986, 15.

31. Masaru Muzuno, *Shuzeikyokucho no 1300 Nichi: Zeisei Bappon Kaikaku he no Ayumi* [1300 Days of the Director of the Tax Bureau] (Tokyo: Ōkura Zaimu Kyōkai Zeino Shirube Sōkyoku, 1993), 95.

32. Ibid., 96.

33. Based on the agreement between the MPT and MOF, the Cabinet finalized the tax reform plan for the fiscal year 1987, including 20% flat tax on interest income with special exemptions limited to accounts held by the elderly and single mothers, income tax reduction, and value added tax. In mid-January 1987, related bills were sent to the Diet. However, due to opposition parties' opposition to value added tax, the bills were stalled, and the LDP separated bills for the revision of interest income tax from value added tax and passed them in September 1987. Zenkoku Ginkō Kyōkai, *Ginkō Kyōkai 50 Nenshi*, 396–397.

34. *Asahi Shimbun*, December 6, 1992, 7.

35. Zenkoku Ginkō Kyōkai, *Ginkō Kyōkai 50 Nenshi*, 399.

36. *Asahi Shimbun*, August 21, 1992, 3.

37. At a meeting of the GTSRC's subcommittee on taxation on income from interest and capital gains in October 1992, the MPT's Postal Savings Bureau chief appealed for the increase of the limit to ¥7 million. However, most members of the subcommittee opposed the increase, citing that it gave preferential treatment to the wealthy elderly, and some of them even called for its abolition. The subcommittee's final report issued in November concluded that the increase in the tax exemption limit was unnecessary, and this became the official position of the MOF. *Asahi Shimbun*, Evening Edition, October 10, 1992, 3; November 24, 1992, 1.

38. *Asahi Shimbun*, December 12, 1992, 2.

39. *Asahi Shimbun*, December 15, 1992, 2.

40. *Asahi Shimbun*, December 17, 1992, 2.

41. *Kinyū Zaisei Jijyō*, June 4, 1984, 16–17.

42. The liberalization of deposit interest rate for very large deposits preceded the U.S.–Japan agreement in 1984. Collected Deposits with the minimum of ¥500 million whose interest rate was not subject to the MOF's regulation began in 1979. See Zenkoku Ginkō Kyōkai, *Ginkō Kyōkai 50 Nenshi*, 437–438.

43. *Kinyū Zaisei Jijyō*, January 4, 1988, 92.

44. *Nihon Keizai Shimbun*, August 8, 1985, 1.

45. *Nihon Keizai Shimbun*, September 14, 1985, 1.

46. The MOF divided deposits into three in accordance with the scale of a deposit—large for ¥100 million and over, medium for between ¥10 million and ¥100 million, and small for ¥10 million and under. The MOF planned to liberalize interest rates for large-scale deposits while using different MMCs for small and medium-size deposits from spring 1987. See Zenkoku Ginkō Kyōkai, *Ginkō Kyōkai 50 Nenshi*, 437–438.

47. *Nihon Keizai Shimbun*, March 8, 1986, 3.

48. *Nihon Keizai Shimbun*, May 23, 1986, 3.

49. *Nihon Keizai Shimbun*, December 2, 1986, 3.

50. *Nihon Keizai Shimbun*, September 18, 1987,

51. *Nihon Keizai Shimbun*, January 18, 1988, 5.

52. *Nihon Keizai Shimbun*, May 29, 1988, 1; *Nikkei Kinyū Shimbun*, May 30, 1988, 1.

53. This agreement set the upper limit of each interest rate. The upper limit for the three-year MMC would be long-term government bond interest rate minus 0.7%. The upper limit of the three-month MMC's interest rate would be the CD interest rate minus 1.75% (per year) and that of the two-year MMC would be the CD interest rate minus 0.5%. The ratio to be subtracted from CD's interest rate for six-month and one-year MMCs was respectively 1.25% and 0.75%. See *Kinyū Zaisei Jijō*, December 19, 1988, 6.

54. The interest rate of the *teigaku* deposit increased after six months, after one year, after two years, and after three years, and the rate was highest after three years. The agreement in December 1988 set the cap on the highest *teigaku* interest rate. Also, the agreement stipulated that the lower limit of the *teigaku* interest rate be 3% per year. See *Nihon Keizai Shimbun*, Evening Edition, December 8, 1988, 1; and Zenkoku Ginkō Kyōkai, *Ginkō Kyōkai 50 Nenshi*, 468.

55. *Nihon Keizai Shimbun*, Evening Edition, December 8, 1988, 1.

56. Small-scale MMCs went through further changes before their abolition in June 1993 with the liberalization of fixed deposit interest rates. In November 1990, the MPT and banks further diversified small-scale MMCs based on the deposit amount—¥3 million and above and under ¥3 million—and abolished special rules for interest rate determination. In April 1991, the minimum deposit was reduced to ¥500,000. See Zenkoku Ginkō Kyōkai, *Ginkō Kyōkai 50 Nenshi*, 468.

57. *Nikkei Kinyū Shimbun*, April 12, 1990, 3.

58. *Nihon Keizai Shimbun*, September 1, 1990, 1.

59. *Nihon Keizai Shimbun*, September 1, 1990, 1.

60. *Nihon Keizai Shimbun*, December 23, 1990, 1; Zenkoku Ginkō Kyōkai, *Ginkō Kyōkai 50 Nenshi*, 469.

61. Zenkoku Ginkō Kyōkai, *Ginkō Kyōkai 50 Nenshi*, 439.

62. From April through November 1991, the PSF increased by about
    ¥8.4 trillion. See *Nihon Keizai Shimbun*, October 26, 1991, 7;
    December 26, 1991, 7.
63. Zenkoku Ginkō Kyōkai, *Ginkō Kyōkai 50 Nenshi*, 470.
64. *Kinyū Zaisei Jijō*, January 13, 1992, 12–13.
65. Zenkoku Ginkō Kyōkai, *Ginkō Kyōkai 50 Nenshi*, 471.
66. *Nihon Keizai Shimbun*, June 13, 1993, 38.
67. *Nihon Keizai Shimbun*, May 22, 1991, 7.
68. *Kinyū Zaisei Jijō*, July 15, 1991, 6; Zenkoku Ginkō Kyōkai, *Ginkō
    Kyōkai 50 Nenshi*, 469.
69. Zenkoku Ginkō Kyōkai, *Ginkō Kyōkai 50 Nenshi*, 480.
70. Ibid., 471.
71. Ibid.
72. After liberalization suspecting the maintenance of a cartel among banks
    regarding interest rates, Ueda Shozo, an economics professor emiritus,
    filed a request for investigation with the Fair Trade Commission in
    Kinki (Osaka) area in June 1994. Although the Commission did not
    impose any final ruling, it eventually became active in examining banks'
    interest rate setting. See *Nihon Keizai Shimbun*, July 8, 1994, 39;
    Nikkei Kinyū Shimbun, November 30, 1994.
73. Zenkoku Ginkō Kyōkai, *Ginkō Kyōkai 50 Nenshi*, 471.
74. In the report on the liberalization of liquid deposits issued in
    December 1993, the MOF's FIRG concluded that the rule not per-
    mitting checking accounts to have interest be maintained. *Nihon
    Keizai Shimbun*, December 23, 1993, 7.
75. *Nihon Keizai Shimbun*, November 5, 1993, 7.
76. *Nikkei Kinyū Shimbun*, April 10, 1994, 3.
77. Specific rules on the determination of PSF ordinary interest rates
    during the time of low interest rates at banks were as follows. When
    the market-determined average interest rate of banks' ordinary savings
    was lower than the higher of the three-month CD interest rate multi-
    plied by 0.16 and the product of the three-month CD interest rate
    and 0.35 minus 1.0, PSF ordinary savings interest rate would be the
    higher of these two plus about 1 (all figures in annual percentage). See
    Kinyū Zaisei Jijyō, April 18, 1994, 26.
78. According to the agreement, the PSF's special savings interest rate
    would be linked to the average interest rate of banks' counterparts, but
    the MPT and MOF would negotiate if the latter rates were deemed to
    be too low. See *Nikkei Kinyū Shimbun*, April 10, 1994, 3.
79. Zenkoku Ginkō Kyōkai, *Ginkō Kyōkai 50 Nenshi*, 472–473; *Nihon
    Keizai Shimbun*, September 16, 5.
80. Just before the December 1994 agreement, the MPT gave up a
    planned increase in the PSF savings interest rate in response to the
    MOF's request in November. See *Nihon Keizai Shimbun*, November
    5, 1994, 1. In March 1995, the MPT reduced the interest rate by

0.05% to 1.30% annual rate. This was the first time PSF interest rate reduction was done preceding the reduction of the official bank rate by the Bank of Japan, and the interest rate difference with banks' savings rate was reduced at the time of the reduction. (Since banks lowered their savings interest rate accordingly, the interest difference soon came back to the same level.) See *Nikkei Kinyū Shimbun*, April 24, 1995, 2. The MPT further reduced the PSF ordinary savings interest rate two weeks later. See *Nihon Keizai Shimbun*, April 29, 1995, 4.

81. *Asahi Shimbun*, January 10, 1989, 9.
82. *Asahi Shimbun*, April 2, 1991, 9.
83. Of course, other factors, such as the burst of the bubble economy and declining interest in stock investment among the public in the early 1990s, contributed to the continued increase of the total PSF deposit until the end of the 1990s. Yet, the aforementioned maximum PSF deposit increase was a necessary condition for this PSF expansion.
84. *Asahi Shimbun*, December 28, 1991, 7.
85. A *Yū Yū* Loan allows the *teigaku* depositor to borrow up to 90% of the *teigaku* deposit but below the limit of ¥1 million. This system, established in 1973, enabled *teigaku* depositors to borrow money at a low interest with their *teigaku* as collateral. See Zenkoku Ginkō Kyōkai, *Ginkō Kyōkai 50 Nenshi*, 473.
86. *Asahi Shimbun*, December 27, 1991, 3.
87. ATM refers to automated machines that handle any transaction. In Japanese terminology, an ATM means a machine that handles various transactions and a cash dispenser referred to as CD is a machine that is used only for cash withdrawal. A common term for these machines is CD-ATM in Japanese. CD-ATMs began to operate in 1967 and by the Sumitomo Bank in 1969; the number of CD-ATMs at banks increased to about 30,000 in March 1983. See Zenkoku Ginkō Kyōkai, *Ginkō Kyōkai 50 Nenshi*, 791.
88. Ibid., 473–476.
89. The MPT also tried to establish an organization to promote the use of the dual-use card in 1986, but, due to commercial banks' opposition, the MPT abandoned this the next year. See Zenkoku Ginkō Kyōkai, *Ginkō Kyōkai 50 Nenshi*, 476.
90. *Asahi Shimbun*, June 13, 1986, 8.
91. *Asahi Shimbun*, September 2, 1986, 9.
92. Commercial banks planned to issue a statement against the issuance of PSF dual-use Visa cards, but the MOF prevented them from doing it for fear of friction with the United States, the home country of Visa International.
93. *Asahi Shimbun*, September 19, 1996, 11.
94. Security firms were not able to make a decision because banks did not make clear if they were going to approve network connection with

securities firms. Also, since the MOF had not approved the MPT's budget request for connection expense, the firms were not certain about the prospect of its connection with PSF networks. See *Asahi Shimbun*, December 19, 1996, 10.

95. *Asahi Shimbun*, October 26, 1996, 1.
96. As of November 1999, about 500 financial institutions had network connections with the PSF. *Asahi Shimbun*, November 11, 1999, 14.
97. Yusei Mineika Mondai Kenkyū Kai (*Yūsei 3 Jigyō [Kokuei or Min-ei]: Sono Zehi wo tou* [The Three Postal Businesses (Government owned or Private?): Questioning Its Validity] (Tokyo: Nippon Rīdāzu Kyōkai, 1997), 70–78.
98. Ibid., 79–82. *Asahi Shimbun*, July 24, 1987, 9.
99. *Asahi Shimbun*, February 25, 1993, 9.
100. *Asahi Shimbun*, November 16, 1996, 11.
101. The Ministry of Transportation maintained a prefecture-based carrier license system. Yamato's expansion required obtaining license in the prefectures where Yamato did not have a license. Yet, the Ministry, seeking to prevent new entrants, kept Yamato's application pending for five years. Yamato sued the Ministry in court and pressed the Ministry to issue the license.
102. *Asahi Shimbun*, Osaka Edition, March 6, 1990, 10.
103. *Asahi Shimbun*, June 21, 1995, 2.
104. *Asahi Shimbun*, October 16, 1996, 14.
105. *Asahi Shimbun*, April 18, 2000, 12.

Chapter 5   Reforms in Transportation

1. Nihon Dōro Kōdan 30 Nenshi Henshū Iinkai, *Nihon Dōro Kōdan 30 Nensh* [The Japan Highway Corporation's 30-Year History] (Tokyo: Nihon Dōro Kōdan, 1986).
2. Gerald Curtis and Masumi Ishikawa, *Doken Kokka Nippon: "Sekai no Yūtōsei no Tsuyomi to Yowami"* [Construction State Japan: The Strong and Weak Points of "the World's Honor Stundent"] (Tokyo: Kobunha, 1983), 17–18.
3. In general, a nominated bidding system is used in choosing a contractor. Based on expertise and past construction experience, the government preselects a pool of construction companies, and only these preselected companies are allowed to participate in bidding. By manipulating the preselection process, LDP politicians can influence the bidding process. For example, Suzuki Muneo, an old guard politician from a rural area in Hokkaido, allegedly pressed the local government to limit the contractor to his locality so that his supporters would get the contract.
4. Since the government decided not to infuse funds into JH from the fiscal year 2002, JH canceled the 13 expressway construction projects

in December 2001, including one in Shimane prefecture—the district of HC director general of the LDP, Aoki Mikio. Aoki was furious and, along with other *dōro zoku* LDP politicians, demanded that JH proceed as scheduled. Conceding to the pressure from the LDP, JH resumed the construction of the projects. *Mainichi Shimbun*, January 24, 2002, 2.

5. Masako Yoneda, *Tanaka Kakuei to Kokudo Kensetsu: "Rettō Kaizōron" wo koete* [Tanaka Kakuei and National Land Development] (Tokyo: Chuō Kōronsha, 2003), 143–144.

6. Nikkei Bijinesu, *Fujii Haruho Den: Dōro Bōchō no Sengoshi* [Biography of Fujii Haruho: A Post-War History of Road Expansion] (Tokyo: Nikkei Bpsha, 2003), 52.

7. The Ministries of Construction and Transport, along with other two agencies, was incorporated into the Ministry of Land, Infrastructure, and Transport in January 2001.

8. *Mainichi Shimbun*, July 9, 2002, 5.

9. *Mainichi Shimbun*, December 25, 2001, 2; December 26, 2001, 2.

10. *Mainichi Shimbun*, November 23, 2001, 3.

11. *Nihon Keizai Shimbun*, May 13, 2003, 7; December 28, 2003, 3.

12. Tsutomy Kuji, *Tōkyo-wan Akua Rain no Kenshō* [An Examination of Tokyo Bay Aqua Line] (Tokyo: Ryokufu Shuppan, 1999).

13. Ibid.

14. Kazuaki Tanaka, a member of the Committee for the Promotion of the Privatization of Public Highway Corporations established by Prime Minister Koizumi, points out that the new expressway construction arrangement after the privatization of JH will be similar to the arrangement of building the Tokyo Bay Aqua Line, and argues that the new arrangement will continue to accumulate government deficit from expressway construction. Masatake Matsuda, another member, went so far as to say that under the new arrangement, the privatized JH would be like a child who was given a credit card and told to buy anything with it, since the JH, like the Aqua Line Authority, would not have to be worried about paying back the debt from constructing expressways. Masatake Matsuda and Kazuaki Tanaka, "Dōro Kōdan Uragiri no Mineika Zenuchimaku" [The Deceived Privatization of the Japan Highway Corporation: The Entire Inside Story]," *Bungei Shunjū* 82, no. 2 (2004): 98–99.

15. Yoshiyuki Kasai provides a comprehensive description of labor relations in JNR, based on his personal experience. My analysis of labor politics in this section is based on his book. Yoshiyuki Kasai, *Mikan no "Kokutetsu Kaikaku"* [The Unfinished "Japan National Railways Reform"] (Tokyo: Tōyō Keizai Shimpō-sha, 2001).

16. Since changes in JNR's labor conditions, such as wage, required Diet approval, preliminary agreements between the JNR management and unions were often overturned in the legislative process.

17. Taro Yayama, *Kokutetsu ni Nani wo Manabuka: Kyodai Soshiki Fuhai no Kōzō* [What to Learn from Japan National Railways: The Structure of the Corruption of a Big Organization] (Tokyo: Bungei Shunjyū, 1987), 12–15.

18. Ryōhei Kakumoto, *Kokutetsu Kaikaku: JR 10 nenme karano Kenshō* [JNR Reform: Perspective after JR's 10 Years] (Tokyo: Kōtsū Shimbunsha, 1996), 30–31.

19. Ibid., 7.

20. Airline services provided a much shorter ride time than the bullet train between Tokyo and Osaka. However, since airports were located away from city centers, passengers needed to spend more time on transit to and from airports, lessening airlines' advantage over bullet trains.

21. *Nihon Keizai Shimbun*, April 9, 1987, 11.

22. *Nihon Keizai Shimbun*, January 10, 1986, 31.

23. *Nihon Keizai Shimbun*, December 28, 1987, 3.

24. *Nihon Keizai Shimbun*, January 18, 1989, 1.

25. Besides the Nagano bullet line, the Yamagata bullet train service (in 1992) and Akita bullet train service (in 1997) began to operate from the Tokyo station. Yet, these trains ran on existing bullet train and ordinary train lines without the need to construct new lines.

26. *Nikkei Sangyō Shimbun*, January 9, 1993, 9.

27. *Nihon Keizai Shimbun*, July 8, 1994, 5.

28. *Nikkei Sangyō Shimbun*, December 18, 1996, 28.

29. *Nihon Keizai Shimbun*, December 4, 1998, 5.

30. Unyu-shō, *Unyu-Sho 50-Nenshi* [The 50-Year History of the Ministry of Transport] (Tokyo: Unyu-Sho 50-Nenshi Hensan Shitsu, 1999), 139–142, 220–224.

31. *Nihon Keizai Shimbun*, August 8, 1984, 5.

32. *Nihon Keizai Shimbun*, August 8, 1985, 5.

33. *Nihon Keizai Shimbun*, September 18, 1985, 5.

34. In August 1986, Japan's Fair Trade Commission issued a warning to the three carriers, suspecting collusive price-setting activities supported by the MOT. *Nihon Keizai Shimbun*, Evening Edition, August 22, 1986, 15.

35. *Nihon Keizai Shimbun*, April 26, 1993, 5.

36. Discount tickets needed to be purchased from two months to four weeks before the departure date, but their prices were just 25% to 36% lower than respective ordinary airfares. *Nikkei Ryūtsū Shimbun*, March 16, 1995, 16.

37. *Nihon Keizai Shimbun*, March 4, 1996, 2.

38. International airfare was significantly reduced as a result of U.S.–Japan airline negotiations in 1998. The Japanese government agreed to deregulate the international airline market and abolish restrictions on international airfare. *Nihon Keizai Shimbun*, Evening Edition, January 31, 1998, 1.

Chapter 6   Telecommunications Regulatory Reform

1. *Yomiuri Shimbun*, March 8, 1989, 31.
2. When Prime Minister Hashimoto pursued government reorganization in 1997, the MITI lobbied to take over jurisdiction over telecommunications from the MPT. The initial government reorganization plan split the MPT into telecommunications and postal service, giving the MITI jurisdiction over telecommunications.
3. See Chapter 2 for the explanation of reciprocal consent as an important feature of politics in developmental networks.
4. For the analysis of the MPT's *amakudari*, see Koichi Nakano, "Becoming a 'Policy' Ministry: The Organization and Amakudari of the Ministry of Posts and Telecommunications," *Journal of Japanese Studies* 24, no. 1 (1998): 95–117.
5. *Jyu-kyū chōsei* is similar to the price mechanism that Japanese agricultural producers use to maintain price levels. In Japanese agriculture, the Japanese Agricultural Association orders farmers to stop shipping (and usually throw away) over-supplied agricultural products when price levels are falling and seem likely to reach unprofitable levels.
6. Vogel, *Freer Markets, More Rules*, 163–164.
7. *Nikkei Communications*, October 3, 1988, 61–65.
8. *Nikkei Communications*, January 18, 1993, 48.
9. Hajime Fujii, *Bunkatsu: NTT vs Yōseishō Taiginaki Tatakai* [Breakup: The Battle without Noble Cause between NTT and MPT] (Tokyo: Daiyamondosha, 1996), 13–19.
10. *Nikkei Communications*, January 2, 1995, 133–136.
11. *Ekonomisuto*, March 27, 1990, 28–29.
12. *Nikkei Communications*, January 2, 1995, 136.
13. *Nikkei Communications*, January 2, 1995, 136.
14. *Nihon Keizai Shimbun*, March 20, 1990, 5.
15. *Nikkei Communications*, January 2, 1995, 129–133.
16. Erik Bohlin, "Restructuring Japan's Telecommunications," *Telecommunications Policy* 21, no. 2 (1997): 81.
17. *Ekonomisuto*, November 28, 1995, 49–50.
18. Fujii, *Bunkatsu*, 145.
19. *Nihon Keizai Shimbun*, November 10, 1995, 3.
20. Fujii, *Bunkatsu*, 76–85, 121.
21. Yoshio Suzuki, "Yūseisho to NTT ga Enshutushita 'Inakashibai'" [The MPT and NTT-Directed Theatrics], *Ekonomisuto* 75 (1997): 35.
22. Fujii, *Bunkatsu*, 140–144.
23. *Nihon Keizai Shimbun*, December 7, 1996, 3.
24. Hidenori Fuke, *Jōhō Tsūshin Sangyō no Kōzō to Kisei Kanwa* [Structural Change and Deregulation in the Telecommunications Industry] (Tokyo: NTT Shuppan, 2000), 72–86.

25. Ibid., 62–68.

26. NTT DoCoMo's formal name was NTT Idōtsūshinmō until the company adopted NTT DoCoMo as its name in 2000.

27. According to NTT DoCoMo President Ōboshi Kōji, after DoCoMo's spin-off from NTT, other divisions of NTT stopped raising objections to changes in mobile communications services. See *Shūkan Daiyamondo*, September 21, 1996, 38–40.

28. Fuke, *Jōhō Tsūshin Sangyō*, 36–37.

29. *Asahi Shimbun*, June 21, 1997, 13.

30. *Nihon Keizai Shimbun*, December 10, 1998.

31. Keiko Tsuyama, *NTT&KDDI: Dōnaru Tsūshin Gyōkai* [NTT and KDDI: What Will Become of the Communication Industry?] (Tokyo: Nippon Jitsugyo Shuppansha, 2000), 35–36.

32. *Nihon Keizai Shimbun*, March 27, 1997, 13; Tsuyama, *NTT&KDDI*, 83–84.

33. *Nihon Keizai Shimbun*, October 2, 1999, 10; *Nikkei Ryūtsū Shimbun*, October 5, 1999, 15.

34. *Nihon Keizai Shimbun*, July 28, 1998, 5.

35. *Nihon Keizai Shimbun*, December 11, 1999, 9.

36. *Nihon Keizai Shimbun*, December 17, 1999, 3.

37. *Nihon Keizai Shimbun*, October 3, 2000, 11.

38. For an overview of the WTO agreement, see Chantal Blouin, "The WTO Agreement on Basic Telecommunications: a Reevaluation," *Telecommunications Policy* 24 (2000): 135–142.

39. *Nihon Keizai Shimbun*, January 22, 2000, 9; and *Nikkei Sangyō Shimbun*, June 9, 1998, 6.

40. *Nikkei Sangyō Shimbun*, July 8, 1999, 7; and Tsuyama, *NTT&KDDI*, 146–147.

41. Tsuyama, *NTT&KDDI*, 94–98.

42. *Nihon Keizai Shimbun*, March 10, 1999, 29.

43. *Nikkei Sangyō Shimbun*, May 15, 2000, 5.

44. Tsuyama, *NTT&KDDI*, 133–134. As a result of the acquisition of shares by takeover bid, Cable and Wireless increased its share of IDC to about 98%, and renamed it Cable & Wireless IDC in June 1999. See *Nihon Keizai Shimbun*, June 17, 1999, 11.

45. *Nikkei Sangyō Shimbun*, April 27, 1999, 32.

46. *Nikkei Sangyō Shimbun*, December 20, 2000, 32.

47. *Nikkei Sangyō Shimbun*, April 27, 2000, 7. This arrangement was short-lived. Both British Telecom and AT&T's shares were sold to Vodafone in 2001. See *Nikkei Sangyō Shimbun*, May 2, 2001, 1.

48. Global One Communications, jointly established by Sprint, French Telecom, and German Telecom, gained the status of common carrier in 1998. See the MPT Press Release, dated November 27, 1998; http://www.soumu.go.jp/joho_tsusin/pressrelease/japanese/denki/981127j603.html.

49. *Nihon Keizai Shimbun*, January 27, 1995, 5.

50. *Nihon Keizai Shimbun*, February 29, 1996, 5.
51. *Nikkei Sangyō Shimbun*, June 9, 1998, 6.
52. *Nihon Keizai Shimbun*, Evening Edition, June 20, 1997, 1.
53. The U.S. government claimed the interconnections charges that NTT collect from NCCs was not set in accordance with WTO rules. For a more detailed analysis of the interconnections charge dispute, see Eiji Kawabata, "Still Bilateral after All These Years: US–Japan Trade Negotiations in Telecommunications," *International Relations of the Asia Pacific* 5 (2005): 97–99.
54. Interviews with LDP Diet members, June 2001.
55. International Telecommunications Union: http://www.itu.int.
56. Communications Division, Telecommunications Council, *IT Kakumei wo Suishin suru tame no Denki Tsūsin Jigyō ni okeru Kyōsō Seisaku no arikata ni tsuite no Dai Ichiji Tōshin—IT Jidai no Kyōsō Sokushin Puroguramu* [The First Report on the Format of Competition Policy in Telecommunications for the Promotion of the IT Revolution: Competition Enhancement Programs in the Age of IT] (2000).
57. *Keidanren* (Keizai Dantai Rengō Kai: Federation of Economic Organisations) released a report, which emphasized IT as the most important economic activity that would promote economic development. See Keizai Dantai Rengo Kai, *IT Kakumei Suishin ni Muketa Jōhō Tsūshin Sei no Sai Kōchiku ni Kansuru Dai Ichiji Teigen* [The First Proposal for the Reconstruction of the Telecommunications Law System for the Promotion of the IT Revolution] (Tokyo: Keizai Dantai Rengo Kai, 2000); http://www.keidanren.or.jp/japanese/policy/2000/012/index.html.
58. *Nihon Keizai Shimbun*, July 17, 2000, 2.
59. IT Senryaku Kaigi, *IT Kihon Senryaku* [IT Basic Strategy] (2000).
60. Tsuyama, *NTT&KDDI*, 73–78.
61. *Nikkei Sangyō Shimbun*, January 29, 2001, 3.
62. *Nikkei Sangyō Shimbun*, February 16, 2001, 3.
63. *Asahi Shimbun*, November 28, 2000, 13.
64. *Nihon Keizai Shimbun*, February 7, 2001, 5.
65. *Nihon Keizai Shimbun*, February 16, 2001, 3.
66. *Nikkei Sangyō Shimbun*, March 19, 2001, 3.
67. *Nihon Keizai Shimbun*, April 12, 2001, 13.
68. *Nihon Keizai Shimbun*, Evening Edition, April 18, 2001, 1.
69. KDDI President Okuyama Yuzai said the company might file a law suit against the MPT, challenging its approval of the L-mode. See *Nikkei Sangyō Shimbun*, April 20, 2001, 5.
70. *Asahi Shimbun*, August 9, 2001, 8.
71. *Nikkei Sangyō Shimbun*, January 29, 2001, 3.
72. Kawabata, "Still Bilateral after All These Years," 98.
73. Interview with an MPT official, September 2001.
74. Interview with an MPT official, September 2001.

75. Its formal name was the Special Department for Desirable Pro-Competitive Policies Telecommunications Field for Promoting the IT Revolution.
76. See http://www.joho.soumu.go.jp/policyreports/japanese/telecouncil/it/00905s02.html.
77. Ministry of Posts and Telecommunications (2000), *Kyōsō Seisaku Shōiinkai ni Okeru Shuyō Ronten* [Major Points of the Competition Policy Subcommittee] (2000); http://www.joho.soumu.go.jp/policyreports/japanese/telecouncil/it/PDF/001020d21101.pdf.
78. Ministry of Posts and Telecommunications, *Yunibāsaru no Genjō to Kadai* [The Current Status and Issues of the Universal Service] (2000), 4; http://www.joho.soumu.go.jp/policyreports/japanese/telecouncil/it/PDF/000918d21206.pdf.
79. See http://www.joho.soumu.go.jp/policyreports/japanese/telecouncil/it/00905s02.html.
80. Masayuki Funada, "IT Kakumei Suishin no tame no Denki Tsūshin Shingikai Dai Ichiji Tōshin ni Tuite (Jō)" [On the First Report of the Telecommunications Council for the Promotion of IT Revolution], *Jurisuto* 1197 (2001): 52–58.
81. Telecommunications Council, *IT Kakumei wo Suishin suru tame no Denki Tsūsin Jigyō ni okeru Kyōsō Seisaku no arikata ni tsuite no Dai Ichiji Tōshin—IT Jidai no Kyōsō Sokushin Puroguramu* [The First Report on the Format of Competition Policy in Telecommunications for the Promotion of the IT Revolution: Competition Enhancement Programs in the Age of IT] (2000).
82. Ibid.
83. Ibid.
84. Keiazai Dantai Rengo Kai, *IT Kakumei Suishin.*
85. They included the relaxation of regulations on NTT regional companies and the establishment of the universal service fund.
86. Kyūshū Tsūshin Network Kabushiki Gaisha et al., *IT Kakumei wo Suishin suru Tame no Denki Tsūshin Jigyō ni Okeru Kyōsō Seisaku no Arikata ni tuite* [On the Desirable Competition Policy in Telecommunications for the Promotion of the IT Revolution] (2000).
87. *Nippon Denshin Denwa Kabushikigaisha* (2000), 8–9.
88. Telecommunications Council, *IT Kakumei wo Suishin suru tame no Denki Tsūsin Jigyō ni okeru Kyōsō Seisaku no arikata ni tsuite no Dai Ichiji Tōshin (Sōan) ni Taisuru Iken Oyobi sore ni tsuite no Kangaekata* [Opinions on (the draft of) the First Report on the Format of Competition Policy in Telecommunications for the Promotion of the IT Revolution and the Council's response] (2000).
89. *Nihon Keizai Shimbun,* November 8, 2000, 1.
90. *Nikkei Sangyō Shimbun,* March 28, 2001, 1.
91. Interview with an LDP Diet member, June 2001.

92. LDP's telecommunications subcommittee was reorganized into the administrative affairs subcommittee in conjunction with government reorganization.
93. *Asahi Shimbun*, March 9, 2001, 11; April 11, 2001, 11.
94. *Nihon Keizai Shimbun*, March 27, 2001, 5.
95. Interview with an MPT official, September 2001.
96. *Nikkei Sangyō Shimbun*, March 28, 2001, 1.
97. *Nihon Keizai Shimbun*, Evening Edition, June 15, 2001, 1.
98. Interview with LDP Diet members, June 2001.

Conclusion

1. Some attribute the railroad accident in May 2005 that killed more than one hundred passengers to JR West's business strategy to speed up train service to stay competitive against rival railways in the Osaka area.
2. *Asahi Shimbun*, March 22, 2004, 3.
3. *Nihon Keizai Shimbun*, February 13, 2002, 5.
4. Representative publications include Peter Hall and David Soskice, eds., *Varieties of Capitalism: The Institutional Foundations of Comparative Advantage* (New York: Oxford University Press, 2001); J. Rogers Hollingsworth and Robert Boyer, eds., *Contemporary Capitalism: The Embeddedness of Institutions* (New York: Cambridge University Press, 1997); Kozo Yamamura and Wolfgang Streek, eds., *The End of Diversity? Prospects for German and Japanese Capitalism* (Ithaca, NY: Cornell University Press, 2003).
5. Margarita Estevez-Abe, Torben Iversen, and David Soskice, "Social Protection and the Formation of Skills: A Reinterpretation of the Welfare State," in *Varieties of Capitalism: The Institutional Foundations of Comparative Advantage*, ed. Peter Hall and David Soskice (New York: Oxford University Press, 2001).

Index

Administrative Management Agency, 75
administrative reform, 71–6, 98, 105, 148, 154
Administrative Reform Committee (ARC), 71–9, 199–200
Advisory Council to Consider the Modalities of the Three Postal Businesses, 80, 82
agencification, 23, 25, 195
Ageo Station riot, 135
agriculture, 126, 128, 181, 211
All Nippon Airways (ANA), 142–3
amakudari, 151, 211
antitrust law, 123
Aqua Line, *See* Tokyo Bay Aqua Line
Aso, Taro, 83
automated teller machines (ATMs), 118–19, 207

Bank of Japan, 110, 207
The Basic Law for the Reform of Central Government Organizations, 78, 200
Britain, 5, 13, 17, 19, 22–5, 28–9, 31–4, 36–7, 39–40, 42, 45, 57, 65, 67, 179, 185, 188–9, 194–5
  Big Bang, 28
  centrism, 36
  civil service reform, 23–5, 195
  deregulation, 28, 33
  equity financing, 42
  government reform, 13, 17, 31–3, 35, 179: state

decision-making structure, 32–3; state embeddedness, 32–3
  parliamentary system, 5
  post–World War II political economy, 19, 22, 37, 194
  regulatory reform in, 28–9
  telecommunications reform, 28
budget deficit, 19–22, 53, 61, 66, 69, 88, 99, 134, 136, 138–9, 147, 180, 202
bullet train, 61, 138–41, 145–6, 182, 186, 210
Bundesbank, 20, 35
bureaucracy, 1, 5–6, 8, 12–14, 22–5, 31, 34, 36, 50, 52, 55–7, 61, 70–1, 123–4, 179
bureaucrats, 3–4, 6–11, 13–15, 43–4, 53, 56, 65, 67, 70–3, 75–6, 87–8, 90–3, 97–8, 128, 146, 182, 185
  and reform, 65, 91
business, 1–6, 8, 11–13, 19, 26, 32, 50
  actors, 26, 36, 147, 151
  leaders, 3, 5, 7–9, 13, 17, 36, 53–4, 67, 69–70, 73, 91, 93, 166, 171
  and reform, 65, 91

capitalism, 22, 40, 41, 50–2, 94, 187–91
  comparative, 187–91
  German, 21, 194, 196

capitalism—*continued*
  Japanese, 50–2
  organizational, 51
civil service reform, 14, 18, 22–6,
  30, 37, 194–5
classical economics, 18–19
Clean Government Party, 49, 84,
  86–7
commercial banks, 2, 28, 36, 42,
  60, 80, 94–5, 97–101, 105–6,
  113, 118, 122–3, 146,
  202, 207
Committee for the Promotion of
  the Privatization of Public
  Highway Corporations, 89–90
Communist Party, 22, 40, 44,
  49, 134
comparative capitalism, 187–91
comparative political economy, 13,
  17–38, 188
competition, 1, 3, 6–7, 9–10, 12,
  15, 19–20, 26–30, 32, 46,
  51–2, 55, 63, 68, 81, 83, 111,
  149, 153–4, 157–8, 162, 165,
  172, 179–80, 188, 191
  private sector, 26, 51
  post–World War II restriction of,
    19–20
construction companies, 7, 11, 55,
  57, 66, 88, 91, 95, 125, 128,
  182, 190
Council on Economic and Fiscal
  Policy, 84
credit card companies, 119, 207

Daini Denden Incorporated (DDI),
  160–1, 167–8
  DDI–IDO alliance, 161
data communications, 159, 165
deficit, *See* budget deficit
Democratic Party of Japan (DPJ),
  84–5, 87
Democratic Socialist Party, 49, 134
deregulation, 6, 12, 15, 17, 24,
  26–30, 33, 39, 58, 61–2, 65,
  71, 91, 125, 142–7, 155–6,
  159–60, 165–6, 174, 178,
  180, 183, 186, 190–1, 195,
  197, 210
Derthick, Martha, 27, 195
development, 4, 7–15, 21, 26, 28,
  37, 39, 41–3, 45–57, 59, 62–3,
  66–8, 70, 74, 92, 95, 128, 138,
  147, 191, 211, 213
  bureaucracy, 50, 52
  business groups, 50, 52
  government spending, 55, 57
  Japan's national interest, 53
  LDP, 46–7, 50, 53–4, 56
  management–labor relations, 53
  mechanism, 7–11, 13
  pre–World War II Japan, 54
  post–World War II Japan, 45, 53
  rural areas, 56
  social problems, 48
  tax increases, 66
  telecommunications, 15, 68, 74
  urban centers, 54, 56
Diet, xi, 11, 45, 53, 56, 59, 60–1,
  68–70, 75–6, 78, 82–3, 86–8,
  90–1, 96, 99–100, 102, 107,
  113, 126, 128, 133, 136–9,
  151, 155–6, 171, 174, 176–7,
  179–80, 184, 200, 202–4, 209
distribution, 4, 7–15, 37, 39, 41–3,
  49–50, 54–8, 60–3, 66, 70, 73,
  75, 79, 91–5, 125, 131, 141,
  144–7, 150, 158, 181–3,
  189, 191
  bureaucracy, 37, 50, 55–7, 75
  business groups, 37, 50
  farmers, 54
  government, 55
  LDP, 15, 47–50, 54, 56–8, 93
  post–World War II, 54
  (re)distribution, 41, 50
  of wealth, 62
Doko, Toshio, 67–8, 198
domestic transportation, *See*
  transportation
dōro zoku, 88–90, 182, 209
downsizing, 23–5, 53, 75

dual state, xi, 7, 9, 12, 14–15, 17,
   38–9, 43–63, 65, 92, 146, 191
   formation of, 43–50
   and government reform, 39,
      65–92
   structure of, 50–7
dōro tokutei zaigen (gasoline tax
   revenue), 126–7, 130, 131,
   139, 144

economic activities, 6–7, 18–21,
   32–4, 37, 46, 56, 58, 60, 62,
   105, 125, 156, 179, 186,
   188–9, 191, 213
   actors, 32, 62, 188–9
   competition, international, 14, 22
   government involvement in,
      32–3, 37, 58, 105, 179, 186
   nonliberal market interventionist
      approaches to, 19
   private sector (Japan), 46, 60
   social aspects, 188
   transportation, 125
economic development, *See*
   development
economic distribution, *See*
   distribution
economy, Japanese, *See* Japanese
   economy
embeddedness
   See state embeddedness in
      economy
employment, 19, 128, 189–90
European Union (EU), 28–30
exports, *See* Japanese economy,
   exports

Fair Trade Commission, 113, 154,
   206, 210
Federal Communications
   Commission (FCC), 28, 75,
   165, 172, 176
Financial Issue Research Group
   (FIRG), 109, 111–12, 206
financial liberalization, *See*
   liberalization

Fiscal Investment and Loans
   Program (FILP), 11, 50, 55,
   61, 70–1, 77, 87–8, 95–6, 125,
   127–9, 137, 140, 181, 185
fragmentation, 31, 35–6, 39, 42,
   160, 165, 184–5, 191
France, 13–14, 17, 20, 22, 24–5,
   28–32, 34, 36–7, 40–3, 46, 81,
   179, 188, 194, 196, 201
   and bureaucracy, 34, 36–7
   civil service reform, 24–5
   deregulation, 29
   development and distribution,
      41, 46
   France Telecom, 29
   French Republicanism, 24
   government reform, 13, 17,
      31, 34–5, 179: state
      decision-making structure,
      34; state embeddedness in
      economy, 34, 36–7
   interventionist policy, 20, 41
   post–World War II political
      economy, 20, 22, 34, 37,
      40–2
   privatization, 29
   regulatory reform, 24, 28–30
   social security system, 20, 42
   Socialism, 40–2
   statism, 14, 22, 28, 31–2, 34,
      36, 41
   telecommunications reform,
      29–30
Fujii, Haruho, 90, 131, 202
Fujio, Masayuki, 102, 203

General Agreement on Tariffs and
   Trade, 46
Germany, 13–14, 17, 20–2,
   24–5, 29–32, 34–5, 37,
   40–3, 45, 81, 126, 188,
   194–6, 201
   Autobahn, 126
   civil service reform, 25
   cooperative federalism, 42
   deregulation, 29–30

Germany—*continued*
  development and distribution,
    41–3
  fiscally conservative, 22
  German capitalism, 21, 194, 196
  government reform, 13, 17, 31,
    34–5: state decision-making
    structure, 34–5; state
    embeddedness in economy,
    34–5
  long-term economic perspective,
    20, 42
  political stability, 43
  privatization, 29
  regulatory reform, 29–30
  social market economy, 14, 32, 42
  social welfare, 42–3
  society-led embeddedness, 37
  state–business–labor relations, 42
  telecommunications reform,
    29–30
  (West) German post–World War
    II political economy, 20–2,
    37, 40–3, 194
ginkō zoku (banking policy tribe), 97
Glass-Steagall Act of 1933, 28
Gotoda, Masaharu, 103
government
  actor, 20, 151, 155
  bureaucracy, *See* bureaucracy
  bureaucrats, *See* bureaucrats
  business, 19, 32, 53
  control of market activities, 27
  corporations, 3, 10, 14, 28, 33,
    55, 61, 67–8, 71, 77, 79,
    87–8, 91–2, 134, 136–7,
    149, 158, 180, 183, 185,
    187: privatization of, 67, 91;
    special government
    corporations reform,
    87–8
  expansion, 18–22, 37–8,
    40, 62
  Japan, *See* Japanese government
  ministries, 14, 25, 29, 71–5,
    77–9, 87, 90, 92, 197

  monopoly, 19, 26, 30, 57–8, 80;
    telecommunications, 19,
    30, 58
  operations, 26–8, 57, 60, 70, 75,
    77, 107, 179
  protection, 8, 63, 191
  reduction of, 39, 71
  regulation, 3–4, 7–8, 15, 19–22,
    26–30, 55, 69, 151, 179–80,
    199; *See also* regulatory
    reform
  reorganization, 17, 65, 72–3,
    91–3, 181, 190, 199;
    See also Hashimoto reform
  revenue, 27, 66, 98–9, 125,
    154–5, 181
  role in post–World War II political
    economy, 19
  service, demand for, 26, 71
government reform
  civil service reform, 14, 18, 22–5,
    37, 194
  comparative perspective, 17–38
  Japanese, *See* Japanese
    government reform
  patterns of, 18, 30–7
  post–World War II government
    expansion, 18–22, 40
  regulatory reform, 14, 18, 25–30,
    37, 194
  structural reform, 14
government spending, 3, 7, 19–22,
  50, 54–6, 63, 67, 125–6, 146,
  180–1, 193, 197–8
Government Tax System Research
  Council (GTSRC), 99,
  101–2, 204
the Great Depression (1929), 18, 19
Green Card System, 99–101,
  108, 116
Gross Domestic Product (GDP),
  3, 41
gross national product (GNP), 2
Gyōkakushin (Advisory Council for
  the Promotion of
  Administrative Reform), 70–1

Hanshin earthquake, 71, 199

Hanshin Expressway Public
    Corporation, 88, 127

Hashimoto, Ryutaro, 5, 9, 69,
    72–3, 76, 79–80, 141, 143–4,
    156, 184, 187, 211
  and administrative reform,
    72–9, 141

Hashimoto reform, 14–15, 25, 35,
    65, 70–80, 91, 93, 141, 143–5,
    147, 156, 186, 211

health care, 19, 21, 42–3, 49, 53,
    195

highway system, 48–50; *See also*
    national expressway (toll way)
    system

highway system holding
    organization, 89–90

Honshu-Shikoku Bridge Authority,
    88, 129

Honshu-Shikoku Bridges, 128–31

horizontal communications, 37

horizontal groups, 51
  keiretsu, 51

horizontal integration, 160

Hosokawa, Morihiro, 71

House of Councillors (HC), 76, 79,
    86–7, 96, 201–2, 109, 175

House of Representatives (HR), 72,
    82, 84–7, 90, 156, 197, 201

Ikeda, Hayato, 45–6

i-mode technology, 157, 168–9

imports, 46, 48, 129

Income Doubling Plan, 46

income tax reform, 101

industrial competitiveness, 20

industries (infrastructure), 27

inflation, 20–1, 50, 195

Information Technology (IT),
    165–7, 181
  Committee for IT Strategy, 167
  IT Committee, 171–4, 214
  IT Revolution, 167, 213–14

interactions, 7–10, 13–14, 32, 36,
    63, 65, 92–4, 98, 103, 118,
    124–5, 145–6, 148, 151,
    157–9, 165, 171, 177
  bureaucracy and, 13, 36, 124
  dual state, 14, 36
  developmental-distributive, 63,
    65, 92
  inter- and intra-network, 7–10
  nonliberal and liberal
    economies, 32
  MPT-NTT, 151, 157–9,
    165, 171
  reformers-old guard, 93–4, 145–6

interest income, 98, 101–3, 107,
    115–16, 146, 203–4

interest rate, 30, 94–5, 98, 105–12,
    116, 202, 204–7

Internet, 74, 148, 152, 155, 157–9,
    162, 165–72, 177

interventionist policy measures,
    20, 41

Japan Airlines (JAL), 142–3

Japan Highway Corporation (JH),
    12, 25, 55, 62, 88–90, 93, 95,
    126–8, 129–32, 139, 145, 147,
    182–3, 186, 202, 208–9
  and toll roads, 126–31

Japan National Railways (JNR), 3,
    11, 25, 57, 60–1, 67–70, 92–3,
    133–5, 137–8, 180, 182–3,
    185, 198, 209–10
  deficit, 67, 138–9, 147–8,
    150, 198
  JNR Reconstruction
    Administrative Committee,
    69–70, 139
  See also privatization, JNR;
    unions, JNR

Japan Railway Construction Public
    Corporation (JRCPC), 137

Japan Socialist Party (JSP), 44–6,
    70, 134

Japanese deregulation, 197
  airline, 143–4, 146–7, 210
  telecommunications, 59, 156,
    165, 180, 183, 186, 211

Japanese economic reform, 193

Japanese economy, 1–8, 10–12, 14, 17–18, 21, 26, 43, 45–53, 66, 70, 79, 93, 98, 105, 128, 131, 143, 179, 191, 193–4
  bubble burst, 143, 193, 207
  bubble period, 1–2, 122
  budget deficit, *See* budget deficit
  and bureaucracy, 52–3
  business, 2, 47, 52
  business–bureaucracy relations, 52
  business–labor relations, 43
  capitalism, 50–2
  currency appreciation, 21
  current problems, 3–5, 12, 17, 79, 193
  development and distribution, 43, 51
  doru shokku (dollar shock), 48
  export-oriented, 43, 66, 179
  fiscally conservative stance, 21
  and government, 3–4, 18, 26, 52, 70, 79, 93
  history of, 51
  imports, 66
  individual deposits, 99
  industrial policy, 2, 12
  and LDP leaders, 53
  and national security, 51
  and oil prices, 48, 66, 128
  oiru shokku (oil shock), 48, 131
  post–World War II political economy, 21–2, 43, 51; fiscally conservative stance, 21–2
  rapid development period, 1, 3, 11, 21, 47–52, 62, 95, 98, 105, 127, 180
  raw materials, 48, 66
  and the state, 51
  trade surplus, 66
  and U.S. economic environment, 48
  See also exports, imports, Income Doubling Plan

Japanese exports, 1, 9, 21, 43, 46–8, 52, 66

Japanese government, 3–5, 18, 21, 40, 46, 51, 65–6, 70, 79, 93–4, 99, 105, 113, 120, 125–6, 128–9, 132, 159, 184
  budget deficit, 66, 99
  business–government relations, 51
  downsizing of, 3
  and economy, 3–4, 18, 21, 70, 79, 93, 105
  history of, 51
  occupation forces, 65
  pre–World War II, 40
  and PSF, 94
  spending expansion, 21
  and transportation, 125

Japanese government reform, xi–xii, 3–15, 17–18, 21–2, 25, 30, 35–9, 46, 53–4, 57, 60–2, 65–92, 120, 179–91, 195, 203
  bureaucracy, 36, 43–4, 53
  civil service reform, 25, 195
  comparative perspective, 17–38
  development-distribution nexus, 65
  dual state, 65–92
  economic problems, 4–5, 17
  Green Card system, 99–101
  post–World War II political economy, 21–2, 35–7, 39–40, 43–51, 197
  postal business, *See* postal business reform
  privatization as part of, 84
  problems with, 184–7
  state decision-making structure, 36–9
  state embeddedness in economy, 36–9
  state-society networks, 37
  success, 6–7, 17
  telecommunications, *See* telecommunications reform
  transportation, *See* transportation reform

vertical administration, 37
See also Hashimoto, Koizumi,
Nakasone reforms; *Rinchō*
Japanese policymaking, 36, 43–4
Japanese political economy,
12–13, 50
See also dual state
Japanese politics, 50, 126
Japanese state, 36–7, 51, 197
bureaucracy-business nexus,
36–7, 46
state decision-making
structure, 36
state embeddedness in economy,
36–7
JR East, 164
JR West, 89, 215
JRs, 70, 135–6, 140–1, 145,
180, 215
jyu-kyū chosei (supply and demand
adjustment), 152, 211

Kanemaru, Shin, 102–3, 203–4
Kansai Airport, 144
KDDI, 161–3, 212
Keidanren (the Federation of
Economic Organizations),
67, 149, 154, 158, 166–7,
172–4, 213
keiretsu groups (horizontal), 51
keiretsu groups (vertical), 52
Keynesianism, 19–22, 194
Kinyū Jiyūka Taisaku Shikin
(the fund for coping
with financial liberalization),
107
Kishi, Nobusuke, 45
Kobe, 2, 49, 71, 127
Koizumi, Junichiro, 5–6, 9, 12, 14,
77–92, 104, 110, 123–4,
129–32, 141, 145–6, 184,
200–1, 209
reforms, 12, 14–15, 25, 35,
65, 77–91, 93, 97, 130–2,
145, 147, 181, 186,
193, 200

kokudō (ordinary government
roads), 127
Kokusai Denshin Denwr (KDD),
160–2, 165, 167
KDD Law, 160
KDDI, 212–13
Korean War, 1, 21
Koso, Kenjii, 96

labor, 19–20, 23–5, 32, 42–4, 47–8,
53, 61, 67, 69–71, 73, 87,
180, 209
Leftist movements, 48, 50, 54, 67,
134–6, 145
Letter Delivery Service bill (LDS
bill), 81–3
Liberal Democratic Party (LDP), 3,
5–9, 11, 13–15, 35–6, 39–40,
44–50, 53–4, 56–63, 66–72,
75–6, 79–91, 93, 95–104, 123,
125–31, 133–5, 137–41, 145,
149–51, 154–5, 158, 165, 168,
175–6, 178, 182–4, 186,
190–1, 197–8, 200–4,
208–9, 215
bureaucracy, 56–7
development, 46–7, 56
distribution, 47–9, 56–8
fragmentation, 184
LDP General Affairs
committee, 82
LDP government, 21, 39, 44, 46,
62, 66
LDP leaders, 65–71, 87, 93, 98,
102, 104, 150, 154–5,
184, 204
LDP politicians, 14, 53–4, 56–7,
60–2, 65, 75–7, 81, 88–90,
93, 100–3, 128–30, 133,
137–8, 145, 149, 154, 165,
178, 186, 204, 208: and
reform, 63, 77, 91; and
tokutei, *See tokutei*; *See dōro
zoku*, old guard politicians,
yūsei zoku politicians
LDP politics, 14, 40, 79

Liberal Democratic Party
    —continued
    LDP Tax System Research
        Council (LTSRC), 101–2,
        104, 203
    and Postal Savings Fund,
        99–102
    and tax reform, 99–103, 204
liberalization, 10, 15, 28–30, 34,
        46, 58–9, 61, 77–8, 80–3, 94,
        98, 103, 105–7, 109–18, 120,
        124–5, 143, 145–9, 151–2,
        158, 160, 162, 164, 174, 178,
        201, 204–6
    commercial banks, 113
    deposits, 105–7, 204–5
    EU energy markets, 30
    financial markets, 94, 98, 103,
        105–6, 115–16, 120,
        124, 146
    fixed deposit interest rates, 105,
        109–15, 205
    interest rates, 109–16, 205
    liquid deposit interest rates, 105,
        111–16, 206
    logic of, 149
    Postal Savings Fund operation, 107
    postal service, 80–3, 201
    telecommunications markets, 10,
        15, 28–30, 58–9, 147–8,
        151–2, 158, 160, 162, 174,
        178
L-mode controversy, 167–70, 213
local governments, 127, 132
Lockheed scandal, 50, 76, 126
long-term profit, 20, 42, 188–9
LTSRC, *See* LDP Tax System
    Research Council

macroeconomic policy, 19–20, 27,
        32–3
Management and Coordination
    Agency, 76, 199
managerial flexibility, 23–5, 59–61,
        68, 83, 143, 149, 157, 194

market competition, 1, 3, 6–7, 9–10,
        12, 15, 19–20, 22–3, 26–8, 47,
        52, 112–13, 146–8, 150–4,
        162, 166, 168, 171–7, 180
    restricted, post–World War II,
        19–22, 47
market economy, 26, 188–9
    coordinated, 188–9
    liberal, 188
market entry/exit regulation, 7,
        15, 27, 55, 81–2, 152–3,
        157, 159
maruyū, 99, 101–2, 107–8, 203
Meishin Expressway, 127
Metropolitan Expressway Public
    Corporation, 88, 127
microeconomic management, 20,
        22, 26, 33
Ministry of Agriculture, 74–5, 78
Ministry of Communications, 94
Ministry of Construction, 74–5, 78,
        90, 126–8, 131, 139, 199
Ministry of Defence, 78
Ministry of Economy, Trade, and
    Industry, 78, 197
Ministry of Education, 73–4, 78
Ministry of Finance (MOF), 11, 60,
        66, 69, 71–4, 77–8, 95,
        97–118, 123–4, 127–8, 141,
        146, 154–5, 158, 204–8
    Banking Bureau, 97, 109,
        114, 119
    banking regulation authority,
        73–4
    bribery scandals, 72
    General Affairs Bureau, 103
    Investment Fund Account, 95
    national expressway system, 127–8
Ministry of Foreign Affairs,
        73–4, 78
Ministry of General Affairs, 75
Ministry of Health and Welfare, 72,
        74, 77–8
Ministry of Home Affairs, 75,
        78, 141

Ministry of Land, Infrastructure,
and Transport (MLIT),
11–12, 78, 88–90, 129–31,
146, 185, 202
Ministry of Land Development,
74–5, 199
Ministry of Land Maintenance,
74–5, 199
Ministry of International Trade and
Industry (MITI), 46–7, 52, 59,
69, 73–5, 78, 150, 154, 193,
197, 199–200, 211;
telecommunications, 59, 69, 75
See also Ministry of Economy,
Trade, and Industry
Ministry of Justice, 73–4, 78
Ministry of Posts and
Telecommunications (MPT),
10–11, 15, 59–60, 68–9,
73–80, 91, 94, 96–120, 122–4,
146, 148–62, 164–78, 183,
185, 187, 193, 199–200,
202–4, 206–8, 211, 213
MPT Telecommunications
Council, 165
regulatory policymaking, 167–77
MPT-MOF negotiations, 103,
107, 109–10, 113, 115, 146
NTT privatization, 68–9, 199
postal business, 60, 120–3
Postal Savings Bureau, 103, 204
Postal Savings Fund, 99–107, 123
and private sector, 60
regulation, 158
telecommunications policymaking,
76, 91, 164, 200
Ministry of Public Management,
Home Affairs, Posts and
Telecommunications
(MPHPT), 78–80, 83, 117,
148, 169–70, 175–8, 180–1,
200–1
Ministry of Transport (MOT),
69–70, 74, 78, 122, 134,
140–5, 208, 210

Miyazawa, Kiichi, 71
MMCs, See money market
certificates
mobile communications, 157,
160–1, 167–8, 180
money market certificates (MMC),
105–12, 114–15, 205
Mori, Yoshiro, 79, 167
MPT/MPHPT, 80–1, 169, 175,
177–8
Murayama, Tomiichi, 71–2
Muto, Kabun, 76, 199

Nakasone, Yasuhiro, 5, 9, 11, 35,
66, 68–70, 73, 102, 139, 186
reform, 11, 14, 17, 25, 60,
65–70, 73, 91, 93, 145,
147–8, 185
national airline, 15, 61, 125, 137,
141–5, 210
National Banking Association,
114, 119
national expressway (toll way)
system, 126–33, 137, 141,
146, 181, 185, 190
construction, 57, 61–2, 90,
125–33, 146, 208–9
kokudō (ordinary government
roads), 127
national railway, 55, 61, 68, 125,
133–41
national security, 26, 165, 171, 176
nationalization of industries, 19
natural monopoly, 10, 26–7, 197
neoconservative economic ideology,
39, 57, 63, 65, 67, 147
neoliberal economic ideology,
185–9, 191
new common carriers (NCCs),
148–9, 151–2, 154–5,
157–60, 164, 168–70, 172–4,
176–7, 213
New Deal, 19
new public management (NPM),
24–5

Next Steps initiative, 23–5, 33, 195
Nihon Ido Tsushin (IDO), 160–1,
　　167–8
Nippon Telecom, 161–5, 168
Nippon Telegraph and Telephone
　　(NTT), 3, 10, 15, 25, 30,
　　57–60, 67–70, 72, 91–3, 105,
　　133, 147–50, 152–65, 167–78,
　　180, 183, 185–7, 189, 198–9,
　　211–14
　　breakup of, 154–6, 158–9, 177,
　　　187, 189
　　family firms, 59, 149, 198
　　NTT Communications, 157–8,
　　　160, 162, 164, 173, 175
　　NTT DoCoMo, 157–8, 160–2,
　　　168–9, 173, 175–6
　　NTT East, 156
　　NTT Law, 168–70
　　NTT West, 157
　　NTTEW, 158, 168–70, 172–3
　　privatization, *See* privatization,
　　　NTT; reorganization, 154–8,
　　　161–2, 167, 170–1, 178
Nonaka, Hiromu, 82–3

Obuchi, Keizo, 79, 204
occupation forces, 43–5, 54, 65
oil prices, 1, 21, 48, 98, 128, 131
old guard politicians, 7, 9–11, 14,
　　37, 57, 61–3, 80, 84, 87–8,
　　90–4, 97, 123, 125, 130,
　　131–2, 141, 145, 147, 182–3,
　　189–90, 201, 204, 208
Organization of Petroleum
　　Exporting Countries
　　(OPEC), 48

patterns of government reform, 18
pensions, 43, 53
Plan for the Remodeling of the
　　Japanese Archipelago, 49
policy actors, 36, 167
Policy Affairs Research Council
　　(PARC), 69, 73, 83, 102,
　　104, 203

policy deliberation councils
　　(*shingikai*), 36
policymaking, 8–10, 12–13, 18, 36,
　　43–4, 49, 53–4, 73, 84, 97–8,
　　104, 150, 162, 165, 167, 185
　　See also civil service reform
political actors, 26, 36, 69, 93,
　　146, 150
political instability, 20, 40–1,
　　44, 48
political stability, 14, 18, 39–41,
　　46, 194
politicians, 3–4, 6–10, 12–14, 49
post–World War II
　　air transport, 141
　　government expansion, 18–22,
　　　62, 98, 194
　　political economy, 13, 18–22, 31,
　　　40–1, 50, 62, 94, 97–8, 105,
　　　138, 182, 194
　　road construction, 126–8,
　　　136, 144
　　social stability, 4–5, 18
postal business, 4, 10–11, 35, 58,
　　60, 73, 75, 78, 82, 94–7,
　　122–5, 151, 178, 182,
　　200, 208
　　reform, 11, 35, 39, 60–1, 63,
　　　76–87, 122, 146–7
postal life insurance (PLI), 15, 60,
　　75, 80, 84–6, 94–5, 120–4,
　　181, 186, 200–1
postal office service networks,
　　84, 118
Postal Savings Bureau, 103, 204
Postal Savings Fund (PSF), 11,
　　14–15, 30, 35–6, 55, 60–1,
　　70–1, 75, 77, 80, 84–5,
　　93–103–24, 146–7, 181,
　　185–6, 200–4, 206–8
　　world's largest consumer bank,
　　　11, 55
　　deposits, 108, 110
　　and distributive sector, 55, 94
　　expansion of, 116–23, 207
　　"Japan's second budget," 11

interest rates, 95, 98, 113–14, 206
and MPT, 95, 99–100
personal banking, 30, 35, 94, 97, 123
PSF Dual-Use Card, 119, 124, 207
reform, 71, 147
source of government finance, 94
tax exemptions, 94, 99–100, 203
taxation, 98–104, 107, 116, 123, 204; *See also Teigaku*
Postal Savings Law, 94
postal service, 14–15, 26, 55, 57, 60, 75, 84, 94, 122–4
poverty, 40–1
price competition, 21, 143, 153
price controls, 7, 19, 28, 55
private sector companies, 30, 46–7, 51–2, 60, 69, 71, 77, 81–2, 84, 87, 95, 97, 120–4, 132–4, 136, 143, 145, 149, 180, 186, 200, 202
automobiles, 46
importance in economic development, 52
life insurance, 120–2, 124
logic, 30
management, 22–3, 25–6, 65, 77, 194
NTT, 69, 199
and postal business, 60, 71, 81–2, 200
and Postal Savings Fund, 97, 202
zaibatsu (family-run), 51
privatization, 3, 6, 10–12, 14–15, 17, 23–30, 33, 39, 55, 57–62, 65, 67–70, 72–3, 75, 77, 79–93, 105, 123, 125, 129–32, 135–6, 139, 142–3, 145, 147–50, 152, 154, 159, 177, 180–3, 185–7, 190, 198–202
Britain, 28, 33
five principles for, 84
France, 29
Germany, 29
of government corporations, 14, 26–7, 58, 65, 67, 181
Japan, 29
of JAL, 143, 145
of Japan Post, 79–87, 190
of JH, 12, 62, 93, 130–2, 147, 181–2, 185–6, 209
of JNR, 11, 15, 55, 61, 67–70, 92–3, 135–6, 139, 142, 145, 147, 180–1, 185–6; JR carriers, 70, 135–6, 140–1, 145, 180
of NTT, 10, 15, 30, 55, 57, 59, 67–70, 72–3, 92–3, 105, 142, 147–50, 152, 154, 159, 177, 180–1, 183, 185–7, 198–9
of PHCs, 88–91, 202
of postal business, 60, 79–86, 92, 123, 200–1
of public highway corporations, 129–31
United States, 28
PSF Dual-Use Card, 119, 124, 207
public (the), 3, 5, 67, 70–2, 79, 186
Public Affairs Research Council (PARC), 72
public highway corporations (PHCs) privatization of, 88–92, 202
public sector management, 22–3, 29, 194
public utilities, 26, 28, 30
public works, 55, 76, 98, 126

quality competition, 21
Quirk, Paul, 27, 195

radical movements, 41–3
railway transportation reform, 17, 67
See JNR, Nakasone reform
"reciprocal consent," 8, 52, 151, 211
redistribution, 7, 22, 193, 197
reform, *See* government reform

reform politics, 57–62, 93–4,
146, 158
reformers, 10, 15, 22, 39, 57, 59,
62, 67, 77–80, 84, 90–4, 98,
100, 124–5, 136, 139, 145–7,
178, 181, 184–6, 189, 191, 194
reformist politicians, 3, 5, 8–9, 17,
37, 39, 71, 77, 84, 87, 89, 93,
123, 151, 187, 202
Reagan, Ronald, 17, 67, 185
regulation, *See* government
regulation
regulatory reform, 14, 18, 24–30,
37, 194–5
See privatization, deregulation
Rinchō (the Second Provisional
Administrative Reform
Commission), 66–73, 198–9
Rōjin Maruyū, 103–4
rural areas, 7, 10–11, 49–50, 54–5,
57, 61, 67, 80, 83–5, 88, 95,
128–9, 131, 133, 136–7, 141,
144, 173, 181–3
dependent on government
spending, 55, 181
postmasters, 57, *See tokutei*

Samuels, Richard, 8, 52, 193, 197
Sato, Eisaku, 49, 197
Sato, Koko, 76, 199
Shikoku, 62, 128–9
shinsho (correspondence), 122–3
social costs, 8, 18, 55, 144
Social Democratic government, 21
German, 21
Social Democratic Party (SDP), 71,
141, 156, 199
social instability, 39–40, 48
social market economy, 14
social stability, 4–5, 18, 21–2, 27,
37, 40, 50, 189
and basic infrastructure
industries, 27
post–World War II, 4–5, 18,
21–2, 37, 40; and
capitalism, 22

social welfare, 19–21, 34, 41–3,
49–50, 103, 194
Japan, 49–50
Socialist Party, 40–2, 44–7, 134
societal actors, 13–14, 19–20, 31,
33–4
society-centered approach, 12–13
special government corporations, 95
reform, 87–8
state, 12–14, 31–8
approaches, 12–14
decision-making structure, 18,
31–8
embeddedness in economy, 18,
31–8
fragmentation, *See* fragmentation
structural reform, 14, 35, 79
Suzuki, Muneo, 208
Suzuki, Zenko, 66–8

Taiju, 96
Takkyūbin (express home delivery
packages), 122
Tanaka, Kakuei, 49–50, 85, 96,
126, 128, 137–8, 201, 209
tax
evasion, 99–101
exemption, 94, 98–103, 107–8,
146, 203–4; bank accounts,
See maruyū
increases, 66–7, 79
reform, 98–103, 115–16, 120,
146, 204
taxation, 98–103, 107, 123, 126–7,
203–4
on bank deposits, 107
on capital gains, 204
of gasoline, *See dōro tokutei zaigen*
on interest income, 98, 101–4,
107, 115–16, 203–4
on PSF, *See* Postal Savings Fund,
taxation
on wage income, 98, 102
technological development, 26–7,
47, 52, 59, 69, 138, 149, 152,
157, 160, 172, 174, 181

teigaku (fixed long-term rate account), 94, 100, 106–8, 110–11, 115–16, 202, 205, 207
telecommunications, 4, 6, 10–11, 15, 26, 28–30, 55, 58, 68, 73–4, 147–51, 157–78, 183, 185, 187, 197, 211
    integration, 159–62, 167, 177
    internationalization, 157–60, 162–5, 167, 177
    Internet, 165–7, 177
    and national security, 165, 171, 176
    after privatization, 148–52
    reform, 10, 17, 26, 28–30, 35–6, 39, 57–60, 63, 66–70, 92, 150–2, 167, 171, 197
    regulation, 166, 170
Telecommunications Business Law, 159, 170
Telecommunications Council, 169, 171, 174–6, 214
telecommunications-related laws (TRLs), 170–1, 175–7
Thatcher, Margaret, 5, 17, 23, 67, 185
    reform, 17, 23, 28, 67
Toa Domestic Airlines (TDA), 142–3
tokutei (special) local postmasters, 11, 60, 75–6, 83–4, 86, 95–7, 103, 182–3, 190, 202–3
Tokyo, 2–3, 36, 48–9, 54, 56, 62, 88, 118, 126–8, 131, 133, 135, 138, 142, 144, 161, 164, 210
Tokyo Bay Aqua Line, 131–3, 209
Tokyo (Narita) International Airport, 144
Tomei Expressway, 127
Trans Tokyo Bay Road Authority, 132–3
transportation, 4, 6, 10–11, 15, 30, 50, 58, 61, 88–9, 93, 125, 133, 136
    reform, 39, 61–3, 125–46, 198

unemployment, 2–3, 21, 42–3, 189–90
unions, 47–8, 69, 87, 134–6, 141, 145, 150, 156, 187, 189
    JNR, 48, 69, 134–6, 150, 209: Dōrō, 134–5: Kokurō, 134–5; Tetsurō, 134
    postal, 48
United Kingdom, 67
United States, 1–2, 9, 13, 17, 19, 22, 24–8, 31–7, 39–45, 48, 53, 56–7, 60, 65–7, 75, 81, 99, 105, 109, 13–14, 13–32, 141–3, 159, 162, 164–5, 179, 185, 188–9, 195–6, 201, 207, 210, 213
    civil service reform, 24, 195
    and currency exchange rate, 48, 66
    and deregulation, 27–8, 195
    Enron scandal, 28
    equity financing, 42
    Federal Reserve, 33
    government involvement, 33
    government reform, 13, 17, 24, 31, 33–5, 67, 179: state decision-making structure, 33–4; state embeddedness in economy, 33–4
    and liberalization, 105
    monetary policy, 33
    occupation forces, 43–5, 54, 65, 133
    pork barrel politics, 3, 56
    post–World War II political economy, 19–20, 22, 37, 40–1
    and privatization, 28
    protectionism, 9
    regulatory reform, 28
    social welfare, 20, 41
    special interest groups, 196
    and taxes, 99
urban areas, 48–9, 54, 56, 81, 87, 127, 173

U.S.-Japan interconnection charge
    dispute, 170, 213
U.S.-Japan agreement on
    liberalization of Japanese
    market (1984), 98
U.S.-Japan peace treaty, 141–2
U.S.-Japan Security Treaty, 45,
    47–8
U.S.-Japan Talks (1995), 164
U.S. Treasury, 105, 114

vertical administration (*tatewari
    gyōsei*), 37, 70–1, 179, 181,
    185, 199
vertical communications, 37
vertical integration, 160
Virtual Private Network, 153
Vogel, Steven, 26, 194–6

wealth redistribution, 22, 47, 49, 55
welfare programs, 19, 21

(West) Germany, *See* Germany
World Bank, 126–7, 138
World Trade Organization, 162,
    164, 212–13

Yamato Transport, 81–2, 122–3,
    208
the yen, 1, 48, 66
Yoshino, Yoshihiko, 103
Yū Yū Loan, 118, 207
yūsei zoku, (postal tribe) politicians,
    60, 75, 77, 79–84, 86, 97,
    100, 103–4, 123, 125, 151,
    175–6, 178, 190, 200,
    203–4

zaibatsu (family-run conglomerate)
    groups, 51
zoku (policy tribe) politicians, 56–7,
    69, 79, 82, 93, 125, 130–1,
    139, 140–1, 155, 182–3